BUFFALO
LAKE CITY IN NIAGARA LAND

Marina Sunset. Photo by Gertrude Maloney, 1979

BUFFALO

Lake City in Niagara Land

An Illustrated History by Richard C. Brown & Bob Watson

with picture research by Clyde Eller Helfter
and editorial coordination by Margaret Colvin Tropp
Produced in cooperation with the Buffalo and Erie County Historical Society

WINDSOR PUBLICATIONS, INC.

Library of Congress Cataloging in Publication Data

Brown, Richard Carl, 1919-
   Buffalo, Lake City in Niagara Land.

   "Sponsored by the Buffalo and Erie County
Historical Society."
   Includes index.
   1. Buffalo (N.Y.) — History. 2. Buffalo (N.Y.) —
Description. I. Watson, Bob, 1914-
II. Buffalo and Erie County Historical Society.
III. Title.
F129.B857B76   974.7'97   81-52014
ISBN 0-89781-036-8   AACR2

Supervisory editor: Barbara Marinacci
Coordinating editor: Margaret Colvin Tropp
Business-history editor: Karen Story
Business historians: Ann Podd and Tim Murray
Editorial assistance: Phyllis Rifkin and Criss E. Cannady
Picture editors: Teri Greenberg and Jana Wernor
Indexer: Roberta Goodwin
Designer: John Fish
Art production supervisor: Dee Cooper
Production supervisor: Shirley Leuin
Compositors: E. Beryl Myers and Barbara Neiman
Proofreader: Doris Malkin

TABLE OF CONTENTS

Facing page
Buffalo's impressive City Court building stands in Niagara Square. City Hall can be seen in the background. Photo by Paul Pasquarello.

INTRODUCTION

Happy 150th Birthday, dear Buffalo, on your Sesquicentennial celebration, 1982! Many pleasant hours to you, dear reader, when perusing this book that portrays 150 years of our Queen City's history and collective cultural memory.

The Buffalo and Erie County Historical Society is delighted to offer this commemorative volume to you, planned expressly for popular readership, yet based on careful scholarship. As 1982 approached, we felt duty-bound to publish a large, beautifully illustrated book that would honor this milestone in Buffalo's progress. The task seemed too formidable and costly for us to undertake on our own, so we turned to an experienced outside source for assistance, Windsor Publications, Inc. They approached individual business firms and institutions in our locality to interest them in helping to produce the book by adding their own biographies to the history of our city and partially assuming the cost of manufacture. The joint venture of sponsoring organization, publisher, and the generous Buffalo community has been wonderfully cooperative and eminently successful.

We were especially fortunate in securing two excellent co-authors: Dr. Richard C. Brown, long a distinguished professor at State University College at Buffalo, and Bob Watson, a former financial editor and columnist for the Buffalo *Evening News*. Watson agreed to write the 19th century portion of the volume, since he was already familiar with that period from writing his book *A Law Firm and a City*. Brown, knowledgeable about modern social history in America, undertook the 20th century in Buffalo. Together they have employed their considerable research and creative talents to tell the tale of Buffalo's evolution.

The Buffalo and Erie County Historical Society contributed its rich picture resources to illustrate this volume. Several other sources also provided illustrations. Finally, the city's photographers, both professional and amateur, responded enthusiastically to the Society's invitation to submit photos for possible inclusion in the book. We are indebted to all who

Above
Artist John Rother painted January Morning, Lafayette Square in 1895. Rother made the preliminary sketches of the Buffalo Public Library as seen in a snowstorm from a window of the German-American Bank. Courtesy, Buffalo and Erie County Historical Society.

gave time and effort to evaluating the project as it developed and turning it into this splendid book.

As the title suggests, *Buffalo: Lake City in Niagara Land* explores an overall theme. Waterways—lake, river, and canal—were main factors in creating a special city in a unique setting. Waterways also enabled Buffalo to be joined commercially and spiritually to communities elsewhere, especially within the "Niagara Land" on both sides of the international border between the U.S. and Canada.

To read this book is to journey through a century-and-a-half of time. To look at its impressive collection of pictures is to enrich one's sense of the reality of the past and assist in understanding and measuring change.

Robert B. Meech
President
The Buffalo and Erie County Historical Society

Above
Built as the only permanent structure at the Pan-American Exposition, the New York State Building was dedicated as the permanent home of the Buffalo Historical Society in 1902. The building, designed by Buffalo architect George Cary and built at a cost of $175,000, is an example of the American Renaissance or Neoclassical Revival style of architecture—a style officially inaugurated at Chicago's Columbian Exposition in 1893. Courtesy, Buffalo and Erie County Historical Society.

AUTHORS' FOREWORD

Compared with other cities in the northeastern United States, Buffalo is quite young. During the War of 1812, Buffalo—then just a small village—was destroyed by fire. Since its rebirth, the face of Buffalo has been changed many times. During the 19th century, more often than not, these changes were the result of decisions arrived at by leaders in the Western New York and Canadian community. Such conscious alterations became less true in the 20th century, when external forces exerted pressures that local leadership could do little to guide or resist. Nowhere are these changes more evident than in Buffalo's central areas and on its waterfront.

Waterways have figured significantly in Buffalo's history. Buffalo Creek, Lake Erie, Buffalo's harbor, the Niagara River, and the Erie Canal all played major roles in the city's development as a successful international trade center. Today, these waterways serve as popular recreational areas as well.

Buffalo has much to boast about. During much of its existence, Buffalo has been the second-largest metropolis in the Empire State, surpassed only by New York City in wealth and population. At the same time, within the international region often called "Niagara Land," Buffalo is more populous than any city in the Canadian province of Ontario with the exception of Toronto, which has taken the lead in the last quarter century.

Above
This bronze statue of Abraham Lincoln by Niehaus was presented to the Buffalo and Erie County Historical Society by the Lincoln Birthday Association and the Julius E. Francis estate in 1902. Photo by Dr. Joseph Manch.

From its very beginning Buffalo has been a community in motion, having taken part in many of America's most important events—the Civil War, the Pan-American Movement, World Wars I and II, and the era of mass migration. And today the city is a part of America's trend toward advanced technology. Frequently, in striving for a prosperous future, the city has been a leader and an innovator.

How does this history differ from previous books, such as Henry Wayland Hill's *Municipality of Buffalo*, Josephus Larned's *A History of Buffalo and Erie County*, and *History of Erie County, 1870-1970*, edited by Dr. Walter Dunn, Jr.? The date of publication is one answer. *Buffalo: Lake City in Niagara Land* is up-to-date and gives a strong emphasis to the latest decade of Buffalo's history—the beginning of the city's renaissance. The book will deal with the present and the city's potential for the future, as well as its important past.

Moreover, *Buffalo: Lake City in Niagara Land* was written for popular, not scholarly, readership. It covers major aspects of Buffalo's development at a lively pace. Fitting facts into interpretative themes makes this possible, involving selection rather than an exacting but dull cataloging of names, events, and dates. Readers of this book will also find that there is great attention devoted to Buffalo's economic, social, and cultural life. The abundant and carefully chosen illustrative materials, integrated with the text, add vital ingredients in making *Buffalo: Lake City in Niagara Land* a unique presentation of the community's history.

Above
The majestic Art Deco Buffalo City Hall overlooks Niagara Square. Photo by Paul Pasquarello.

Part I. Buffalo in the 19th Century, by Bob Watson

CHAPTER I

FRONTIER VILLAGE

Although the day is long since forgotten and its significance lost in time, October 26, 1825, was the biggest day in the history of Buffalo. That was the fine Indian summer day when the Erie Canal, more than seven years in the making, finally opened in Buffalo. The canal magically transformed an off-the-beaten-path frontier village into a strategically positioned city, triggering an explosive growth in Buffalo that gathered momentum through the rest of the 19th century and on into the 20th.

For whatever other reasons there may have been later on, it was the canal that ignited the dazzling fireworks of urban expansion that made Buffalo to the 19th century what such Sunbelt cities as Houston and Atlanta are to the last half of the 20th century.

Spectacular as was the growth of the city after the coming of the canal, Buffalo's start had been painfully slow. There was no reason for it to have been otherwise. French explorers La Salle and Father Louis Hennepin in the 17th century and the Joncaires in the mid-18th century had seen the unbroken, lakefronted wilderness from which Buffalo would one day be carved. During the American Revolution, British troops occasionally camped along the mouth of the waterway that would become the Buffalo River. But the visits of these or any other white men had no permanency.

Facing page
Red Jacket, a leader of the Seneca tribe of the Iroquois federation, enthusiastically greeted United States Commissioner Colonel Thomas Proctor, who came to the Indian settlement in 1791 to solicit the Seneca's help in persuading their more hostile brethren in Ohio to become peaceful. Painted in 1867 by Thomas Hicks. Courtesy, Buffalo and Erie County Historical Society (BECHS)

Then after the American Revolution, in the 1780s and 1790s, came the first white men seeking the loneliness of frontier life in its most primitive state. And they stayed as long as the primitive environment prevailed. They were loners and drifters, most of them, and not even adventurers of a very high order. They enjoyed the company of the Indians who populated the place, but they suffered phobias that caused them to feel hemmed in when the number of their fellow whites multiplied to much more than a half-dozen.

They were a miniature melting pot in the beginning, just as Buffalo has been a melting pot on a larger scale ever since. Among them was Cornelius Winne, a Dutchman from Hudson River country who came to establish a post for trading with the Indians. There was Captain William Johnston, of British origins, who mingled with the Indians and married one. He built a sawmill that furnished the Indians with board and plank, and they thanked him by giving him land—two square miles of it. Their generous gift not only made him the first landowner when all the others were squatters, but it later made him useful to Buffalo's founder, Joseph Ellicott, in gaining title to the site on which Ellicott's dream city would be laid out.

Winne's and Johnston's neighbors included "Black Joe" Hodge and Jesse Skinner, who had grog shops of a sort, and Martin Middaugh, a German immigrant who worked at odd jobs and was more fluent in Indian dialects than in English. Middaugh and his son-in-law, Ezekiel Lane, built the first log house in the settlement. The site of their double house, when street names emerged, was on Exchange Street a little east of Washington. Winne's trading post was not far away, down what would become Washington Street.

A strange bedfellow of this strange lot was Asa Ransom. Ransom, several cuts above the others intellectually and in the social graces, is credited with having brought "the first simple refinements of civilized life" to the frontier outpost. A silversmith, he came in 1797 to fashion earrings and trinkets for which he found a ready market among the Indians.

Visitors to the ragged settlement were rare. One of the rare ones, in 1791, was Colonel Thomas Proctor, a United States Commissioner. The only white man Proctor later spoke of seeing was Winne. No doubt he took pleasure in the Dutchman's rum and had reason to remember him. Proctor's business, however, was not with Winne but with the Indians. His mission, under President Washington's orders, was to solicit the help of the Indians in persuading their more hostile brethren in Ohio to simmer down and keep the peace.

The Senecas gave Proctor a rousing welcome to their council house on Buffalo Creek, firing in his honor a two-pounder swivel gun loaded with what the colonel remembered as "an

Above
Father Louis Hennepin's account of the area that would include Buffalo is among the earliest and is impressive in its description of the Niagara. (BECHS)

Facing page, top
This first view of Niagara Falls, engraved by J. van Vienen and published in the 1697 Dutch edition of Hennepin's Nouvelle Decouverte, is known as the Hennepin view and is distinctive because of the flat appearance of the Falls. (BECHS)

Facing page, bottom
These pieces of silver jewelry, buttons, beads, and flint were excavated from the Joncaire site in Lewiston, New York. (BECHS)

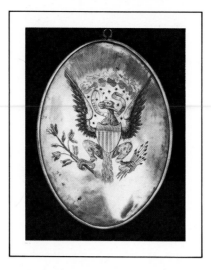

uncommon charge." Proctor might have known what was coming if he had chanced to observe that the fuselier had prudently taken shelter inside the council house while he lighted the fuse with a long stick which he poked through chinks between the logs.

The ensuing recoil of the piece "upset it entirely," and presumably upended the colonel as well. To the startled United States Commissioner, the sly Indian leader, Red Jacket, cordially explained that the bombastic salute was the Indians' way of thanking the Great Keeper for the colonel's safe arrival. Proctor, after recovering his equilibrium, stayed nearly a month and thoroughly enjoyed himself. His mission failed, though—not because of any recalcitrance on the part of the Indians but because of a foul-up in arranging their peace-keeping transportation to Sandusky, Ohio.

The deafening gun salute in Proctor's honor seems to have inadvertently started a long tradition. For more than 100 years, the citizens of the village and then the city of Buffalo would show the same predilection for ear-splitting artillery fire on splendid occasions as had their Indian predecessors. They fired at least one cannon when the digging of the Buffalo end of the Erie Canal began, and they fired not one but many when it was finished. They fired another to welcome the first transmission of electric power from Niagara Falls to Buffalo. And the firing of a cannon when President McKinley arrived in their city for the Pan-American Exposition nearly blew the presidential train off its tracks.

Six years after Proctor came to curry the favor of the Senecas on their home turf, the Indians surrendered that turf and nearly the whole of Western New York to the white man. And they surrendered it not in battle but in negotiations around their council fires, where they bargained away to Dutch speculators 1.3 million acres of their land for $100,000.

The right to strike a deal with the Indians for their Western New York land was a valuable commodity in the 1790s. This sole right was held by the Commonwealth of Massachusetts, which finally wound up selling it to Robert Morris of Philadelphia, the financial genius of the American Revolution. Morris, in turn, sold it to the Holland Land Company. But the crafty Dutchmen attached a provision that it was Morris who would have to tackle the ticklish job of persuading the Indians to sell, and to sell on acceptable terms.

So it was that the agents of Morris, on behalf of the Dutch speculators, went head to head with Red Jacket and other Indian notables at Big Tree (Geneseo) on the Genesee River in

Above and Facing page
George Washington presented this medal to Red Jacket in 1792 as a symbol of diplomacy. (BECHS)

1797. There, in 20 days of dickering around the council fires in August and September, they extracted the Indians' agreement to sell and arrived at the $100,000 selling price.

Red Jacket was opposed to the sale and at one crucial point stomped out the council fire as a signal that the deal was off. But the signal was not as irrevocable as it first seemed. Red Jacket was convinced of the error of his ways by a personal gift of $600 in cash and the promise of an annual honorarium of $100. When the deal was struck, all that was left to the Indians in Western New York was something less than 200,000 acres of reservations on which they would henceforth confine themselves.

Joseph Ellicott, already on the scene as the representative of the Holland Land Company, worried that the Indians might insist that one of their reservations intrude upon the site north of Buffalo Creek upon which in his vivid imagination he saw a new city rising.

To Ellicott's rescue came Captain William Johnston. The land that had been given to him by the Indians was on the site where Buffalo would eventually grow, and it was easy for Johnston to persuade his Indian friends to exclude those lands from their reservation. Conveniently, he then traded his two square miles of land to the Holland Land Company for a choice lot or two in the new town.

Ellicott, relieved, then began the tedious job of leading a 130-man crew in surveying all the Western New York lands so recently acquired. By the time he finished, around the turn of the new century, Ellicott had been promoted to the post of resident agent for the Holland Land Company. Ellicott then began laying out a plan for the city of his dreams.

"The building spot," he wrote his Dutch employers, "is situated about sixty perches from the lake on a beautiful bank about twenty-five feet above the water. From the top of the bank, there are few more beautiful prospects."

He plotted a grid system of streets but with some east-west avenues striking off at acute angles, radiating from a public square (Niagara) like spokes from a hub. If the layout resembled that of Washington, D.C., it was meant to. Washington's street plan was the pattern for Buffalo's. Joseph Ellicott had been influenced by working with his older brother, Andrew, one of the principals in laying out the nation's capital city. Except for three or four major streets that have been sacrificed on the altar of urban renewal, the Buffalo street plan remains pretty much as Joseph Ellicott designed it.

Ellicott named his new town New Amsterdam to please his Dutch employers. And to

please them even more, he attached their names to many of New Amsterdam's principal streets—names such as Willink, Van Staphorst, Schimmelpennick, Vollenhoven, Busti, Cazenovia, and Stadnitski.

Ellicott reserved for himself a large tract on the east side of the main thoroughfare on which he planned to build a house befitting a town planner. In the street itself, midway between Swan and Eagle, he fashioned a semicircular arc. His house was to front precisely on that curving jog in the street. The main street below the arc he called Willink Avenue; above the arc, the street became Van Staphorst Avenue.

Old-timers in the place were horrified by this early-19th-century urban planning and showed their disdain for it. Cornelius Winne, as soon as he got wind of what was coming, vanished into thin air. So did Jesse Skinner, who was casually dismissed anyway as "a person of no note." Asa Ransom, by far the most creditable of the lot, snapped at an invitation from Ellicott to establish a tavern out in Clarence Hollow to entertain prospective land buyers on their way into the new town. In moving out to Clarence Hollow, Ransom negotiated the first land purchase from the Holland Land Company—150 acres at two dollars an acre.

Above
Joseph Ellicott, a representative of the Holland Land Company, did not want the Indians to settle on the site north of Buffalo Creek. This was where he envisioned a new city rising. (BECHS)

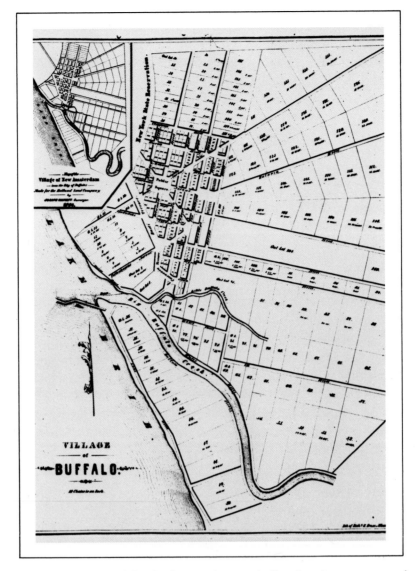

Martin Middaugh, who had built the settlement's first log house, stayed until the first newcomers arrived in response to Ellicott's beckoning. Then he sold the house and moved down to the solitude of the uninhabited island that separates Lake Erie from Buffalo Creek, where he lived contentedly as a squatter to an old age. His son-in-law, Ezekiel Lane, and Black Joe Hodge followed their Indian friends out to one of the reservations, but Lane eventually came back to die at the age of 102 in what was by then a fast-growing city.

More permanent homesteaders took their places. Ellicott finished the job of laying out the town in 1801 and, though the land was cheap and the terms easy, waited three years to make his first sale. It took time for word of his bargains to trickle back into the rest of upstate New York and on into New England. It was November 1804 before he negotiated his first land sales in the town, at about $20 a lot.

Most of the newcomers came to traffic in one way or another with the Indians. One of the first was Captain Samuel Pratt, who brought his wife and a large brood of children from Vermont to New Amsterdam in 1804. His sons and grandsons would become bankers and manufacturers, but Sam Pratt, Sr., made his living trading merchandise to the Indians for their

Above
The inner and outer lots of the village of New Amsterdam as it was when Ellicott surveyed it in 1804 are shown on this map. (BECHS)

furs and pelts. While honoring him with a name that meant "Honest Dealer," the Indians tried to trick him by filling the claws of beaver they sold him with lead. Pratt quickly caught on and quietly clipped off the claws with his hatchet before weighing the pelts.

Pratt bought two lots from the Holland Land Company, plunking down $30.45 in gold. On one of the lots, covering half the block between Main and Washington streets on the south side of Exchange Street, he built the first frame house of substance in the village, with his store attached to it. Today the descendants of Pratt are in their 10th generation as a Buffalo family.

Already in the village when the Pratts arrived was John Crow, an innkeeper. The street where Crow had his tavern, which later became Exchange Street, was known at first as Crow Street. Very early, the tavern was taken over by Joseph Landon, another newcomer, and its name was changed to Landon's Tavern. Rebuilt and expanded many times, it eventually became the Mansion House, a Buffalo landmark throughout the rest of the 19th century.

Landon's Tavern was as much a community center as a hostelry. The first court sessions in the village were held there. The Presbyterians, before they had a church, held some of their early meetings and performed some of their earliest baptisms in the tavern. De Witt Clinton, however, who stayed overnight at Landon's in 1810 while scouting a route for what would be the Erie Canal, complained that he was "indifferently accommodated."

Dr. Cyrenius Chapin, who arrived early as the town's first physician, was a competent enough doctor for his times. When the good doctor lost a patient, he was not necessarily through with him. A versatile man, he could switch hats and conduct the funeral.

Ebenezer Walden came to the village from central New York in 1806 as its first lawyer. His name endures in Walden Avenue, which runs through the city's east side and out into its eastern suburbs. Walden was followed in by several other lawyers—among them, Jonas Harrison, Heman B. Potter, and John Root.

In the diary he kept on his visit to the village in 1810, De Witt Clinton thought it was worth noting that he had found "five lawyers and no church." The reason was simple enough. There wasn't that much law to be practiced, but the lawyers were quicker than the clergy to sniff the sweet smell of profits to be had in real estate. Walden reaped a considerable profit from his dealings in real estate, and so did many of his colleagues at the bar.

The law in the frontier village was simple at both bench and bar. One of the early newcomers, Zenas Barker, wore the professional mantle of judge. But for Barker, the bench was a mere sideline. His more serious businesses were a ferry service across Buffalo Creek and a tavern. Some of the other early judges—Samuel Wilkeson, Augustus Porter, Erastus Granger, and Samuel Tupper, to name a few—were no more practiced in the law than was Barker.

Juba Storrs came into the village as a lawyer, but he was quickly offended by "the crudity of the legal process" and turned to merchandising. Joining Storrs and Sam Pratt, among others, on the roster of tradesmen were Abel Grosvenor and Reuben Heacock, partners, and Charles Townsend and George Coit, who arrived together with 20 tons of merchandise to set themselves up in business. David Rees came in as a blacksmith.

Erastus Granger, in 1803, was the first to arrive in town as the beneficiary of political patronage. The brother of President Jefferson's postmaster general, he came in as postmaster, collector of the port, and superintendent of Indian affairs, duties that were more honorary than demanding and gave him ample time to double in brass as a judge. Granger later bought

Facing page
Buffalo's first lawyer was Ebenezer Walden. His name endures in Walden Avenue, which runs through the city's east side and into its eastern suburbs. Courtesy, Buffalo Savings Bank-Roy Nagle Collection. (BECHS)

land for a farm in what is now Forest Lawn Cemetery, near its Main Street entrance, where he built himself a large frame house.

William Hodge came in 1805 but backtracked a little from the village out to what is now Main and Utica streets. He built what came to be known as the Brick Tavern on the Hill, a popular watering place, and had such other diverse interests as a brick plant, a nursery, a store, and the manufacture of screens and sieves for milling flour.

A neighbor of all these early settlers was a colorful Frenchman, Louis Le Couteulx, who had the first drugstore in the village. Le Couteulx gave the place a unique air of elegance. He went about the streets in silver-buckled shoes, knee britches, and long stockings, wearing his hair in a neatly braided ponytail tied with a bright ribbon. He carried a jeweled snuffbox that was a gift from Louis XVI. A public benefactor, Le Couteulx donated the land for what became St. Louis Church, the first Roman Catholic church in Western New York. He was still alive when Buffalo was elevated from village to city status in 1832. The first city directory, published in that year, listed all the male citizens by trade or occupation. Le Couteulx was identified simply as "gentleman."

By 1811 the village had between 400 and 500 citizens. Its buildings were mostly of wood, painted white, but there also were a goodly number of brick structures. Brick plants and sawmills were among the earliest businesses, and log houses never were long in vogue. The village's northern boundary was Chippewa Street, and there was little except thick forest to the east of Oneida (Ellicott) Street and to the west of Cayuga (Pearl) Street. Within those rather tight boundaries were numerous houses, four taverns, eight stores, a courthouse, a jail, and a weekly newspaper.

The newspaper was the *Buffalo Gazette*. Smith H. Salisbury and his younger brother, Hezekiah, who had learned the printer's trade in Canandaigua, came to Buffalo in the late summer of 1811 and opened a printing office at Pearl and Seneca streets. The first edition of the first newspaper in Buffalo hit the streets on October 3.

The name of the weekly newspaper was ample evidence of the liberties that local residents were taking with names dear to resident agent Joseph Ellicott. With considerable unanimity, the citizens early on had determined that Ellicott's name for their town, New Amsterdam, simply would not do. They preferred Buffalo, and that's what they called it.

There are theories galore about the origin of the name, but there were those among the early arrivals who were convinced that the name was that of a half-breed Indian, Buffaloe, who had been hounded out of his Far West tribe because of the white blood that flowed in his veins. The Indian, so the story went, had come east and found peaceful solace on the banks of a creek, where he pitched permanent camp. Early travelers, finding him there and knowing no other name of the place, dubbed it Buffaloe's Creek. When a village started to rise beyond the creek, its citizens clung to the "Buffaloe" name, refusing to do any more than shorten it to Buffalo.

Besides rejecting New Amsterdam as the village's name, the villagers also straightened the main thoroughfare, removing the spacious arc that Ellicott had designed as a pleasant vista fronting the grand house he planned to build. Ellicott took all this as a personal affront and decided against building a house there or coming in at all from the Holland Land Company's headquarters in Batavia, 30 miles away, except on official business. Buffalo, if that's what they wanted to call it, would be deprived of his residential presence. "God has made Buffalo and I must try to make Batavia," was his parting message to the villagers.

The villagers thereupon were emboldened to begin scrapping the Dutch street names

Facing page
St. Louis Church (pictured here) burned in 1885, but was later rebuilt. The St. Louis Church that survives today is a Gothic structure and a landmark. It reflects the growth of the German population in the parish at that time. (BECHS)

that stuck in their throats. It took some time to accomplish, but the village trustees, following the dictates of their constituents, eventually renounced the Dutch names once and for all. Willink and Van Staphorst became Main Street. Vollenhoven became Erie Street. Stadnitski became Church Street. Schimmelpennick became Niagara. Cazenovia (named for Holland Land Company's general agent in Philadelphia, Cazenove) became Court Street. Cazenovia Terrace became simply the Terrace. Busti became Genesee.

Some of the Indian names—Chippewa, Huron, Mohawk, Delaware, and Seneca—stayed as they were. But the villagers, in a spirit of no hard feelings, gave Ellicott's name to what had been Oneida Street. And they changed the name of Onondaga to Washington, Cayuga to Pearl, and Tuscarora to Franklin. Swan and Eagle they decided to leave alone.

A little more than two years after the Salisbury brothers began publishing the *Gazette* as Buffalo's first newspaper, they hastily moved their printing press out to Williamsville. Their temporary move was not a minute too soon. The War of 1812 was closing in on Buffalo. Everybody knew it, but not everybody was as timely in taking leave of the place as the Salisburys had been after the publication of their December 21 edition in 1813.

The *Gazette* earlier had helped beat the drums for a buildup in military forces in Buffalo, publishing the plea of a brigadier general in a camp near Buffalo for volunteers. "Will you stand with your arms folded?" the general scolded the holdouts. "Are you not related to the men who fought at Bennington and Saratoga? Has the race degenerated? Shame, where is thy blush?" The *Gazette*'s Hezekiah Salisbury was one of those who answered the call.

In the dwindling days of 1813, a force of militia and Indians numbering about 2,000 had gathered in Buffalo and Black Rock to defend the two villages. Their commander was General Amos Hall of Canandaigua, whose battlefield command had been limited to a sergeancy during the American Revolution. He reviewed his troops on December 26 and pronounced his approval of their "martial appearance" and their "alacrity in flying to arms."

The British, across the Niagara River in Canada, did not hear his words, or were unimpressed if they did. In the early morning darkness of December 30, 1813, 800 British troops, many of them regulars, and 400 to 500 Indians crossed the river to Black Rock in two detachments. The corner of what would be Niagara and School streets became the main battleground.

The firing of British musketry from nowhere and everywhere in the darkness, the crack of rifles, the sound of bugles, and the bloodcurdling screams of the Indians were too much for the American forces. Unprepared for such close-quarter fighting, they frantically gave way. Not even General Hall, hurrying to Black Rock over the Guide Board Road (North Street), could repair the disarray.

Most of the Americans panicked and fled for their lives. Some took cover in the surrounding forest, where the Indians pursued them and finished them off. The British and their Indian cohorts then pushed on the two miles into Buffalo, where they found the going easy.

Two cannon, manned by a few sailors, were planted at Main and Niagara streets. They spit out only a brief, feeble protest before they were abandoned. The sailors elected to take to their heels as the British and their Indian allies closed in. Dr. Cyrenius Chapin, the physician and sometime conductor of funerals, by this time wearing the hat of a colonel, attached a handkerchief to his cane and frantically waved a makeshift flag of surrender.

Chapin and the British officers conversed for awhile, and Chapin thought he had exacted an agreement that public property would be seized but private property would be spared. In any case, the British reneged, disputing Chapin's claim that he had authority to negotiate. The best that can be said of Chapin's effort is that he stalled for time and gave the villagers a chance to get out of town. Civilians joined the fleeing soldiers taking off in all directions, especially clogging the road out to Williamsville.

The British had come to Buffalo not to possess it but to emasculate it. And on this next to the last day of 1813, they applied the torch. Then they went back to Black Rock, leaving behind a pall of murky smoke hanging over the town that had been Buffalo.

New Year's Day, 1814, dawned bright and clear. Unexpectedly, the British and their Indian friends came back to Buffalo to celebrate the holiday by burning whatever they might have missed the first time. When they were through, there was nothing left except the house of Mrs. Margaret St. John, the stone jail, David Rees's blacksmith shop, and a building the carpenters had not yet finished. The only sign of life was a cat gingerly pawing its way through the smoldering ruins.

Above
On December 30, 1813, the British burned Buffalo. This wood engraving depicting the tragic event appeared in Taylor's Universal History. *(BECHS)*

While most of the other villagers fled in wagons, on horseback, and on foot, Mrs. St. John had stayed behind with her daughters to save their house. Miraculously, the family and their home remained unscathed. A neighbor, Mrs. Joshua Lovejoy, had similar intentions, but she was not so lucky. The Indians took her life and her scalp.

There were few other heroes. One of the villagers still on the scene when the British came back a second time sought to save his own skin by informing one of the officers that two miles away was Hodge's Brick Tavern where there was $50,000 of public property which "you can destroy as well as not."

"Depend upon it," replied the officer. "If you are leading us into an ambush, you are the first man to die."

But there was no ambush, and the British troops ravaged Hodge's Tavern, too.

The prisoners taken on that grim New Year's Day in 1814 were put aboard a boat at Black Rock. An Indian squaw, herself bedecked in war paint, serenaded the American prisoners in song:

> Buffalo, Buffalo, Happy New Year
> Buffalo, Happy, Happy New Year
> Buffalo, Happy New Year for the Yankee.

By the following spring, Black Rock's General Peter B. Porter had recruited a new force of Indians and militia and Generals Jacob Brown and Winfield Scott had been sent to bring order out of chaos in the war effort at Buffalo. To show they meant business, Generals Brown and Scott ordered that four court-martialed deserters be publicly shot in Niagara Square. The drama of the execution must have sent shivers up the spines of the troops, particularly if thoughts of desertion had ever lurked in their minds.

Actually, there was a fifth man sentenced to be shot. The life of the fifth was spared because he was young and impressionable and was thought to have been unduly influenced by his older comrades. But he was not told of his reprieve. Like the other four, he was blind-folded and his arms pinioned as he knelt before his own coffin. When the volleys rang out, only the fifth man did not receive the bullet. But he thought he had, and he fell in a dead faint.

Discipline instilled in the troops was effective. American forces redeemed themselves in battle across the river in Canada, sometimes heroically, but without ever clinching a clear-cut victory. As it turned out, the war was almost over anyway. It ended with the treaty at Ghent in December 1814, and nowhere was the futility of the sorry episode more evident than on the Niagara frontier.

Down but not out, Buffalonians did not wait for the war to end but started straggling back into their burned-out village as soon as the coast was clear of their British tormentors. Like the Phoenix of Egyptian mythology, the village renewed itself from its own ashes.

Appropriately enough, it was the proprietor of the Phoenix Tavern at Main and Seneca streets who did the first rebuilding, announcing in the *Gazette* on February 22, 1814, that he was "again erecting his tavern among the ruins of Buffalo" and that on March 1 he would be ready "to receive and wait on company." Hodge's Brick Tavern out at Main and Utica streets was the next to reopen. Troops that had been sent in to beef up the war effort had money to

Facing page
Jacob Brown, a brigadier general in the War of 1812, was placed in command of the New York frontier. Brown was later promoted to major general and given command at Niagara. He began a campaign into Canada in 1814, crossing the Niagara River and taking Fort Erie. (BECHS)

spend, and their cash would help nourish the town's recovery. There wasn't a moment to lose in reopening the taverns.

All of the survivors of the holocaust, showing their spunk, came back to pick up the pieces. At first they put up make-do shanties. But when they rebuilt more permanently, what they built was better than what they had left behind when they fled.

Token financial assistance came from several sources. New York City, not so impoverished as it would be a century and a half later, magnanimously sent $3,000 to aid in Buffalo's reconstruction. The city of Albany sent $1,000, and the state legislature voted a grant of $40,000 to the stricken village. The federal government, to the village's dismay, was less charitable.

Proof of the village's resiliency was to be found in the number of its citizens. Within two years after the war ended, the prewar population of 500 had doubled to 1,000, and in the next four years it doubled again. To accommodate the growth in potential readership, a second newspaper, the *Niagara Journal*, began publication in 1815.

In 1816 a splendid new courthouse of light-colored brick was built on Washington Street, where the expansive plaza in front of the Buffalo and Erie County Library is now. The courthouse had a shining cupola on top and six fluted columns along the front. Across the street a pleasant park ran down toward Main Street.

Since 1808 Buffalo had been a part of Niagara County. In 1821 the state legislature carved Niagara into two parts, creating a new Erie County with Buffalo as its county seat. Samuel Wilkeson, neither a lawyer nor a judge but full of wisdom, became Erie County's first common-pleas judge. Heman B. Potter, every inch a lawyer, was the first district attorney. Wilkeson was a busy man with diverse interests, but the new courthouse was at least his occasional domain.

In the same year the courthouse went up, Gaius Kibbe built a spacious three-story Georgian-style tavern and adorned it with his own name. He sold it three years later to entrepreneur Benjamin Rathbun. Rathbun renamed it the Eagle Tavern and made it the finest stagecoach stop and public gathering place west of New York City. The Eagle was on the west side of Main below Court Street. Across Main from the Eagle there blossomed Buffalo's first theater. It was called simply The Theatre, and if nothing else, it was an amenity serving notice that a more refined urban life was in the making.

On side-by-side Main Street lots, separated by what appropriately became known as Church Street, the Episcopalians built St. Paul's Church in 1819-1820 and the Presbyterians erected the First Presbyterian Church in 1823. The lots were given to them by the Holland Land Company and soon became choice pieces of real estate.

The Methodists built the first meetinghouse in Buffalo, on Franklin Street, in 1819. Then, taking a cue from the Episcopalians and the Presbyterians, they went hat in hand to Holland Land soliciting free real estate and came away with a lot on Niagara Street, upon which they built a church in 1823.

If they were slow, in De Witt Clinton's view, in getting their first churches, Buffalonians moved too far too fast in opening their first bank, the Bank of Niagara, in 1815. Buffalo was growing, but it hadn't grown enough yet to support a bank. The financial spark at the Bank of Niagara sputtered and then was extinguished. Its sponsors, good citizens such as Ebenezer Walden, Jonas Williams, Augustus Porter, Samuel Tupper, Charles Townsend, Oliver Forward, and Smith Salisbury, were not at all dismayed. They had erred only in being premature.

Although the rebirth of Buffalo was constantly in the making, there were wartime scars that did not quickly heal. De Witt Clinton, visiting in 1816, wrote of seeing from his tavern window "the remains of a house destroyed in the general conflagration of this place." Millard Fillmore, who hitchhiked from Cayuga County on a summer vacation in 1818, wrote in his diary of seeing "cellars and chimneys without houses." To young Fillmore, visiting Buffalo for the first time, the sight was proof of how thorough had been the wartime arson.

But Fillmore was taken with the spirit of the place, and he came back in 1822 to study law as a clerk with lawyers Asa Rice and Joseph Clary. Asa Rice, one of Fillmore's law teachers, had given up a successful law practice in Eagle village in the town of Manlius for what he was convinced would be more fertile ground for a lawyer in a rebuilding Buffalo. He was so satisfied with his move that he persuaded his lawyer brother-in-law, Joseph Clary, to come to Buffalo from Cherry Valley. It was in the Rice and Clary law office, on the east side of Main Street a little above Lafayette Square, that Fillmore prepared himself for the law, supporting himself in the meantime by teaching in the newly built Cold Spring district school out on Main Street about where the Sixth Precinct police station is now. He received $20 a month for teaching school and, as was the custom, was furnished board by the parents of his students. Twenty-eight years later, Fillmore was President of the United States.

Asa Rice came to Buffalo in the summer of 1817, amid a dizzying pace of events. He had hardly unpacked his bags when the President of the United States came to town. Shortly after that presidential visit, Joseph Bonaparte, ex-king of Spain and Napoleon's brother, stopped off in Buffalo on his way to see Niagara Falls.

Buffalonians learned of President Monroe's approaching visit in a one-paragraph notice in the *Buffalo Gazette* of July 29, 1817: "A meeting of the citizens of this village is requested at Mr. Kibbe's Tavern on Wednesday evening at 7 o'clock for the purpose of making suitable arrangements for the reception of the President of the United States."

No 19th-century equivalent of Air Force One brought the President to Buffalo. He rode horseback from Niagara Falls to Black Rock, where the citizens of Buffalo were waiting to meet him and to escort him the rest of the way to a reception in their village at Landon's Tavern. At Landon's, President Monroe got a respectful welcome but also an earful of discontent from citizens upset by government foot-dragging in compensating them for their wartime property losses.

For Buffalonians, the presidential visit further buoyed their already rising spirits. But the biggest boost to their morale had already come a month earlier, when news reached them that, at Rome, New York, the digging of the Erie Canal had begun. The news gave rise to a hope and a prayer that the canal might someday be dug all the way to Buffalo.

Above
In the spring of 1814 General Winfield Scott (shown here) and General Jacob Brown ordered the public execution of four court-martialed deserters. (BECHS)

CHAPTER II

THE
E-RI-E CANAL

The Erie Canal, if it touched off soaring hopes in Buffalo, also triggered a controversy of monumental proportions. Latter-day controversies among Buffalonians over where to build such 20th-century accoutrements as a new football stadium, a new university campus, a new downtown rapid-transit station—all pale by comparison with the controversy in the early 1820s over where to put the western terminus of the new canal.

Much to Buffalo's delight, the state legislature in 1819 authorized a westward extension of the canal to Lake Erie. But, unfortunately, the legislature was no more specific than that. Would it end at Black Rock, squeezing out Buffalo? Or would it end at Buffalo, making Black Rock a way station? The choice was a prerogative of the canal commissioners. Buffalo and Black Rock signaled the commissioners without subtlety, battling each other ferociously as though locked in mortal combat—which indeed they were.

The stakes were high. Whichever village won the nod as the western terminus of the canal would be the port of entry into the canal. And whichever was the port of entry would become "the city," at the expense of the other. Buffalo and Black Rock fought like tigers. Their mudslinging filled the columns of the local newspapers and even attracted national attention.

Facing page
The locks at Lockport lifted the canal up and over the escarpment onto the Erie plain. John W. Barbour made this 1841 hand-colored engraving of the locks. (BECHS)

Black Rockers sneered at Buffalo, pointing out that Buffalo had no harbor and claiming that no harbor could be built there. Black Rock, a smaller village than Buffalo, did have a harbor of sorts, protected by a huge black stone that jutted into the Niagara and gave the town its name. Buffalonians sneered back at their neighbors, saying any shipping at Black Rock would be swept down the swift and uncompromising Niagara.

The Black Rockers were absolutely right when they said that Buffalo had no harbor. Buffalo did have its otherwise navigable Buffalo Creek that would make a fine inner harbor, except that its mouth into Lake Erie was effectively blocked to traffic by a sandbar of such proportions that canoes crossing over it sometimes went aground.

But the Black Rockers were totally wrong when they said of Buffalo that no harbor could be built there. Buffalonians knew full well that without a usable harbor, their chances of getting the terminus of the Erie Canal were slim or nonexistent. So, with no handouts from any government other than a $12,000 loan from the state that had to be guaranteed for twice that amount, Buffalonians began to build a harbor. And they chose Samuel Wilkeson, with no credentials for what he was about to do, to build it.

Wilkeson recruited a work force in the village and the surrounding countryside and, in the summer of 1820, began building a pier that would ultimately extend about 800 feet into the lake and discourage the flow of sand toward the sandbar. This protective pier he sturdily fashioned from timber cribs filled with stone and rock nestled in massive cushions of brush. The breakwater was scarcely finished when it was exposed to a sudden September gale. The villagers cheered as the pier held fast. Proving its seaworthiness, it held fast that winter, too, and for many winters and summers thereafter.

But the pier, although an essential part of the harbor-making enterprise, did not itself create a harbor. The offending sandbar off the mouth of Buffalo Creek still had to be dealt with. Wilkeson daringly proposed to deal with it by moving the mouth of the creek 60 rods to the south, away from the obstruction. And he proposed to move its mouth by forcing the creek itself to dredge its own new channel. His idea was to dam the creek at exactly the right place and let the force of the current gouge its way through sand and gravel, straight out to the lake.

The orthodontic surgery he was performing on the mouth of Buffalo Creek was tricky and complex, and Wilkeson could ill afford any distractions. But just when the operation seemed to be going well, Nature dealt him a blow to the midsection that would have discouraged a

Above
Samuel Wilkeson was responsible for establishing Buffalo's harbor. Since his time, numerous volumes have been written about the history of the harbor. (BECHS)

less resolute man to the point of drowning his sorrow at the nearest tavern. A freak wind and then a torrential rainstorm that did odd things to the water levels in both creek and lake suddenly threatened to undo everything Wilkeson had accomplished so far.

Wilkeson, keeping his head, sent out a hurried call for volunteers, and the villagers, responding, all ran down to the waterfront. Drenched to the skin in the unceasing rain, they labored feverishly through the day and by torchlight through the night to make the rising floodwaters work to Wilkeson's advantage instead of washing away his handiwork.

Triumphantly, if not miraculously, the raging current in Buffalo Creek was made to gouge the new channel, straight and true, into the lake. The deepened channel, nurtured to permanency, gave Buffalo a navigable harbor. Boats forever after would enter and leave it with splendid ease. The job, from pier to channel, had taken 221 working days. Wilkeson was convinced that Providence was as determined as he was to create a harbor in Buffalo and that the flood that delivered the finishing touch had been divinely dispatched.

The harbor-making effort bore the stamp of an entire village working in concert. It was a stirring example of rarely surpassed civic resolution. But it was Wilkeson who conceived the plan and kindled the enthusiasm of the villagers. The Latin inscription chiseled into the headstone over his grave in Forest Lawn Cemetery tells it all: *Urbem Condidit.* (He Built the City.)

The labor of love that brought forth the harbor put a new head of steam on the battle between Black Rock and Buffalo to get the nod as the Erie Canal's western terminus, and Buffalonians believed it gave them a leg up in getting a decision in their favor. The argument between the two neighboring villages reached its climax on a hot summer's day in 1822, when the canal commissioners came to Buffalo to listen to Buffalo and Black Rock fight it out in a debate in the Eagle Tavern's dancing hall.

General Peter Porter, polished and persuasive and Black Rocker to the core, pleaded the case for Black Rock. Sam Wilkeson, not much of a public speaker but all heart, peeled off his jacket and in his shirt-sleeves sensibly if not as eloquently argued on behalf of Buffalo.

The canal commissioners heightened the drama by doing nothing to dispel the impression that the Porter-Wilkeson debate was the climactic finale of the competition for the canal's western terminus. Actually, they were already tilting toward Buffalo because of economic considerations. The waters in the lake at Buffalo were at a higher level than in the Niagara at Black Rock, and every inch gained in the elevation from which water would be drawn into the canal would produce a saving in the cost of excavation.

Above
Major General Peter Porter pleaded Black Rock's case to become the western terminus of the Erie Canal. (BECHS)

The commissioners finally hinted their preference before they left Buffalo, and the next winter they made it official. Buffalo would get the canal. Buffalo would become the city, and Black Rock would gradually fade as a separate entity. Whether or not it took that long for hard feelings to be calmed, it would be another 32 years before Black Rock finally and formally was merged into Buffalo.

Once their decision was made, the canal commissioners lost no time in awarding contracts for the digging of the canal's western end, and they set August 9, 1823, as the day when the digging would begin in Buffalo. As usual, it was a day of celebration and ceremony—the gun salute, the sermon, the turning of the first spadeful of earth by Judge Oliver Forward.

But this groundbreaking was more than ceremonial. All the villagers were invited to it, and those who had them were encouraged to bring their oxen and help dig. On the morning of the groundbreaking, a dozen yokes of oxen hitched to plows were gathered on the boggy flatland below the Terrace, waiting for the signal to "go lang buck."

Amid the noisy exhortations of their drivers, the oxen joined the Irish diggers in turning the earth for at least a half-mile down the path that had been laid out as the course of the canal. Those who had nothing with which to dig except their hands joyfully dirtied them to

Above
The Erie Canal Basin and Elevator as they appeared circa 1872. (BECHS)

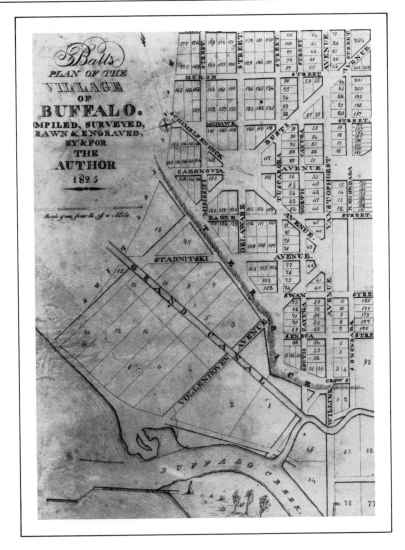

carry away the sod as it was turned by digger and plow.

Not only in the spirit of celebration but in a devilishly clever plot to raise the level of productivity of those who dug, the contractors set out barrels of pure rye whiskey along the path of the canal. Beyond the first barrel, just far enough away to be sniffed, was a second. Beyond the second was another, and then another. The rye was on the house. Tin dippers were furnished, and all who came upon the rye were expected to stop long enough to liberally partake of it.

What the contractors lost in time out for refreshment they more than made up in the frenzy of digging to get on to the next barrel. It was a ploy the contractors did not hesitate to use on other occasions when they felt an urgent need to extract the last drop of sweat from the brows of the diggers.

On August 9, 1823, it provided a bountifully boozy beginning to the building of the western end of the Erie Canal. Eight hundred and nine days later, wild horses could not have stayed the villagers as they crowded the Buffalo waterfront to see the finished canal and the gala beginning of its navigation on October 26, 1825.

Above
*Sheldon Ball compiled, surveyed, drew,
and engraved this 1825 Plan of the
Village of Buffalo. (BECHS)*

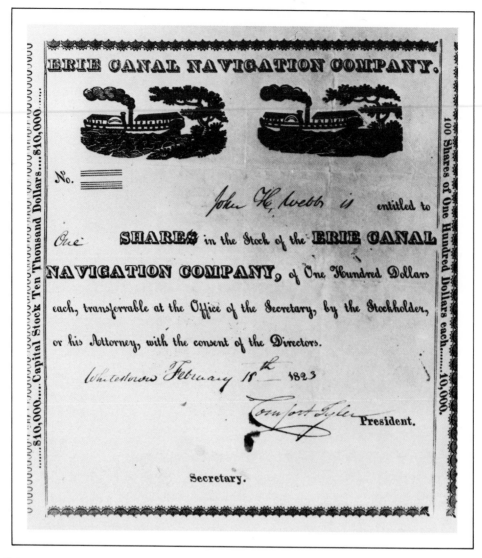

Buffalonians, all 2,412 of them, who toasted in the New Year on the last night of 1825 must have felt a genuine reluctance to watch the old year slip away. Without question, it had been their best yet, a mind-boggling humdinger full of crowd-pleasing razzle-dazzle.

Blotted out were the nightmarish memories of New Year's Eve a dozen years before, when all that remained of the village were the smoldering ruins of a British and Indian attack. Now, a scant 12 years later, the Erie Canal was changing Buffalo overnight from an outpost of little consequence into a boomtown straddling the threshold to the nation's emerging new frontiers.

Ceremonially, at least, the upbeat year of 1825 began on a fine June day when the Marquis de Lafayette, the French hero of the American Revolution and a Buffalo favorite, visited the village. The whole town turned out to parade him up Main Street and then to wine and dine him at the Eagle Tavern.

Buffalo and its neighbor, archrival Black Rock, jockeyed for position as they vied for the pleasure of the Frenchman's company. Buffalo snagged him first. Bowing and waving in response to vociferous applause, he rode in an open carriage up Main Street to the Eagle

Above
This share of stock in the Erie Canal Navigation Company took on added value as construction on the western end of the Erie Canal began on August 9, 1823. (BECHS)

*When the Erie Canal opened in 1825, a
Memoir illustrated with George Catlin
drawings of Buffalo and the canal was
published in celebration of its completion. These two views are entitled
Buffalo Harbour From the Village (top)
and Buffalo From the Light House (bottom). (BECHS)*

Tavern, where he was put up for the night and royally entertained at a reception and then at a banquet hosted by the Eagle's proprietor. The village that night was illuminated in Lafayette's honor.

The Indian Red Jacket was on the guest list for the reception. With an unofficial steering committee of responsible citizens at his elbow to keep him in tow and reasonably sober, the old Indian came to greet the equally aging French warrior. Red Jacket admired the Frenchman's full head of hair and told him so, having no notion that it was a wig. To the guest of honor, Red Jacket bared his own balding pate and wistfully allowed that time had dealt more kindly with Lafayette.

The next morning, Lafayette was routed out of bed at daybreak and whisked off to Black Rock for breakfast. Whether or not he enjoyed the pulling and tugging between the two villages, he tolerated it good-naturedly. What he really wanted most of all was to see Niagara Falls, which he finally managed to do.

Latter-day Buffalonians, like their forebears, seem never to have ceased their hero worship of Lafayette. They gave his name to one of the principal downtown public squares, a hospital, a public high school, two churches, a hotel, a movie theater, and one of their splendid residential avenues. On everything except the demolished theater, the Lafayette name endures. This is more than has ever been done to perpetuate the name of Buffalo's own Samuel Wilkeson, a hometown hero who, by virtue of his having built the harbor, built the city.

Scarcely 10 days after the Lafayette visit and before the villagers had time to catch their breath, there was a ceremonial bonus that turned out to be the biggest crowd-gatherer of them all. The three Thayer brothers, having been convicted of "a most awfully and too successfully premeditated murder," were publicly hanged from a scaffold erected in Niagara Square.

For the grisly but congenial ceremony that disposed of the Thayer boys simultaneously and economically, the village cloaked itself in all the trappings consistent with any host city of a Super Bowl 150 years later. An estimated 20,000 of the curious, 10 times the normal population of the village, came from far and near to see the deed done at high noon and then to fill the coffers of merchants and tavernkeepers.

Doughty old Red Jacket, breasting the tide of white men descending upon the village for the hanging-bee, explained why he instead was fleeing it. "Fools enough there now," he grumbled to Judge Ebenezer Walden. "Battle is the place to see men die."

Above
As a result of Lafayette's 1825 visit to the United States, his likeness was applied to numerous items such as this half-pint flask. (BECHS)

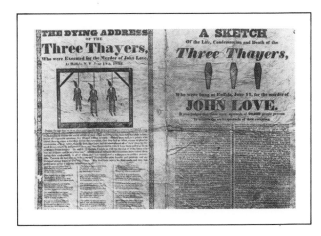

The Thayer brothers—Isaac, Israel, and Nelson—were a vulgar, irreverent, and profane lot who lived several miles out of Buffalo in the town of Boston. Protective Boston mothers knew them well enough to cover their children's heads with their aprons whenever they came upon the shouting and cursing Thayers.

The brothers had become indebted to one of their sometime neighbors, a miserly itinerant peddler named John Love, and Love was squeezing them to pay up. The Thayers mercilessly but not uncharacteristically solved the problem of their pressing debt by putting a bloody and definitive end to Love with rifle and meat ax. The brothers then compounded their crime and thoughtlessly focused attention on themselves by forging powers of attorney which they successfully used to collect money from others who were in Love's debt. When the three boys began flashing large sums of money, suspicions were aroused about both the Thayers and the whereabouts of Love.

When a town of Boston magistrate offered the princely sum of $10 to spur a hunt for the missing Love, local residents looked first on the Thayer property. They found him quickly and easily, buried in a grave so shallow that his toes peeked out.

At a standing-room-only trial in Buffalo's courthouse on April 21, 22, and 23, it was charged that the Thayer brothers, "moved and seduced by the instigation of the Devil," had dispatched the hapless Love to oblivion. Sheldon Smith, one of the prosecutors, reminded the jury in 1825, "it is to be feared that the age in which we live is becoming more and more corrupt; that the perpetration of crimes is becoming more and more frequent." The time had come, he admonished, for the courts and conscientious juries to stem the tide of excessive permissiveness.

The Thayers must have fidgeted in their seats when they heard their own lawyer, Thomas C. Love (no relationship), lavishly praise the district attorney and his staff for a prosecutorial job well done and admit to "embarrassment" at having to address the jury in his own role as defense attorney. In his plea on behalf of the defendants, who had not yet confessed, he took a better-safe-than-sorry approach. "It is better that a guilty man escape the punishment due to his crimes," he argued, "than that he should be convicted of an offense upon incompetent proof."

But the jury needed to deliberate only half an hour before finding Isaac and Israel guilty as charged. Nelson's trial began immediately after, and it took the jury only "a few minutes" to arrive at a similar verdict.

The Thayers knew their fate was sealed when Judge Reuben Walworth intoned: "Listen

Above
These broadside accounts of June 17, 1825, tell of the public hanging of the three Thayer brothers for a "successfully premeditated murder." (BECHS)

now to the dreadful sentence of the law and then, farewell forever." Once the sentence of death had been passed, the Thayers confessed to the crime, throwing in a few new gory details for good measure.

The aftermath was their very public hanging in a crowded Niagara Square, on a gallows site that later would be obliterated first by Samuel Wilkeson's house and then by the dazzling Art Deco architecture of Buffalo's City Hall. A military band tootled the mournful "Roslyn Castle," as it led the stars of the show and the supporting actors in a procession from the jail on Washington Street to the square. Vendors moved in and out of the crowd, hawking hastily printed and nearly illiterate ballads reciting the terrible tale of the Thayers' undoing. The militia was abundantly present throughout the town to maintain order.

In their final moments on the gallows, the Thayer brothers set up an eerie wailing that grew louder and louder in a weird sort of crescendo, until the sheriff's rope-cutting blade finally silenced it. But then the wailing monotone was involuntarily picked up by the spectators, and it echoed a thousandfold across the square. After the strange outburst had run its course, the audience turned away, seeking the pleasure of shops and taverns.

Buffalonians who witnessed the hanging never forgot it as long as they lived. But a little more than four months later, the villagers assembled again, and this time there was no room for wailing. This time it was an occasion of pure and unrestrained joy, as they came to celebrate the long-awaited opening of the Erie Canal in Buffalo. They had all dug their hands into the fresh earth to start the digging at their end of the canal; not one of them would have missed indulging in the hoopla that marked its finish.

The first section of the canal was started in Rome, New York, on the Fourth of July in 1817. After agonizing doubts about whether it would ever get to Buffalo at all, digging from the western end began on August 9, 1823. By October 1825, the canal finally stretched all the way across the state to Buffalo, ending below the Terrace not far from the foot of Pearl Street. Although the canal is long gone from Buffalo's waterfront, and gone without a trace, the site of its once-flourishing western terminus appropriately remains a busy, modern-day crossroads of transportation, where the Niagara Section of the New York State Thruway turns, crosses under, and connects with the overhead Buffalo Skyway.

Digging this last section of the canal was easy enough at its Buffalo end and through the

Facing page
George Catlin depicted the process of excavation at Lockport in 1825. (BECHS)

63 miles of soft flatland west of the Genesee River. But carrying it through and over the Niagara escarpment was a technological marvel that was hailed as the finest hydraulic-engineering feat of its time and still commands admiration today. The great locks at Lockport lifted the canal up and over the escarpment onto the Erie plain.

In the waning days of fall in 1825, an expanded labor force, working overtime, was still putting the finishing touches on the locks at Lockport. Finally the builders let it be known that the entire length of the canal would be ready for navigation on October 26. Buffalo, and indeed the whole state of New York, pulled out all the stops to fill with pomp and pageantry the long-awaited opening day, touted by the local press as "one of the greatest events in the recorded pages of history."

De Witt Clinton, who for years had been the driving force behind the canal and had been rewarded for his efforts by being elected governor of New York, came to Buffalo to properly baptize the man-made waterway that finally linked the Great Lakes with the Atlantic.

A flotilla of canal boats gathered in Buffalo on the morning of October 26 to begin that first triumphant trip down the Erie Canal to the Hudson River and then on to New York City. The lead boat in the flotilla was the *Seneca Chief,* drawn by four gray horses and carrying

Above
Sheldon Ball's 1825 View of Buffalo Harbor *was produced totally in Buffalo. It was the first time that a drawing was sketched, plates prepared, and printing done in the village. (BECHS)*

Governor Clinton and a retinue of notables that included Samuel Wilkeson, the builder of Buffalo's harbor. The horses pulling it were bedecked with plumes, ribbons, and silver-plated harnesses, and the horseman wore a gray beaver hat.

Aboard the *Seneca Chief* were two kegs of "the pure waters of Lake Erie," to be ceremoniously mingled with the waters of the Atlantic off Sandy Hook. The kegs, painted red, white, and blue, were prominently displayed on the *Seneca Chief's* foredeck for all along the way to see.

Behind the *Seneca Chief* was the *Noah's Ark*, whose assortment of passengers included two live bears and two lively Seneca Indian boys. Bringing up the rear were the elegant *Superior*, the *Commodore Perry*, and the *Buffalo*. The whole village of Buffalo came down to the new canal to see the flotilla begin its historic trip and then to indulge in a day and night of general merrymaking.

The festive day began with a procession led by Governor Clinton, its ranks swelled by "strangers and citizens" as it marched from the park in front of the Washington Street courthouse to the head of the canal. Jesse Hawley of the visiting Rochester contingent made "a sensible speech of congratulation," reminding Buffalonians that what they were seeing was "the longest canal made in the least time with the least experience for the least money and of the greatest utility of any other in the world."

The speechmaking droned on, but the villagers had waited a long time for what it signified and they were in no mood for restlessness. Besides, they knew that the spectacular finish of the ceremony was worth waiting for. A series of large-caliber cannon had been strategically planted clear across the state to relay the news by gunfire that the flotilla had left Buffalo.

Villagers who crowded along the canal in Buffalo covered their ears with their hands, flinching and squealing in anticipation as they waited for the gunner nearest the boats to fire his weapon when the flotilla cast off. The next gunner, in Black Rock, lighted his cannon fuse when he picked up sound waves from the first earsplitting report. The ritual was repeated by cannoneers strung out all the way to New York City. Buffalonians were sure they heard the first three volleys.

It took just 81 minutes for the thundering cannon to flash the message to New York that the canal flotilla was on its way from Buffalo. It was the fastest transmission of news the world had ever known.

After the Grand Salute, as the cannon firing that reverberated across the state had been billed, the villagers in Buffalo were too hyped to go home. They went back to the courthouse park and simmered down as they listened to a choir sing, to the tune of "Hail Columbia," an ode composed in the canal's honor by a journeyman mechanic in the town.

> Strike the lyre! with joyous note
> Let the sound through azure float
> The task is over, the work complete
> And Erie's waters with ocean meet
> Bearing afar their rich bequest
> While smiling commerce greets the West.

The day of celebration continued with street festivities, a dinner hosted by Judge Ebenezer Walden at the Eagle Tavern, and another party at the Mansion House. The day ended with a grand ball held at the Eagle. Undoubtedly there was as much partying aboard the *Seneca Chief*, now leading the flotilla down the canal. But the flotilla managed to make it to New York in 10 days, receiving a national salute as it arrived at the Battery at 9:00 in the morning on November 4.

But the ceremonies were not over yet. After reaching New York, the *Seneca Chief* turned around and came back to Buffalo loaded with passengers, merchandise, and a kegful of water from the Atlantic. On November 25 the *Seneca Chief* was towed a short distance out of the harbor at Buffalo and, as artillery again fired a salute, Samuel Wilkeson poured the salt water of the Atlantic into the fresh waters of Lake Erie.

Now open all the way, the Erie Canal—"Clinton's Ditch"—was only four feet deep. But that was deep enough to open up an entire nation. And Buffalo, at the canal's western end, stood on the brink of a whole new future as the jumping-off place into America's suddenly accessible interior.

Facing page
This 19th-century view of the Niagara River shows the relation of Buffalo and Black Rock to the river and to Lakes Erie and Ontario. (BECHS)

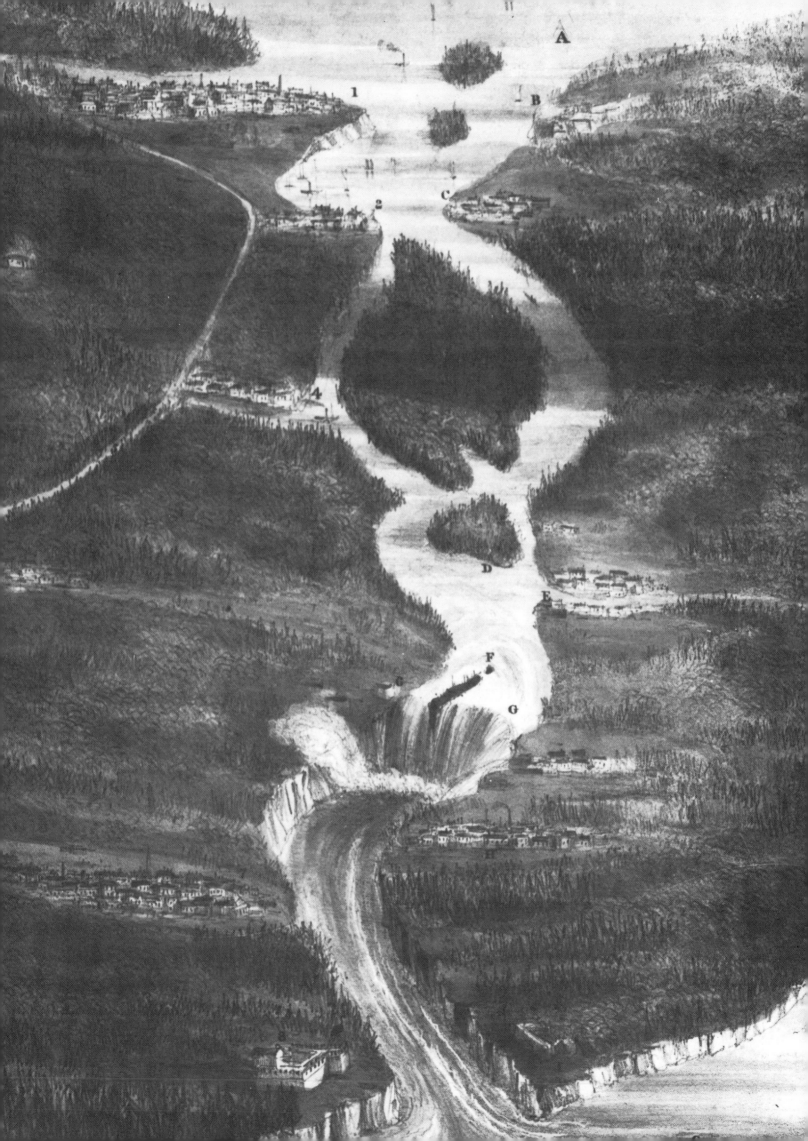

CHAPTER III

A BURGEONING CITY

One 19th-century Buffalonian, wise in the ways of public oratory, touchingly saluted the Erie Canal as "the Good Mother who gave us birth and nursed us through our infancy." His turn of phrase guaranteed him a round of applause. And those who heard it, on the city's 50th birthday, knew that every word of it was true.

The opening of the canal had opened the floodgates in Buffalo. An endless parade of canal boats choked the length and breadth of the narrow, shallow waterway. And the decks of the barges and packet boats were jammed with adventurous Yankees and tens of thousands of immigrants irresistibly drawn to the flame of exciting new frontiers in the Midwest and the West.

Buffalo almost overnight became the greatest inland port of immigration in the country. For the next 15 years after the canal was opened, Buffalo was the funnel through which flowed the multitudes on their way to open up the West. And along with people, the canal boats brought the artifacts of civilization previously denied to Buffalonians, including the first three pianofortes which went on sale at James Sheppard's new Main Street music store.

By the time the westward tide of humanity finally began to slow, the pioneers who had gone west were sending back their crops of grain. The flow of traffic then turned from west to

Facing page
Upon conducting a census in Buffalo in 1825, L.P. Crary found there to be 2,412 inhabitants in the area. This Crary map, which appeared in Buffalo's first city directory, was not published, however, until 1828. Crary had never worked on a venture of this sort and found it to be a "perplexing business" that required many hours of work to complete. (BECHS)

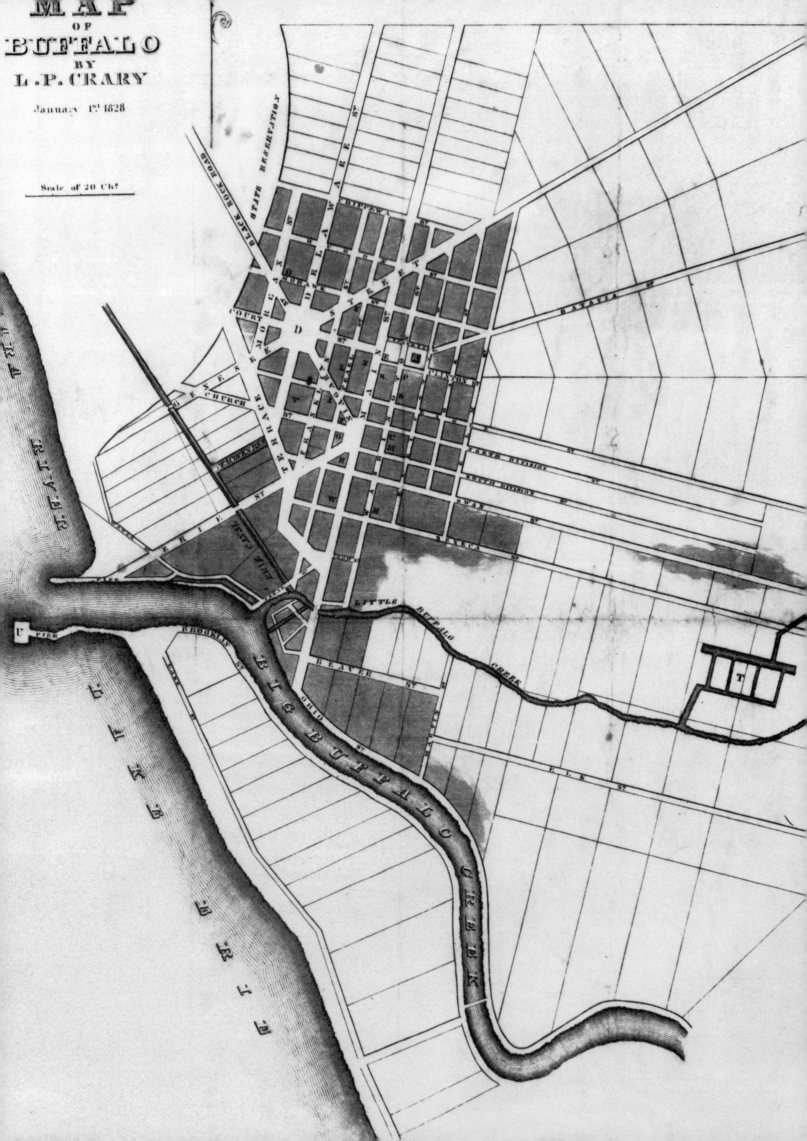

J. D. SHEPPARD,

KEEPS constantly on hand, a complete supply of all all kinds of

𝕸usic, 𝕸usical 𝕴nstruments, &c.

Piano Fortes tuned and to hire, second hand ones taken in exchange for new. Bands and Musical Societies supplied on the most liberal terms.

FANCY GOODS AND TOYS,

a very large assortment. Also, a good supply of genuine

Drugs & Medicines, Perfumery, &c.

a few doors south of the Eagle Tavern, Main st.
Buffalo, August, 1832.

east. The canal became the busiest single wheat-carrying artery of transportation in the nation, and Buffalo the busiest grain-handling port in the world.

Almost from opening day on the canal, the waterfront in Buffalo was noisily, colorfully, and wickedly crowded with newly arrived Yankees and immigrants and the usual contingent of camp followers. Some came to stay and get a piece of the action in a burgeoning Buffalo. Most only paused awhile before moving on to Ohio, Illinois, Michigan, and points west.

Milling about the wharves and nearby streets with the new arrivals were merchants and dockhands, sailors and ship captains, travelers rich and poor, and confidence men who meant to prey upon them all. Bela Coe's and Benjamin Rathbun's stagecoaches added to the bedlam, rumbling to and from the docks with their horns "crowing like chanticleers."

Inns, taverns, and all manner of new businesses were opened to accommodate the throngs. Buffalo instantly emerged from its small-town cocoon and took on the trappings of a city, in fact if not yet in name.

By 1829 Buffalo rated a branch of Nicholas Biddle's United States Bank. By 1830 the time had come for a fire and marine insurance company. Lawyer Ebenezer Walden, who had dab-

Above
This advertisement for Sheppard's musical instruments and other goods appeared in the 1832 Buffalo City Directory. (BECHS)

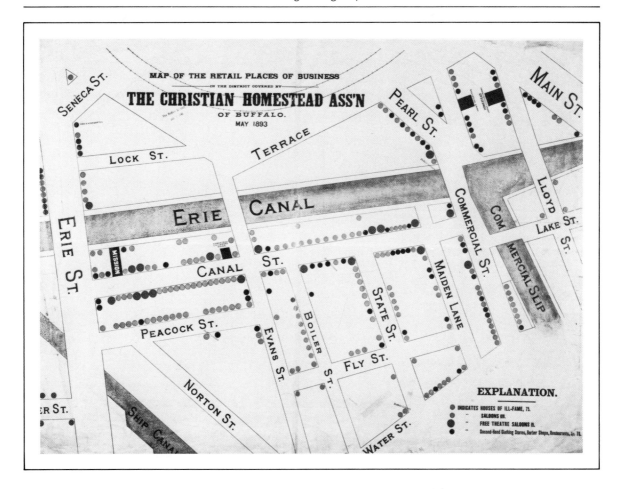

bled profitably in real estate as he waited in the wings for the village to come of age, was the insurance company's president and a director of the United States Bank.

In 1831 a new Bank of Buffalo opened its doors. One of its sponsors and its cashier was Hiram Pratt, son of Samuel Pratt, who had been one of the first to respond to the Holland Land Company's bid for homesteaders. Hiram Pratt, too, opened one of the village's first flour mills.

A sure sign that the town was growing up was the Jubilee Water Works, organized to deliver water through miles of log pipe from the Jubilee Springs out Delaware Avenue just beyond Ferry Street. Jubilee put the town's one-man public utility out of business. For as long as anyone could remember, "Water John" Kuecherer had gone about the streets with a hogshead mounted on a horse-drawn cart, peddling Lake Erie water to housewives who were without wells in their backyards. When Jubilee came into the picture, Water John bowed to progress and retired.

The village, bursting at the seams, was a curious mixture of civility and a total lack of civility. Occasional pockets of elegance, suited to the tastes of the new rich, were surrounded by abysmal inelegance. Nothing was so old yet that it needed to be torn down in the name of

Above
Buffalo's Erie Canal achieved a spicy reputation and attracted a medley of characters. In this Map of the Retail Places of Business, *prepared by the Christian Homestead Association in 1893, note the explanatory key in the lower right corner which shows where the saloons and houses of ill-fame were located. Courtesy, Rare Book Room, Buffalo and Erie County Public Library.*

urban renewal, and new buildings, functional but in good taste, were fast filling up the empty spaces.

New homes were being built, and by the early 1830s as many as 20 of them could be regarded as pretentious and architecturally stylish homes. Picket fences in the front were not so much to prettify them as to exclude the innumerable pigs and cows that roamed the streets as they pleased.

Paved streets were a luxury not yet known to the village, paving being limited to a few hundred feet of Main Street. One newcomer in the 1830s was shocked to find that while Main Street was every bit as wide as Joseph Ellicott had laid it out, most of it was rather deeper than Ellicott had in mind. The mud, at certain seasons of the year, seemed to have no bottom at all.

Sidewalks were nearly as rare as paved streets. Flickering oil lamps provided only the most meager illumination of Main Street after dark. Delaware Avenue, except for one lone estate, was mostly lumberyards and soap factories. Mohawk at Delaware was so treacherously mucky that teams and their wagons sometimes sank nearly out of sight.

The Erie Canal, ending on a waterfront that was as repulsive in odor as in appearance,

Above
Built in 1830, the Jubilee Water Works supplied water to Buffalo and Black Rock until the 1890s, when a system was developed to use Lake Erie water. (BECHS)

was the solid base on which the village's economy was taking root with remarkable ease and speed. But the solidly rooted growth potential was not enough for some. The heady prospects of the canal were so intoxicating as to goad the impatient villagers into the wildest kind of unrestrained speculation. Conservatively or speculatively, fortunes were being made.

The moneymakers dressed the part, carrying gold-headed walking sticks and attiring themselves in gilt-buttoned dresscoats, ruffled shirts, and flowing white cravats as everyday streetwear. Mingling with them on the village streets were immigrants who had not yet discarded their ethnic costumes and moccasined Indians who wrapped themselves in blankets to cover their nakedness.

Though hardly anyone yet lived above Mohawk Street, the boundaries of the village in terms of future growth were being pushed beyond what Ellicott's original street plan had provided. The village leadership, showing its optimism, in 1832 fixed North Street as the northern boundary—even though North Street, then called the Guide Board Road and hidden by groves of chestnuts, was so remote from the rest of the town that it was known, no doubt appropriately, as Lovers' Lane.

Above
Until the Jubilee Water Works was organized in the early 1800s, John Keucherer had a unique business going, whereby he went about the streets of Buffalo with a large barrel mounted on a horsedrawn cart, peddling Lake Erie water to housewives without wells in their backyards. For many years Keucherer was known simply as "Water John." (BECHS)

The census of 1830 put Buffalo's population at 8,680, up from 2,412 when the canal was opened five years before. By autumn of the following year, the number of citizens had passed the 10,000 mark, and the outlook for further growth was staggering. Flexing their muscles, even the most levelheaded Buffalonians began to think of themselves as deserving of something more sophisticated than village status.

In December 1831 a select committee of 18 citizens was appointed to draw up a new charter more suitable to a growing urban center, or to drastically amend the old one. Among the committee members were Samuel Wilkeson, Charles Townsend, Bela Coe, Pierre Barker, William Ketchum, George Webster, and lawyers Millard Fillmore, Joseph Clary, Ebenezer Walden, Henry White, Horatio Shumway, Dyre Tillinghast, and James Stryker.

The committee's decision was to draft a new charter that redefined the village as a corporation to be known as the city of Buffalo—a rare and daring form of municipal government at the time. Buffalo's incorporation as a city and its new charter were approved by the New York State Assembly on April 4, by the New York State Senate on April 18, and by Governor Enos T. Throop on April 20, 1832.

Committeeman Joseph Clary was Millard Fillmore's law partner at the time. He also was the reigning chairman of the village board of trustees, a position that gave him special clout in composing a city charter that reflected not only his own philosophy but his law partner's rigid views on correct social behavior.

Fillmore was a stout defender of decorum and dignity in public places. He once rebuked two of his young law clerks after he and Mrs. Fillmore, riding in their carriage, caught sight of the two clerks walking so fast on an evening stroll that they appeared to be engaged in a foot race and to be wagering on the outcome. At the office the next morning, Fillmore fired off memos of stern reprimand to the offending clerks.

Reflecting the influence of Fillmore and Clary, the new city charter encouraged the common council to prohibit "the rolling of hoops, playing at ball or flying of kites," if the pursuit of such amusements annoyed pedestrians or frightened horses. It banned "the ringing of bells and the blowing of horns and bugles." It spoke out strongly against "horse racing and immoderate riding or driving in the streets," and it took equally strong exception to "the running at large of cattle, horses, swine, sheep, goats and geese."

Not unexpectedly, the charter also empowered the council to "suppress and restrain houses of ill-fame, billiard tables and nine- or ten-pin alleys." All of these restraints, if not ac-

Facing page, top
The elegant Wilkeson home, built in 1824, once stood at Niagara Square. In 1915 the house was razed. Buffalo City Hall was later built on the site. (BECHS)

Facing page, bottom
The wealthier male residents of Buffalo wore silk top hats and carried gold-headed walking sticks. The top hat shown here was made locally by Dunlop and Company and sold at Wippert's of Buffalo. (BECHS)

tually dictated by Fillmore, would have received his enthusiastic endorsement. The citizens of the city must have had moments when they wondered if they hadn't been better off as simple, carefree villagers.

The charter, in addition to laying the ground rules for proper social conduct, authorized the common council to raise $8,000 a year through taxes to defray the expenses of lighting the streets, supporting a night watch, maintaining streets and bridges, and paying the stipends of the official municipal family.

The common council consisted of 10 elected aldermen—two from each of five wards—plus a mayor appointed by them. The council bore the responsibility of appointing a number of other officials, including a clerk, a treasurer, police constables, "common criers," and "scavengers."

Voting privileges in the city were extended to "colored" males so long as they could produce evidence of $250 in net worth, a requirement not demanded of white males. Buffalo's first city directory, published in the year the city was incorporated, treated "colored people" separately. A total of 68 black males were listed, and these and their families were sufficient to warrant the founding of the first black church (a predecessor of the Bethel African Methodist Episcopal Church) in 1831 and the Michigan Avenue Baptist Church in 1836. Slavery had been outlawed in New York State for only five years at the time of Buffalo's incorporation as a city.

Buffalo's first common council, organizing the new city on May 28, 1832, showed rare good judgment in appointing Dr. Ebenezer Johnson as its first mayor. Dr. Johnson was the richest man in town, and he was not at all offended that the charter fixed his salary at $250 a year. Though he was wealthy enough to dismiss the salary as no more than a token honorarium, he was not the kind to have turned it down.

The good doctor was a hard-nosed businessman, so successful in the practice of business that he had long since abandoned the practice of medicine. Real estate was one of his specialties, but he also advertised himself in the first city directory as a buyer of gold. One of his contemporaries characterized him as a strict law-and-order man who religiously obeyed all the laws "except the law against usury." He was also described as "pleasing in countenance, commanding in appearance and decided in his conclusions."

Dr. Johnson owned the whole of the west side of Delaware Avenue between Chippewa and Tupper streets. His 25-acre estate included not only a grand house but a park and a pond

Above
In 1832 the New York State Assembly, State Senate, and Governor E.R. Throop approved the incorporation of the City of Buffalo along with the new city charter. (BECHS)

for fishing, one of his favorite pastimes. A porter's lodge guarded the entrance to the doctor's little empire.

On one Fourth of July when he was mayor, Dr. Johnson stationed himself at Main and Niagara streets to take personal command in enforcing a councilmanic ban on fireworks. When he sighted "fireballs" in the direction of the Mansion House on Exchange Street, the mayor hopped into his carriage and raced down Main Street in a manner that must have violated the council's own rules against immoderate driving. By the time he got to the Mansion House, the miscreants had long since departed and, indeed, were setting off their fireballs back up Main Street where the mayor only recently had been. The mayor raced back up Main Street but, again finding no trace of his tormentors, gave up his role as custodian of the law and went home.

Having a physician, practicing or not, as mayor did no good at all when the city, scarcely a month after it was organized, was struck by an epidemic of cholera that "darted like forked lightning up one street and down another in almost every quarter of the city." The citizens dropped like flies. In July and August of 1832, there were 184 cholera cases, 80 of them abruptly fatal. Henry White, one of the lawyers who helped incorporate the city, went home in good health after an afternoon with an out-of-town client at the Mansion House, and by the next morning he was dead of the dread disease.

The state of the art in epidemiology or even simple medicine was far from adequate to cope with the cholera epidemic of 1832. The coffin makers and the grave diggers had more to do than the nearly helpless physicians. Dr. Cyrenius Chapin did complain, though, of the paperwork that engulfed him as the spread of the disease reached epidemic proportions.

The mayor responded to his first municipal crisis by appointing a board of health to do what it could. On the board, in addition to the mayor himself, were a lawyer, a cattle raiser, and a bookseller. They set up a makeshift hospital "in the hollow between Niagara and Prospect," but corpses were carried out of it daily, including those of one chief nurse after another recruited to staff it.

The citizens were left to shift pretty much for themselves, and this they did in their own way. Even the most rabid teetotalers took to diluting their drinking water with strong brandy. The more practiced tipplers had a once-in-a-lifetime excuse for what one member of the board of health described as "a prolonged saturnalia of bibulous indulgence." All but the most reckless cut their diets to half rations in the hope of lengthening their odds against biting into tainted food.

Above
Millard Fillmore owned this carriage which was constructed in 1854. (BECHS)

The weather that summer was hot and wet, conditions that did nothing to deter the spread of cholera. In its own good time, the disease finally ran its course when cooler autumn weather set in. And the city, after that tragic digression, promptly resumed the more pleasant business of growing by leaps and bounds.

Frightening as the cholera fatalities had been, they scarcely dented the city's population growth. Between 1832 and 1835, the number of Buffalonians rose by 50 percent—from 10,000 to 15,000—and the city was well on its way to a head count of 18,213 by the end of the decade. Incorporating as a city provided more than a psychological stimulus. Real and visible signs of a village growing into a city were everywhere.

On January 1, 1835, Buffalo got its first daily newspaper, the *Commercial Advertiser*, which began publication as a daily version of what had been the weekly *Buffalo Patriot*, a descendant of the old *Buffalo Gazette* that dated back to 1811.

Dr. Thomas M. Foote, a physician turned editor, gave the *Commercial Advertiser* its character and style, sharing or mirroring Fillmore's views as an advocate of Whig political sentiments which most Buffalonians seemed to prefer as long as the Whig Party lasted. The *Commercial Advertiser*, which later shortened its name to the *Commercial*, was a force to be reckoned with in Buffalo journalism until 1923.

In the mid-1830s, with its economy under a full head of steam and unrealistically expanded by speculative excesses, Buffalo got two more banks. The Commercial Bank opened in 1834, the City Bank in 1836.

In 1836 Buffalo's first railroad was built. It went only as far as Niagara Falls, but it was the forerunner of a transportation system that eventually would make Buffalo second only to Chicago as the nation's busiest railroad center. Black Rock's Peter Porter was the force behind the Buffalo-Niagara Falls railroad. While it was being built, a favorite pastime of Buffalonians was to walk down the line and watch the track being laid, trying to imagine what in the world the tracks would look like with a train on them.

In the same year the railroad was built, Buffalo got a new theater. The press hailed the new Eagle Street Theatre as the city's "grandest building, grand enough for a metropolis," and indeed it was.

The Eagle served a dual purpose in the city of 16,000, accommodating not only theatrical

Above
Ebenezer Johnson, Buffalo's first mayor, became one of the wealthiest men in Buffalo. Though a doctor by profession, Johnson found that his business ventures were so successful, he decided to give up his medical practice. Courtesy, Buffalo Savings Bank-Roy Nagle Collection. (BECHS)

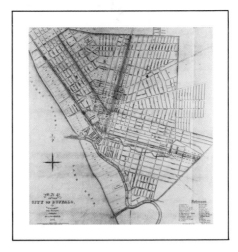

performances but the fashionable balls of Buffalo's social elite. Well-heeled patrons owned their own boxes, which they draped in blue damask and comfortably furnished with upholstered sofas and chairs.

The theater season was in the summer months, when canal and lake were fully navigable and their torrent of business filled the city's streets with pleasure seekers. Theater gave way to the gavotte in the winter months, when the busy navigation season had ended and the social season for the seasonally idled rich was in full swing.

Shakespeare played to full houses during the theater season at the Eagle. But the fare was varied. The theater had a couple of enterprising, audience-wise managers who, after bringing in *Othello* for a week's run, outrageously burlesqued it the following week with *Othello, the Noblest Nigger of Dem All*, and then kept the theatrical pot boiling by staging something as absurdly monstrous and strictly local as *The Three Thieves of Tonawanda*.

Buffalonians loved drama, and if they didn't get it on the stage, they could always find it in the courtroom. Buffalo from its earliest days had a corps of colorful lawyers, and Buffalonians tended to rate their favorites on the basis of their eloquence before a jury and their flair for the dramatic. Word that a lawyer such as George P. Barker or Henry K. Smith was about to appear in court was a guarantee of standing room only in the courtroom.

Barker as a sideline commanded the city militia with the title of general, and he was possessed of a patriotic fervor that was second to none. The Fourth of July traditionally was his day to whoop it up with his city guards in the park in front of the courthouse. The courthouse, meanwhile, was Judge Horatio Stow's domain, and Stow was as zealous in the pursuit of his courtroom responsibilities as Barker was in demonstrating his patriotism. The judge refused to interrupt his court even for the observance of Independence Day.

On one Fourth of July when Barker's city troops and the regimental brass band became so boisterous that they interfered with Judge Stow's court proceedings, the judge sent out a clerk with an order that Barker and his command should move on. Barker, outraged, sent back the message, "General Barker's compliments to Judge Stow and tell him to go to hell." Only Barker's immense popularity with the populace and the intervention of mutual friends at the bar stayed a contempt citation.

By the 1830s and for the rest of the century, the lawyers came as close as any group in Buffalo to constituting an aristocracy. Movers and shakers in the growing city included such big guns in the practice of law as Millard Fillmore, Stephen Austin, Benjamin Austin, Major

Above
Drawn in 1836, the year Buffalo's first railroad was built, this map illustrates the enlarged boundaries of the city in contrast to the boundaries of the village as shown on earlier maps of Buffalo. (BECHS)

Andrews (Buffalo's second mayor), William Moseley, Heman B. Potter, Ebenezer Walden, Philander Bennett, Albert Tracy, Roswell Chapin, George Babcock, Dyre Tillinghast, Solomon Haven, Nathan K. Hall, Orasmus Holmes Marshall, Elbridge Spaulding, and Thomas C. Love.

Many of them found the law to be a stepping stone to political office as well as to positions of wealth and power in the banks, in manufacturing, and later in the railroads. Practiced in the art of persuasion as a result of their courtroom experience, the lawyers quickly learned that they could be equally persuasive when they hit the campaign trail. The voters responded by rather consistently electing them to public office.

None had a more enviable track record in demonstrating the voters' preference for lawyers than did Millard Fillmore, Nathan Hall, and Solomon Haven. These three got together as law partners in 1836. Their law firm, Fillmore, Hall & Haven, was one of the first prestigious law firms in Buffalo, with a reputation and clientele that extended well beyond the boundaries of Western New York and indeed of New York State itself.

Fillmore, Hall, and Haven not only were partners in the practice of law; they were political cronies who rose to high political office on one another's coattails. All three served in the United States Congress. Fillmore and Hall were elected to the New York State Assembly. Haven was mayor of Buffalo in 1846. Fillmore went to Washington as Vice President of the United States and ascended to the Presidency when General Zachary Taylor died midway through his term.

When Fillmore became President, he brought Nathan Hall into his Cabinet as postmaster general. Haven was already in Washington as a member of Congress. Buffalonians, bursting with civic pride, jokingly observed that the Fillmore, Hall & Haven sign ought to have been hanging on the White House.

The three Buffalo lawyer pals saw eye to eye politically as Whigs. They lived within a stone's throw of each other in Buffalo—Fillmore and Hall in neighboring homes on Franklin Street north of Mohawk, and Haven around the corner from Franklin on Genesee Street. They socialized together. They worshiped in the same Unitarian Church on Franklin Street.

The neighborliness and cronyism of Fillmore, Hall, and Haven followed them even to the grave. When they died, they were buried in adjoining family plots in Buffalo's Forest Lawn Cemetery. Incredibly enough, and too late to be accused of illegal advertising, they were buried in the precise order of their old law firm's name—Fillmore on the left, Hall in the middle, and Haven on the right.

Above
Nathan Hall was elected to the New York State Assembly and also served in the United States Congress. (BECHS)

Facing page, top
On January 30, 1836, Erie County District Attorney George P. Barker warned non-Indian residents of the area not to trespass on the lands belonging to the Seneca Indians. (BECHS)

Facing page, right
Dean and M'Kinney's Eagle Street Theatre, which opened in 1835, offered not only theatrical fare, but also provided a suitable setting for fashionable social events. According to this theater program, the building would "vie with any theatre in America" in terms of "permanence of materials, classic elegance of structure, and convenience of accommodation." (BECHS)

Facing page, bottom
Millard Fillmore joined Nathan Hall and Solomon Haven in a law partnership in 1836. The firm was one of the first prestigious law firms in Buffalo. This portrait of Fillmore, who went on to become the 13th President of the United States, was painted by Augustus Rockwell circa 1871. (BECHS)

NOTICE.

To all whom it may concern:

THE undersigned having repeatedly received complaints that persons, not being Indians, are daily committing trespasses upon the lands belonging to the Seneca Tribe of Indians, and known as the Cattaraugus Reservation, in contempt of the laws of this State—I do therefore hereby give notice, that it is my intention to put the law in force indiscriminately, against all, as well those who are trespassing under the color of title from some Indian, as those who do not pretend to have title. And I further caution all persons from leasing from Indians any lands, or buying any wood or timber, standing or lying upon the Indian lands, as such leases and contracts are, by the Statute, utterly void, and no defence to an indictment for a trespass on said lands.

GEO. P. BARKER,

District Attorney for Erie County.

EAGLE STREET THEATRE.

DEAN & M'KINNEY,

Respectfully announce to the citizens of Buffalo that, through the taste and enterprise of Mr. ALBERT BRISBANE, they are enabled to open a building, which for permanence of materials, classic elegance of structure and convenience of accommodation, will vie with any Theatre in America. On their own parts, they flatter themselves that every thing in the way of Scenery, Machinery, Dresses and Decorations, will correspond with the splendor of the house, as they have spared neither pains nor expense in procuring *Artists, Machinists and materials* for that purpose. And if, by constant exertions in their profession, as managers and actors—by keeping a *sterling stock company, competent musicians, attentive and civil officers,* and procuring all the talent and novelty within their power, they succeed in establishing the drama upon a respectable footing in Buffalo, they will feel happy in the conviction that they have accomplished their object and redeemed the pledge made when they first resolved to identify their success with the prosperity of Buffalo.

The Managers have the pleasure of introducing

Mrs. M'Clure

to a Buffalo audience. Her histrionic excellence is too well known to need comment. She will play for the present for five consecutive nights, and occasionally during the season.

The stock Company consists of

MR. M'KINNEY, STAGE MANAGER.

MR. COLLINS, PROMPTER.

MR. DEAN,	MR. FREEMONT,
" M'CLURE,	" MARSH,
" TROWBRIDGE,	" SPRAGUE,
" MARBLE,	" MERRYFIELD.
" WARREN,	
" WALTON,	MRS. TROWBRIDGE,
" CHILDS,	" DEAN,
" F. W. M'KINNEY,	" F. BROWN,
" LENNOX,	" LENNOX,
" FORREST,	MISS WARREN.

S. B. DEAN, Treasurer and Engineer of Gas Establishment.
MR. REED, 2d Engineer of Gas Establishment.
DUKE WHITE AND ALLEN SMITH, Artists.
THOMAS DAINES, Stage Carpenter and Machinist.
MR. FARNHAM, Property Maker,
MR. J. WARREN, Costumer.

ORCHESTRA.

Mr. LE BRUN, Leader.

MR. COOKE, Sen. 2d Violin.	MR. PAPSONS, Horn.
" COOKE, Jr. Trombone.	" BARON, 1st Violoncello.
" KINGSLAND, Flute.	" JOHNSON, 2d do.
" COOPER, Clarinet.	" SAMO, Double Bass.
" DARLING, Viola.	

MONDAY EVENING, JULY 20, 1835.

The evenings entertainments will commence with the recitation by

MR. D. D. M'KINNEY,

OF THE

Prize Address,

Written by AMOS DANN, Esq. of Avon Springs.

MEDLEY OVERTURE,

By the Orchestra, composed expressly for the occasion.

After which J. S. KNOWLES' celebrated Play, entitled

HUNCHBACK.

JULIA,		MRS. M'CLURE,	
MASTER WALTER,		MR. M'KINNEY,	
SIR THOMAS CLIFFORD,		WALTON,	
Modus,	Mr. Lennox,	Thomas,	Mr. F. W. M'Kinney
Fathom,	" Marble,	Lord Tousel,	" Forrest,
Master Milford,	" Marsh,	Simpson,	" Sprague,
Master Heartwell,	" Trowbridge,	Waiter,	" Merryfield,
Gaylove,	" Warren,		
Stephen,	" Childs,	Helen,	Miss Warren.

After the play Mrs. Trowbridge will sing

"SMART YOUNG BACHELORS."

Overture, by the Orchestra, of

"Italiano in Algieri."

To conclude with Shakspeare's admired and laughable Petit Comedy of

Katharine & Petruchio.

KATHARINE,		MRS. M'CLURE,	
PETRUCHIO,		MR. M'KINNEY,	
Baptista,	Mr. Trowbridge,	Grumio,	Mr. Forrest,
Hortensio,	" Marsh,	Nathaniel,	" Merryfield,
Biondello,	" M'Clure,	Sugarsop,	" Sprague,
Pedro,	" F. W. M'Kinney		
Music Master,	" Warren,	Bianca,	Mrs. Lennox,
Tailor,	" Marble,	Curtis,	" Dean.

2d PRIZE ADDRESS, written by Mr. Gates of this city to be delivered on Tuesday.

Miss PHILLIPS is engaged and will appear shortly.

In preparation the Melo-Dramas of the

WATER WITCH & MAZEPPA.

And, as befits the aristocratic nature of the legal profession in their time, their neighbors on the same grassy knoll in Forest Lawn include such of their legal contemporaries as William Moseley, Heman Potter, Thomas Love, and George Babcock. The strange cemetery setting resembles nothing so much as a ghostly meeting of a 19th-century bar association.

Fillmore, Hall, and Haven, and indeed most lawyers, were in an upper class that emerged in Buffalo's social structure in the 1830s and was astonishingly large in numbers, considering the size and the rough-and-tumble character of the city.

For eight months of the year, Buffalonians worked their collective fingers to the bone. The cleverest among them lined their pockets with the riches that dripped from the Erie Canal and the wharves of the harbor. When winter closed the canal and ice choked Lake Erie, those who had been pocketing the proceeds of the business the navigation season brought had no choice but to relax, socialize, and thoroughly enjoy themselves.

They partied. They danced at elegant balls at the American Hotel and the Eagle Theatre. They skated on the nearby frozen waterways. They went off on long rides in brilliantly painted sleighs, some of them scarlet with yellow dashboards and golden swans on either side.

They entertained extravagantly and impeccably in their splendid homes, built with entertaining in mind. Mansions really, their homes had spacious, high-ceilinged rooms with wide folding doors that could be quickly opened to accommodate large numbers of guests. It was not uncommon for a hostess to write 300 to 400 invitations to a single house party.

The house guests drank, and drank the best, but anything resembling drunkenness was regarded as an insult to the host. Champagne, Madeira, sherry, and Bordeaux wines were among their favorites, as was pure cognac for a stronger drink. Whiskey may have been suitable to start the digging of the Erie Canal, but it was frowned upon at house parties as a coarse and vulgar drink. New England rum and gin were popular. So was imported London porter, which the men mixed with ale and called 'alf and 'alf.

It was hard to believe that only a few blocks from all this socially correct gentility was Buffalo's notorious Canal Street. Somebody once called it "the wickedest street in the world." An English visitor, after he was back home, wrote of it as "a corrupt and morally melancholy" place. Its reputation as "the wickedest" of all may have been an exaggeration, but it wasn't much of an exaggeration. The tight little neighborhood of sin, spawned by the Erie Canal, was

in the select company of such infamous seamen's playpens as Shanghai, Calcutta, and the Barbary Coast.

Not even the Danube has inspired more song and prose than did the Erie Canal, but the canal's was more lusty than romantic. One of the popular ballads familiar to Erie Canalers had as its refrain:

> Oh, the E-ri-e is a-risin'
> And the gin is a-gettin' low,
> And I scarcely think we'll get a drink
> 'Til we get to Buffalo,
> 'Til we get to Buffalo.

There was more truth than poetry in that ballad. Every canaler knew that when he sang of getting to Buffalo, what he really meant was setting foot on Canal Street, where the gin flowed freely.

Canal Street, "two tough and torrid blocks of trouble," paralleled the Erie Canal near its end, between Erie and Commercial streets. Actually, it was more than just a street. It was a neighborhood bounded roughly by Main Street, the Terrace, Erie Street, and the harbor. Canal Street was its main thoroughfare, but the overflow spilled over into Maiden Lane and Erie, Fly, Peacock, Le Couteulx, Hanover, and Water streets.

At its best, or worst, the district had 93 saloons, 15 dancing halls, and bordellos too numerous to count. It was a common meeting ground for brawling lake sailors and Erie Canalers, who never got along, and for the girls discreetly referred to by the more genteel up-towners as "soiled doves," and known to Canal Streeters by such flattering names as Pug Nose Cora, Frosty Face Emma, Deadly Dora, and Soapy Kate.

Canal Street, every day of the year, began to come alive at dusk and was just beginning to wind down at dawn. The more unscrupulous of the saloonkeepers thought nothing of drugging a customer's drink, relieving him of whatever valuables he had on his person, and dumping him down a trapdoor to sink or swim in the murky waters of the canal. The police grew accustomed to finding bodies floating in the canal at daybreak.

But Canal Street was not all bad. One of its illustrious contributions to 19th-century American culture was the minstrel show. Other cities no doubt have a more legitimate claim to having originated the minstrel show, but it was on Canal Street in Buffalo that these black-face musical comedies were fine-tuned to an entertainment art form.

Above
Solomon Haven, the third partner of the Fillmore, Hall, & Haven law firm, became the mayor of Buffalo in 1846 and later served in the United States Congress. (BECHS)

POSITIVELY THE LAST NIGHT
FAREWELL CONCERT
AMERICAN HOTEL.
THIS EVENING,
Thursday, Sept. 23d.
CHRISTY'S
Original and well known Band of
MINSTRELS

The man who did it was Ned Christy. Edwin P. Christy came from Philadelphia to Canal Street in 1839 and found ready employment at a time when the least degrading of the cabarets were competing for entertainers. Christy played banjo and did sleight of hand and a song-and-dance routine, all in blackface. Mrs. Harrington's Dance Hall hired him.

Christy was not a great vocalist, but his plaintive singing could bring tears to the eyes, even the bloodshot eyes on Canal Street. His act was the nucleus of what became Christy's Minstrels. Their still-remembered hit song was "Buffalo Gals":

> Buffalo Gals, can't you come out tonight?
> Can't you come out tonight?
> Can't you come out tonight?
> Buffalo Gals, can't you come out tonight?
> And dance by de light ob de moon?

Thanks to Christy, the Canal Street regulars may well have been the first to hear Stephen Foster's "Oh, Susanna!" Christy somehow got his hands on a copy of it—and used it—four years before it was copyrighted and published. For a long time, Christy also sang and took credit for composing Foster's "Old Folks at Home." He bought it from Foster for $50, with the right to put his own name on it.

The Christy Minstrels wowed 'em on Canal Street. Word inevitably leaked out to the more respectable uptowners, who were dying to catch the show but wouldn't have been seen on Canal Street even for a replay of the Resurrection. To their rescue came those show-business wizards who managed the Eagle Street Theatre. Christy's Minstrels were booked into the highly proper Eagle, where audience enthusiasm was every bit as unrestrained as it had been on Canal Street.

Christy and his Minstrels moved on to the big time, landing in New York and on Broadway where, except for a trip abroad and a sellout season in London, they became a long-running institution.

But Canal Street went on long after Christy left it, and it went on well through the century. It eventually died out not because any 19th-century morality cleaned it up but because decent people, most of them newly arrived Italian immigrants, moved into it and by moving in cleansed the wound.

Above
Christy's Minstrels performed at the American Hotel in 1847. The group, which enjoyed enormous popularity in Buffalo, went on to entertain in New York and London. (BECHS)

The Canal Street district was a little world of its own. Outside its limited confines, the man who had the greatest physical impact on Buffalo in the 1830s was Benjamin Rathbun. Rathbun looked more like a clergyman than the master builder he was. Though he kept a low profile, never before or since has there been a builder in Buffalo who matched Rathbun's empirical accomplishments.

Most of Buffalo in the 1830s, in fact, could be said to have been Rathbun-built. In 1835 alone, he put up 99 buildings, 52 of them stores and 33 of them dwellings. He built the first American Hotel on the west side of Main Street below Court Street and in the same year put up the United States Hotel on the Terrace.

He built the jail. He built the four-story Webster Block that began at Main Street and Perry. He built the Darrow Block on Washington Street below Clinton. For Henry Sizer, he built a fine residence on the northwest corner of Niagara Square at Delaware Avenue that years later became the headquarters of Spencer Kellogg & Sons.

For the Unitarians, he built a church at Franklin Street and Eagle that still stands as the headquarters of Abstract Title—the lone remaining monument to the otherwise long-gone Rathbun empire.

To support his seemingly endless building program, Rathbun operated stone quarries, brick plants, and machine shops. But Rathbun was more than just a builder. He owned the prestigious Eagle Tavern. He had grocery stores and dry-goods establishments. He ran stagecoaches and horse-drawn omnibuses. He had his own private bank that issued bank notes over his signature.

But Rathbun, caught up in the speculative excesses that were rampant in the growing city, had moved too far too fast. Not only did he borrow beyond his very substantial means, but he borrowed on notes to which were forged the names of the most affluent Buffalonians. When the smoke of the scandal had cleared and the extent of the skulduggery was sorted out, it was found that Rathbun had a total of $1.5 million in forged notes.

Rathbun had not done the forging himself, but he was aware of it. His brother Lyman masterminded the forging; his nephew, Lyman Rathbun Howlett, was the master forger. Buffalonians, never dreaming that young Howlett was up to no good, knew him as a cute little fellow of 14 or 15 who rode a pony about the streets. Actually, he was so clever that he could execute a forgery under the very eyes of the bankers, and he was riding his pony on what

Above
Master builder Benjamin Rathbun had a great impact on Buffalo in the 1830s. Most of the city's buildings at this time, including the first American Hotel, the jail, and the four-story Webster Block, were constructed by him. Courtesy, Buffalo Savings Bank-Roy Nagle Collection. (BECHS)

turned out to have been his errands of mischief.

Years later, when Buffalonians were eagerly awaiting everything Charles Dickens wrote and *Oliver Twist* finally reached them, they would recognize the Artful Dodger as a devious lad who already had passed their way in the person of Lyman Rathbun Howlett.

By the time the Rathbun bubble burst, young Howlett and his Uncle Lyman were long gone. Benjamin Rathbun took the rap for all of them. While he was awaiting trial, he was incarcerated in the very jail he had built for Buffalo. Found guilty at a trial in Batavia, he was sent to Auburn Prison for five years. When he had served his time, Rathbun went into the hotel business in New York. Buffalonians still thought so highly of him that, to many of them, to stay at any hotel in New York other than Rathbun's was unthinkable.

Rathbun's downfall caused tremors in Buffalo's financial community. And it was devastating to the 2,500 or so employees whose families counted on Rathbun paychecks for the bread on their tables. His shattering collapse in 1836 ended those paychecks and gave Buffalo a head start on the financial panic that swept the country in 1837.

If there were any beneficiaries of those hard times, they were the youngsters of school age in Buffalo. Although school tuition charges were modest, the unaccustomed economic distress in the city caused school attendance to drop. Concerned adults moved with innovation to overhaul the system. Oliver G. Steele, who had made his living in the world of books, provided the academic stimulus and lawyer Nathan K. Hall did the legal work in setting up in Buffalo in 1838 and 1839 the first tax-supported, tuition-free public school system in New York State. Steele became the first school superintendent.

At about the same time, there was further evidence of maturity in the upstart city. As the decade of the 1830s began to wind down, the old Holland Land Company began to wind up its affairs. Its business finished, it closed its books, having netted a bit under $2 million on its investment of $600,000.

Facing page, top
In the 1830s, Benjamin Rathbun ran a stagecoach line. (BECHS)

Facing page, bottom
Benjamin Rathbun owned a private bank that issued bank notes with his signature. He had a hand in many establishments in Buffalo. (BECHS)

CHAPTER IV

THE FABULOUS FORTIES

Buffalo had too much going for it to be more than momentarily stunned by the economic reverses of 1836 and 1837. The rambunctious city was briefly down, but it was never out. It was its port that nursed the city back to health. And it was grain—first a trickle of it, and then a flood—that nourished the port. The grain elevator, which still delights students of architecture, was conceived in the port of Buffalo.

The first wheat cargoes were seen in Buffalo harbor in 1838. Lake ships brought the grain to Buffalo from the Midwest; canal barges moved it on to the East. By 1841, 2 million bushels a year were being unloaded on the waterfront. By the 1850s, grain was a 25-million-bushel-a-year business in Buffalo, and the peak was not yet even in sight. Buffalo became the busiest grain-transfer port in the country, and indeed in the world.

The man who made it all happen was Joseph Dart. When grain began showing up in Buffalo as a newfound cargo of riches, Irish shovelers were sent scrambling into the cargo holds of the incoming lake vessels to scoop it out. Irish stevedores carried the grain in barrels, on their backs, to nearby warehouses. The Irish help was cheap enough. But the system not only was backbreaking, it wasn't fast enough.

Dart revolutionized the system in 1842. He rigged up a series of buckets on a steam-

Facing page, top
This lithograph entitled View of Buffalo, N.Y. from the Old Light House *was made by E. Whitefield in 1847. (BECHS)*

Facing page, bottom
Miller's Livery offered "everything in the Livery Line," including sleighs they would rig out "to the Queen's taste." (BECHS)

VIEW OF BUFFALO, N.Y.

How can a party of young—or even old folks—enjoy an evening's recreation more pleasantly?

☞ If you contemplate getting up a Sleighride Party we will rig you out to the Queen's taste. We have several fine, large Sleighs, of different sizes. We are bound to suit you in the price, and we guarantee satisfaction.

C. F. MILLER'S LIVERY

297, 299 Michigan St., cor. Folsom,

Everything in the Livery Line.

BUFFALO, N. Y.

driven perpendicular belt. The moving belt reached down into the cargo holds and the buckets attached to it scooped up the grain, depositing it in dockside storage houses that came to be known as grain elevators. Dart could unload up to 2,000 bushels of grain an hour. But his fellow grain merchants took a dim view of Dart's mechanical elevator of grain, frowning at the cost.

"It won't do, Dart," one of them told him. "Irishmen's backs are the cheapest elevator ever built."

Dart proved them wrong. By 1855, there were 10 towering grain elevators on Buffalo's waterfront that could unload 22,400 bushels an hour and store more than 1.5 million bushels at one time.

Dart's elevator may have replaced the Irishman's back, but it did not replace the Irishman. Irish labor was plentiful, and the need for it grew rather than diminished as the port grew. The Irish had been the first immigrants to come to Buffalo in substantial numbers—the first of all being Patrick O'Rourke and his wife in 1815. The digging of the Erie Canal was the first big drawing card. The canal contractors advertised for Irish diggers in the Catholic press and in Irish newspapers, and Irish workers couldn't get here fast enough in response to the promised wages of $1.87 a day.

When the canal was finished, many of the Irish settled more permanently in Buffalo, gravitating to the waterfront where they found a ready market for their labor. Their numbers were swelled during the years of famine in Ireland that encouraged emigration, and by 1855 there were 10,000 of them in Buffalo. The waterfront and its businesses were their natural habitat, but later on when the railroads were built, the Irish would help build them.

Buffalo flourished as a grain port for 120 years, with an incredible 225 million bushels being funneled through its elevators in the peak years of the mid-1940s. The glory days in the grain trade ended in the late 1950s, when the newly built St. Lawrence Seaway drastically altered traditional shipping patterns—and altered them at Buffalo's expense.

The long-flourishing grain trade had begun at the moment when Buffalo most needed an economic shot in the arm. Grain did its part in energizing the city, but as it turned out, there was much more that would carry Buffalo to undreamed-of heights of prosperity. The 1840s also ushered in a new free-swinging entrepreneurial age that created powerful captains of in-

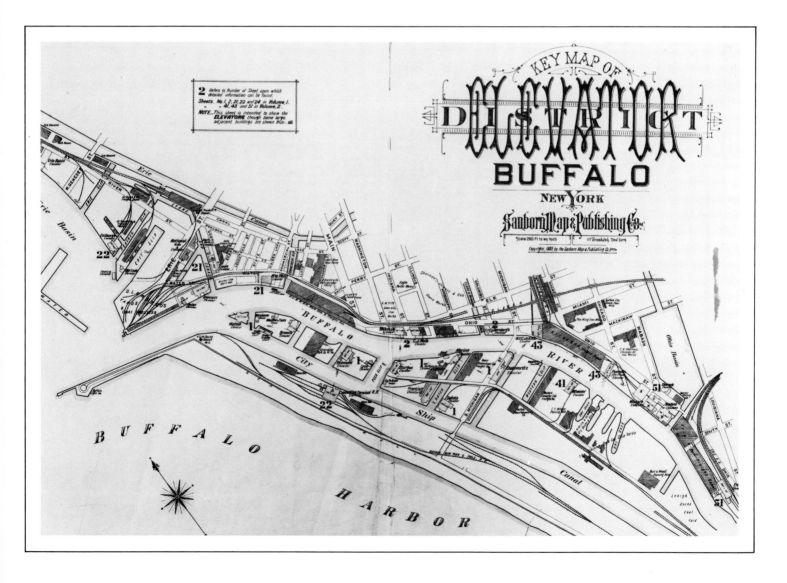

dustry and commerce, the likes of which had never been seen before. Their presence in great numbers meant that for Buffalo, there was no place to go but up.

Three Buffalo entrepreneurs typified the diversity of background from which ambitious young men could propel themselves into positions of wealth and influence: Pascal Paoli Pratt, William G. Fargo, and Jacob Frederick Schoellkopf. All three became millionaires a century and more before millionaires were a dime a dozen.

Pratt, a third-generation Buffalonian and already "old family" in Buffalo, was a veritable symbol of the White Anglo-Saxon Protestant Establishment of the 19th century. Fargo was the poor boy, working when he was 13 years old, who started from scratch and made it big as the Fargo in Wells, Fargo and the Pony Express and as a founder of the American Express Company. Schoellkopf was the young German immigrant who arrived with a few hundred dollars in his pocket and became "King Jacob," founding a family dynasty with almost legendary accomplishments in nearly everything related to capitalism, especially in electric power.

Pascal Pratt started with his brother as a hardware merchant in 1846, but he soon turned to manufacturing, collecting factories as others might collect stamps. Hardware, carriage ware, saddlery, foundries, and ironworking were his consuming interests. Pratt & Company

Above
Pascal P. Pratt began a career as a hard-ware merchant, but soon turned to manufacturing. Several businesses became linked with his name, including Pratt & Letchworth. (BECHS)

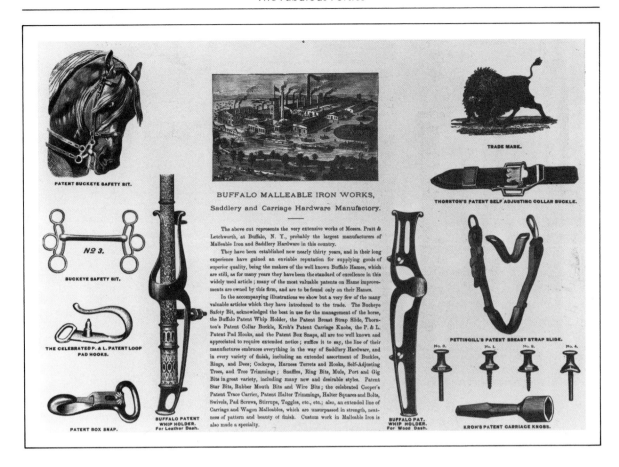

(forerunner of the present Beals, McCarthy & Rogers), Buffalo Malleable Iron Works, the Buffalo Steel Company, Buffalo Iron & Nail Works, and Pratt & Letchworth (still alive and well) were among the businesses with which his name was linked.

When there seemed no more worlds to conquer in the kinds of industry that pleased him, he said enough is enough. And, at the age of 64, he turned to banking. He was by then in a position to start at the top as president of the Manufacturers & Traders Bank, which he had helped found nearly 30 years before. He sat in the presidential chair for 16 years.

The multiplicity of his interests in industry and finance might suggest that he had little time for anything else. Not so. He sat on the Board of Parks Commissioners and was a ringleader in bringing in the great 19th-century landscape architect, Frederick Law Olmsted, to design the park system of nearly 1,000 acres that remains as a glorious monument to the aesthetic goals of 19th-century Buffalonians who were intent upon factoring things of beauty into their industrial city.

Fargo, a Pratt contemporary, came to Buffalo from central New York in 1843 as agent for an Albany-Buffalo express line. He was 25 years old and ready to reach for the stars. The following year, he helped organize a new express line that linked Buffalo with Cleveland and

Above
The Buffalo Malleable Iron Works produced saddlery and carriage hardware such as the Buckeye Safety Bit, Kroh's Patent Carriage Knobs, and Thornton's Patent Self Adjusting Collar Buckle. (BECHS)

Detroit and then with Chicago, Milwaukee, St. Louis, and Cincinnati.

By 1850 Fargo had sufficient stature in the burgeoning express business to be counted among the pioneering giants in the business to sit down at a meeting in the Mansion House on Exchange Street and organize the American Express Company. Fargo at first was secretary but later on took the helm as president of American Express.

With American Express off the ground and running, Fargo and Henry Wells in 1852 organized Wells, Fargo & Co., an express line linking New York and San Francisco that had overland stagecoaches into the West before the railroads were built and ran the Pony Express before there was a communication system. Fargo was vice president.

Fargo also was a vice president of the New York Central Railroad, a prime mover in the building of the Northern Pacific Railroad, and a director of the Buffalo, New York & Philadelphia Railroad. He was wartime mayor of Buffalo from 1862 to 1866. Fargo lived well in a beautiful mansion that covered the entire block bounded by Jersey Street, West Avenue, Pennsylvania Street, and Fargo Avenue on Buffalo's west side.

Fargo and Jacob Schoellkopf came to Buffalo as young men in the same year. Schoellkopf was the supreme example of how fast and how far a hardworking German immigrant could advance himself.

Schoellkopf started modestly enough with a small leather shop on Mohawk Street. Soon he had leather tanneries not only in Buffalo but in Chicago and Milwaukee. He had flour mills in Buffalo and Niagara Falls. And he succeeded in extracting power from the mighty Niagara—something which the visionaries had dreamed of doing for more than half a century, and which four companies before his had tried to do but failed.

Schoellkopf had so many productive irons in the fire that it was left to his perceptive heirs to realize the significance of what "King Jacob" had come upon in tapping into Niagara's power potential. These heirs, generations of them, became leaders of the highest order in electric power.

They also have been manufacturers, notably of chemical dyes. They have been diplomats, Congressmen, bank presidents, and investment bankers. At least one of them, perhaps in the interest of brevity, was quite content to be identified simply as a capitalist, although all of them fully qualified for the same title. The Schoellkopf heirs, down through the years, have been much sought after as directors of such stellar Buffalo companies as the Bell Aircraft Cor-

Above
William G. Fargo, who came to Buffalo in 1843 as an agent for an Albany-Buffalo express line, went on to become a leading figure in the express business. He helped organize the American Express Company and Wells Fargo, served as vice president of the New York Central Railroad, was a director of the Buffalo, New York & Philadelphia Rail-road, and was Buffalo's mayor from 1862 to 1866. (BECHS)

Facing page, top
The estate of William Fargo was comprised of a huge mansion situated in a parklike setting. It covered an entire block on Buffalo's west side. (BECHS)

Facing page, bottom
The Schoellkopf Station, Niagara Falls Hydraulic Power and Manufacturing Company, 1929. The first power station dates back to 1882, and new construction continued until 1925. Shown here are three generators, which at the time were the largest waterwheel-driven electric machines in the world, at 70,000 horsepower each. From the Niagara Mohawk Collection. (BECHS)

poration, the Dunlop Tire & Rubber Corporation, Marine Midland Bank, the American Steamship Company, and Trico Products Corporation.

For at least the first 35 years after the Holland Land Company opened up Western New York to homesteaders, it was the Yankee Anglo-Saxons who had Buffalo pretty much to themselves and its businesses and wealth in the palms of their hands. Even when the city was incorporated in 1832, a good 90 percent of its citizens were of Yankee origin. The remaining slim 10 percent were about equally divided between the Irish and the Germans.

In the 1830s, '40s, and '50s, the ethnic makeup of the city changed dramatically. Both the Irish and the Germans, but especially the Germans, greatly augmented their numbers. By the 1840s, the Germans were the largest foreign-born group in Buffalo and accounted for perhaps one-third of the population. By the mid-1850s, 40 percent of Buffalo's population was of German origin.

The German immigrants who came in great numbers were better educated and equipped

Above
Jacob F. Schoellkopf, a German immigrant, arrived in Buffalo in 1843 and opened a small leather shop. Being a hard working man, Schoellkopf soon had tanneries in Buffalo, Chicago, and Milwaukee, and flour mills in Buffalo and around Niagara Falls. Schoellkopf became the first to successfully extract power from the Niagara and was from then on known as "King Jacob." (BECHS)

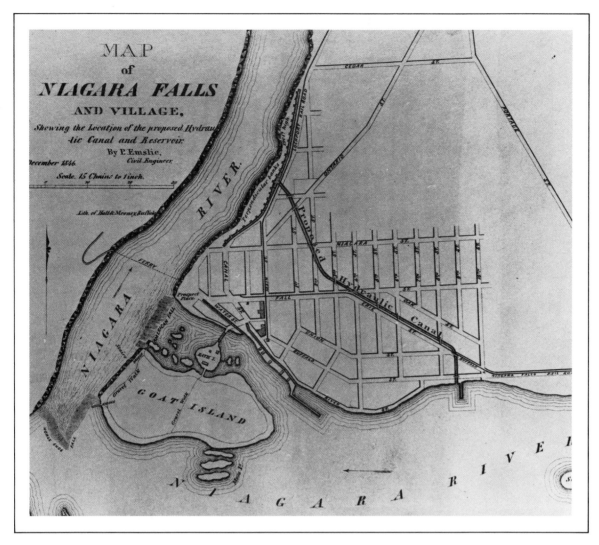

with higher work skills than the Irish who preceded them or the Poles and Italians who followed. And there was scarcely one among them who forgot to bring with him his traditional compulsion for hard work. Jacob Schoellkopf may have best exemplified the German immigrant whose diligent enterprise put an end to Yankee exclusivity in the city's commercial and industrial power structure, but he had plenty of company—among them, tanner George Laub, flour miller George Urban, meatpacker Christian Klinck, brewers Gerhard Lang and Magnus Beck.

Whatever their national origin, the new breed of businessmen in the 1840s gave a new dimension to Buffalo's commerce and industry. And others responded by broadening their own horizons. The 1840s became the Fabulous Forties of the 19th century. The sky seemed the limit as Buffalo got a new railroad, a university, and its first hospital and sent one of its own to Washington where, as things turned out, he would become President of the United States.

Even the Pope was impressed. He granted Buffalo diocesan status and sent Buffalo its first Roman Catholic bishop.

The new railroad, in 1842, was the Attica & Buffalo. It didn't go very far, but it went far

Above
This 1846 map of Niagara Falls and village shows the location of the hydraulic canal and reservoir proposed by Augustus Porter. Porter hoped to sell the right of constructing and using such a canal, but was unsuccessful in his attempt. (BECHS)

enough to connect with the Tonawanda Railroad to Rochester. Beyond that was another and then another link in a chain of small railroads all the way to Albany and then on to Boston. By 1843 the endless chain of railroads was touting 25-hour express service between Buffalo and Albany "in the finest cars." The opening of the railroad was as significant, perhaps, as the opening of the Erie Canal, but it was not nearly as dramatic. There are no records of even a single gun salute.

May 11, 1846, was another red-letter day for Buffalo. On that day, the state legislature authorized creation of the University of Buffalo. Lawyer Nathan Hall, a state assemblyman at the time, saw to it that a special act chartering the university sailed through the legislature without a hitch.

The university at first, and for many years after, was only a medical school. Its first lectures were held in February 1847 in a Baptist church on the northeast corner of Washington and Seneca streets, but the school was moved soon after to Main and Virginia.

Millard Fillmore served as chancellor of the university from its first day until his death in 1874, although the job was more honorary than taxing. His principal duty was to bestow diplomas on departing graduates.

The year after the university began its first medical instruction, the Daughters of Charity of St. Vincent de Paul opened Sisters Hospital, Buffalo's first. The hospital, on Pearl Place, was only a block away from the new medical school. The university had a close relationship with the hospital, as it did with Buffalo General Hospital when Buffalo General began operations 10 years later.

The Buffalo Savings Bank opened its doors in 1846, to be followed by the Western Savings Bank in 1851 and the Erie County Savings Bank in 1854. These were essentially working-men's banks, soliciting the savings of thrifty laborers and lending them money to buy their homes.

On April 23, 1847, the Pope saw fit to create the Diocese of Buffalo. Later that year, the Right Reverend John Timon arrived in town as the first bishop of the new diocese.

Torches, hoisted aloft by the faithful, glowed in the night as the new bishop arrived by train. A coach drawn by four white horses hauled him away for services at St. Louis Church, where he celebrated his first mass the following Sunday morning. St. Louis, whose parishioners were predominantly German, was the first Catholic church in Buffalo, having opened as the Lamb of God in 1832.

Facing page
This structure at the corner of Washington and Seneca streets was originally built as a Baptist church. For a time, between 1836 and 1846, it served as a post office. In 1847 the building became the first home of the newly organized University of Buffalo Medical School. (BECHS)

The new bishop, an affable Irishman, found the Germanic environment a little too confining and, as soon as he could discreetly do so, showed his preference for the friendlier St. Patrick's at Broadway and Ellicott, the first Irish Catholic church in Buffalo.

But within five years, Bishop Timon was breaking ground for a new St. Joseph's Cathedral in Buffalo. The bishop's enthusiasm and persuasiveness were so convincing that the Pope himself donated $2,000 in gold toward the new cathedral and even Unitarian Millard Fillmore volunteered a contribution.

The busy decade of the 1840s began on a political note of strictly local interest. For the first time, the mayor of Buffalo was elected rather than appointed. Captain Sheldon Thompson was the first to win the job at the polls in 1840. Running under the handicap of having once lived in Black Rock, he won by a slim margin of 10 votes—suggesting that while hard feelings still ran strong, Buffalonians were beginning to be more tolerant even of Black Rockers.

Facing page
The Right Reverend John Timon was the first Bishop of the Diocese of Buffalo, which the Pope created in 1847. (BECHS)

Above
In 1843 St. Mary's Church was established by a few German Catholics who had left St. Louis Church. In 1852 St. Mary's started an orphanage for the many children left homeless as a result of the cholera epidemic that swept the area in the preceding years. (BECHS)

Facing page
Bishop John Timon's enthusiasm about St. Joseph's Cathedral persuaded the Pope to donate $2,000 in gold toward its construction. (BECHS)

The decade of the 1840s ended on another political note of considerably greater national import. Millard Fillmore, the Buffalo lawyer, had gone to Washington as Vice President of the United States—quite literally, in his case, a heartbeat away from the Presidency.

Fillmore was nominated in 1848 as General Zachary Taylor's running mate on the Whig ticket. The opposing Democratic ticket was headed by Lewis Cass of Michigan. The election was further spiced, in Buffalo especially, by the emergence of a third party, the Free-Soil Party. Opposed to the extension of slavery into territories conquered from Mexico, the Free-Soilers held their 1848 convention in Buffalo, where they nominated Martin Van Buren as their presidential candidate.

Taylor and Fillmore handily won the three-way race. Buffalo and the rest of Erie County, not surprisingly, gave their overwhelming support to Taylor and their fellow townsman. The Taylor-Fillmore ticket won 7,606 of their votes, Democrat Cass got 3,364, and Van Buren and the Free-Soilers ran a poor third with 2,359.

Thus did Mr. Fillmore go to Washington. And not for a moment did his fellow Buffalonians think he was going to stay very long just as Vice President. Buffalo's crusty old Judge Horatio Stow, as soon as the election was over, predicted that while Taylor may have been

Above
Millard Fillmore presided over the Senate when Henry Clay introduced his plan that became known as the Compromise of 1850. (BECHS)

Facing page
Buffalo's own Millard Fillmore succeeded to the Presidency after Zachary Taylor died in 1850. This photograph of Fillmore was taken by W.J. Baker circa 1870. (BECHS)

pretty good at dodging Mexican bullets in the recent war with Mexico, he didn't stand a chance of surviving Millard Fillmore's luck. The judge was right. Midway through his term, Taylor breathed his last, and in 1850 Fillmore moved into the White House.

Buffalo has intimately touched the lives of four American Presidents. Fillmore was the first. A generation later, Grover Cleveland was in the White House less than three years after he was mayor of Buffalo. Early in the 20th century, President McKinley came to Buffalo to help the city celebrate its Pan-American Exposition and was rewarded for that friendly gesture by being shot. When McKinley died, Theodore Roosevelt came to Buffalo to be sworn in as his successor at the Ansley Wilcox mansion on Delaware Avenue.

When Fillmore assumed the Presidency in 1850, he inherited one of the gravest crises the nation had ever confronted. Slavery, a long-festering sore, was infecting the Union's innards. Fillmore may have reasoned that the nation at that moment needed quiet. At any rate, he walked the tightrope and took a conciliatory approach to the thorny slavery issue. The climax was his support of the Compromise of 1850 and his use of his presidential power to keep the unruly northern Whigs in line on that unpopular bit of fence-straddling.

The most controversial part of the compromise was the Fugitive Slave Act, which gave slaveowners the right to lay claim to escaped slaves and imposed fines and jail terms on those who saw fit to give the escaped slave a helping hand. Ironically, the Fugitive Slave Act was put to one of its early tests in Fillmore's hometown.

The steamer *Buckeye* docked in Buffalo on a summer's day in 1851 with an escaped slave, Daniel, stowed away in the galley as a cook. An agent for the Kentucky slaveowner was waiting at dockside and, with a deputy U.S. marshal in tow, went below to claim the slave. Daniel tried briefly to flee his captors but he was felled, bloodied, and bruised by a billet of wood.

It looked like a simple case of a slave, having tried and failed to gain his freedom, going back to his old Kentucky home. But a lawyer, John Talcott, stepped forward on Daniel's behalf and the case went into the courts. Judge Alfred Conklin found in the slave's favor, ruling that he had escaped before the Fugitive Slave Act became law and that the act was not retroactive. The judge went on to say that disputes involving slaves ought always to be resolved in favor of freedom, citing as his authority for that opinion the Twelve Tables of Rome. It was heady stuff for Daniel.

The slaveowner's agent went back to Kentucky empty-handed, but not before a Buffalo

Facing page
This 1864 broadside offered a "liberal reward" for the apprehension of two runaway slaves. The Fugitive Slave Act, a part of the Compromise of 1850, gave slaveowners the right to lay claim to escaped slaves. The act also provided for the punishment of those aiding runaways. (BECHS)

RUNAWAYS!

Ranaway from the C. S.
Arsenal at Danville, on the 6th inst., two slaves belonging to James A. Eubank, of Middlesex county, named

PHIL AND WASH.

Phil is a dark mulatto, about
45 years old, 5 feet 6 or 8 inches high, quick spoken, and had on, an old suit of homespun cloth and flat top cloth cap.

Wash is black, full round
face, about 5 feet high and 14 years old, had on a suit of black homespun clothes.

A liberal reward will be
paid for the apprehension of these slaves.

T. D. NEAL, Agent
for the owner.

July 8th, 1864.

police magistrate fined him $50 for assaulting the slave. It had not been a good day for slaveowners.

Daniel, head high, walked out of court a free man and triumphantly crossed the border into Canada. He was not the first nor the last to do that. But he was one of the few who did it so openly. The others, 30,000 to 40,000 of them, were more furtively spirited across the border to freedom, thanks to a well-lubricated piece of human machinery known as the Underground Railroad.

Buffalo, being as close as it is to the Canadian border, was one of the main stations on the Underground. Its elusive lines came in by water and up from Pennsylvania and New York's southern tier by land. Buffalo and the surrounding countryside were dotted with the Underground's satellite stations and stationmasters. A Quaker farm in Orchard Park. A home at Utica and Linwood Avenue. The Negro Baptist Church on Michigan Avenue. A porter in the American Hotel. A ferry boat on the Niagara River. Someone patiently standing on a dock.

The country was not well. These were sorry times to be its President. Fillmore's compromise kept the peace for nearly a dozen years, but it did nothing to get at the root of the problem. Yet, as the University of Buffalo's Dean Julius Pratt once put it, without Fillmore

Facing page
The Michigan Avenue Baptist Church was built in 1845 and was later known as a station for the Underground Railroad. (BECHS)

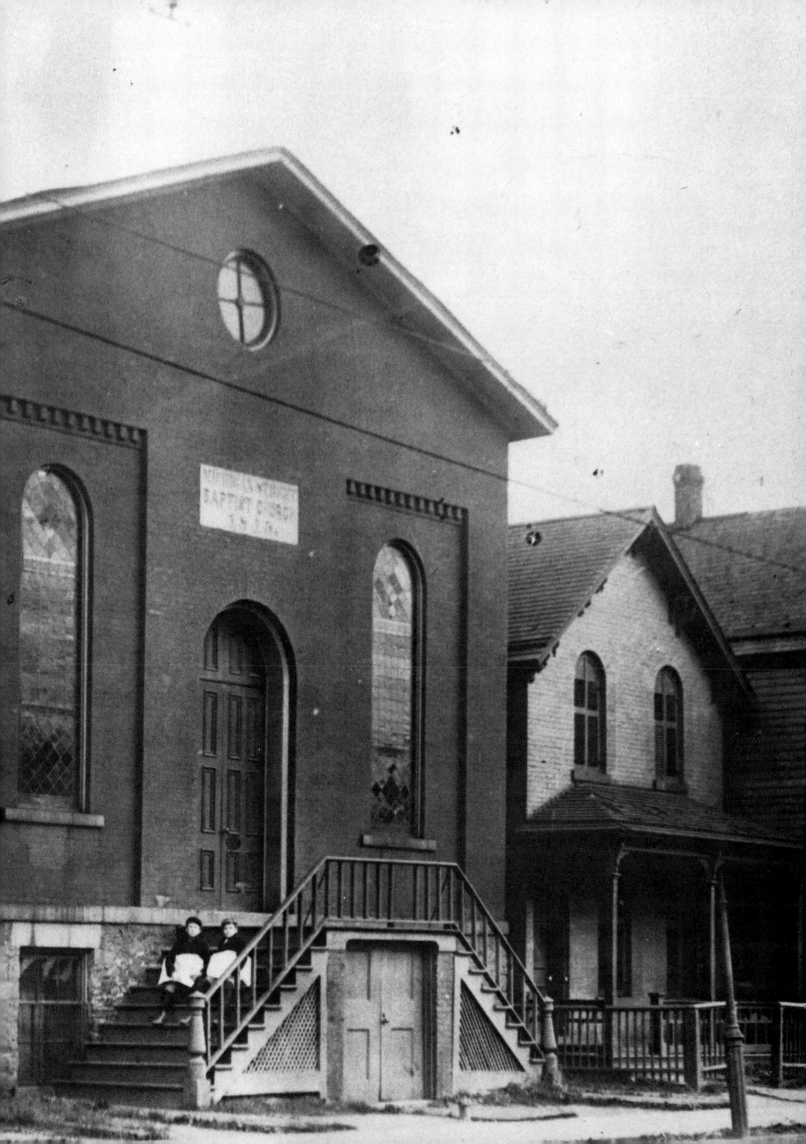

there could have been no Lincoln.

Fillmore's own Whig Party rejected him, denying him the presidential nomination in 1852, and Democrat Franklin Pierce was swept into office as his successor. The Whigs were all but finished. A disillusioned Fillmore came home to Buffalo.

While Fillmore was in the White House, the Buffalo city directories had continued to count him among Buffalo's citizens, listing his occupation as President of the United States and his address not as the White House but on Franklin Street in Buffalo.

When Fillmore was getting ready to come back home, he wondered whether the Franklin Street house was grand enough for an ex-President. Deciding that it was not, he had a new home built on Niagara Square at the northeast corner of Delaware Avenue.

He also worried about how he should make his living now, without demeaning the high office he had attained. He considered a bank presidency briefly but then agreed with old colleagues that he should return to the practice of law, limiting his practice to only the most dignified cases.

It is doubtful that he ever again practiced much law. Having tasted the powers of the

Above
Millard Fillmore purchased this home at Niagara Square in 1858, deciding that his home at 180 Franklin was not grand enough for an ex-President. He lived here until his death in 1874. (BECHS)

highest office in the land, he was persuaded in 1856 to try for it again as head of the Know-Nothing ticket. It was a mistake. He won only in the state of Maryland. Even his hometown failed to rally to his support. Erie County, in the 1856 presidential election, gave approximately 7,500 of its votes to Democrat James Buchanan, 6,700 to Republican John Charles Fremont, and 5,400 to Fillmore.

Fillmore thereafter plunged himself into all sorts of activities that redounded to the benefit of his hometown. He was active in starting the Buffalo Fine Arts Academy, which made Buffalo the fourth American city to have a permanent public art gallery. He was the first president of the Historical Society, and his interest in it sometimes seemed to "possess his life."

He was president of the Grosvenor Library. He participated in the formation of Buffalo General Hospital and served as its president in 1870. He was a founder and first president of the Buffalo Club, a prestigious private club for men. And he always kept an eye on the University of Buffalo as its chancellor.

Fillmore was a bit of a stuffed shirt who never passed up a chance to boast of the regularity of his habits. He once summed up his lifestyle in these words:

Above
This political cartoon, published by Nathaniel Currier of New York City in 1856, shows Millard Fillmore on the Union Rock. If political feelings were running high, the name of the publisher was often left off of the cartoons, as seems to be the case here. (BECHS)

I have taken but one dose of medicine in thirty years and that was forced upon me unnecessarily. I attribute my good health to an originally strong constitution, an education on a farm and a lifelong habit of regularity and temperance. I never smoked or chewed tobacco. I never knew intoxication. I never allowed my usual hours for sleep to be interrupted. The Sabbath I always kept as a day of rest. Besides being a religious duty, it was essential to health.

He is buried beneath a simple obelisk in Forest Lawn Cemetery that tells his name, date of birth, and date of death, but says nothing at all about his having been President of the United States.

Above
At one time, this miniature brass horse and carriage ink stand was used by Millard Fillmore. (BECHS)

Aspects of the city of Buffalo are portrayed in a circa 1840 lithograph. Clockwise from top are views of the lighthouse and harbor, Terrace Market and Liberty Pole, American Hotel, Webster Buildings, and First Presbyterian and St. Paul's churches. (BECHS)

Above
A View of Lake & Fort Erie, from Buffalo Creek, an engraving by John Bluck from a watercolor by E. Walsh, was published on January 1, 1811 at R. Ackerman's Repository of Arts in London. (BECHS)

Top
The Trial of Red Jacket, *painted by John Mix Stanley, portrays the Indian leader on trial for the charge of sorcery. The Seneca Council assembled at Buffalo Creek in 1802 to hear his case. After speaking for close to three hours in his own defense, Red Jacket was found innocent of the charge. (BECHS)*

Top
The Burning of Buffalo, *painted by Raymond Massey, depicts the events of December 1813, when the village of Buffalo was burned. The citizens prepared for a short-lived defense against the British. (BECHS)*

Above
This watch case is designed with typical Seneca Indian beadwork. (BECHS)

Top
The red brick building in this painting from about 1830 is the Eagle Tavern. (BECHS)

Above
In 1833 William Wilgus, at the age of 14, sketched and painted The Johnson Cottage, the home of Mayor Ebenezer Johnson at Delaware Avenue and Johnson Park. (BECHS)

Top
Buffalo from Lake Erie *was painted and engraved by W.J. Bennett from a sketch by J.W. Hill, and it was published by Henry J. Megarey in New York, circa 1836. (BECHS)*

Above
Erie Canal at Buffalo *by R. Stevenson is the center for this blue and white Staffordshire plate with a scalloped lace border. (BECHS)*

Above
The steamer Sultana *in Buffalo harbor is depicted in oils by an anonymous artist, circa 1850. (BECHS)*

Facing page
A portrait of Buffalo's first elected mayor, Sheldon Thompson, was painted by Thomas LeClear, circa 1849. (BECHS)

CHAPTER V

WAR BETWEEN THE STATES

In the dozen years between the Fillmore-endorsed Compromise of 1850 that delayed the War Between the States and the bombardment of Fort Sumter that triggered its start, Northern cities developed the industrial and commercial muscle capable of sustaining a successful war effort. And nowhere was this industrial maturity more evident than in Buffalo.

On the eve of the Civil War, Buffalo had 502 manufacturing enterprises employing a total of 6,000 people. Thirty years before, there had been 40 manufacturers, all of them small in scale and relatively primitive. Most of the newer ones came on strong in the decade of the 1850s, when Buffalo's population nearly doubled again, skyrocketing from 42,000 to 81,000.

The railroads, rinky-dink contraptions in the 1840s, became a new transportation force to be reckoned with. By the mid-1850s, Buffalo was a railroad center of more than casual significance.

The Erie Railroad, hailed as the greatest venture of private enterprise of its time, came into Western New York from the eastern seaboard in 1851, and an independent line, later acquired by the Erie, connected Buffalo to it. President Fillmore and his Cabinet rode the Erie's first westbound train.

Facing page
The Buffalo Starch Factory is representative of manufacturing firms that experienced growth and prosperity in mid-19th-century Buffalo. Established in 1864, it ranked third in world production by 1877 and had a widespread reputation for quality. Pure water was a requisite for production of starch and the Buffalo Starch Factory was located on the banks of the Niagara River. Also convenient for grain-carrying vessels shipping and receiving, it was accessible not only to the Niagara River, but also to the Erie Canal and the railroad. (BECHS)

Two years later, the great New York Central Railroad was put together through a massive merger of tiny railroads across the state, including the Buffalo & Rochester, successor to the embryonic Attica & Buffalo of 1842. Buffalo was the New York Central's western terminus. Dean Richmond of Buffalo helped create the New York Central, becoming its organizational vice president and then its second president. Richmond also figured in the new Buffalo & State Line Railroad that ran southwest along the lakeshore to Erie, Pennsylvania, where it connected with other lines going on to Cleveland and Chicago.

Supportive of expanding industry and the burgeoning railroads were Buffalo's banks, which grew in numbers and in scope. The decade of the 1850s began, in fact, with the formation of the Marine Bank, midway between the waterfront and the Terrace at a location from which it has never strayed very far.

In succeeding generations the Marine would be managed by such illustrious Buffalo families as the Clements, the Rands, and the Knoxes. But in the beginning it was the bank of George Palmer and James Wadsworth, railroad buffs at heart, who would be startled indeed to know that their bank 130 years later was part of the Hong Kong & Shanghai international banking empire. Both Palmer and Wadsworth had financial interests and directorships in the Attica & Hornellsville Railroad, and Palmer was linked with the Buffalo & State Line Railroad.

In the early 1850s, Elbridge Gerry Spaulding brought the Farmers & Mechanics Bank to Buffalo, and in 1856 Pascal Pratt and tannery tycoon Bronson Rumsey founded the Manufacturers & Traders Bank.

But Buffalo was not so absorbed in industry and commerce as to ignore its cultural growth. In 1851, a Jenny Lind concert was booked into the North Presbyterian Church at Main and Chippewa streets. Seats had to be set up outside for the concert overflow, and crowds strained at the church windows to catch the incomparable voice of the Swedish nightingale. The Metropolitan Theatre, later the Academy of Music, joined the roster of the city's theatrical stages in 1852 and stood for 103 years. Ignoble as it was in its later years, in its heyday it played host to the dramatic superstars of the 19th century.

Perhaps the surest sign that Buffalo had grown up came in 1854, when its archrival, Black Rock, was peaceably merged into the city. Black Rock may have ceased to exist as a separate entity, but it has never lost its identity as a proud neighborhood and the Black Rock name goes on.

Despite the economic growth of the 1850s, as the decade wound down the North in

Above
The slogan, "Time and the Erie wait for no man," accompanied this illustration which appeared on a 19th-century trade card emphasizing the punctuality of the Erie Railroad. (BECHS)

Facing page
The name of the Metropolitan Theatre was changed to the Academy of Music in 1868. At the time the latter was thought to be a more fashionable and less offensive name. (BECHS)

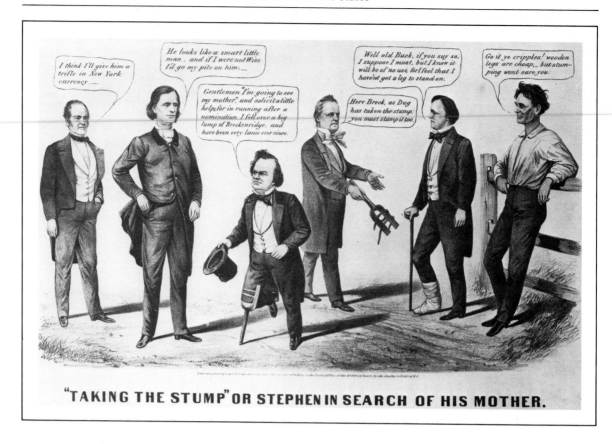

"TAKING THE STUMP" OR STEPHEN IN SEARCH OF HIS MOTHER.

general and Buffalo in particular became disillusioned with the Democrat, Buchanan, they had helped elect to the Presidency. Buchanan had vetoed a measure that would have been helpful to Great Lakes commerce and Buffalonians, like many Northerners, felt discriminated against. "Millions for slavery; no dime for commerce on the lakes" was a frequently heard complaint in Buffalo.

The Democrats were having trouble enough being split on the slavery issue without further alienating the affections of their constituency. The Republicans watched with interest, biding their time until the 1860 election. Buffalo Republicans hoped William Henry Seward would emerge as the Republican presidential candidate at the party's convention in Chicago. They were surprised, but quickly reconciled, when the candidate turned out to be Abraham Lincoln.

Buffalonians voted for Lincoln, but not by any overwhelming margin. They gave him 6,171 votes to 5,733 for Democrat Stephen Douglas. The surrounding towns were more solidly in Lincoln's corner, strengthening his vote in Erie County to 11,767 over Douglas's 10,270.

On his roundabout way to Washington for his inauguration, Lincoln stopped off in

Above
This 1860 Currier and Ives cartoon is entitled 'Taking the Stump' or Stephen in Search of His Mother. Though more Buffalonians voted for Abraham Lincoln than for Stephen Douglas in the 1860 Presidential election, the margin was not an overwhelming one. (BECHS)

Buffalo in February 1861. Fillmore, although he found Republican policy hard to swallow, graciously if somewhat reluctantly welcomed the President-elect and rode with him in an open carriage to the American Hotel, escorted by Company D of the 74th Regiment.

Buffalonians were waiting en masse in front of the American. The eyes of all but the pickpockets were raised to the hotel's balcony, as Lincoln appeared and spoke a few words of no great moment. Across the street, the Young Men's Christian Association had strung a banner, "We Are Praying For You," that caught his eye. That evening he and Mrs. Lincoln hosted a reception at the American, and the next day they attended services at the Unitarian Church with the Fillmores.

Fifteen days later, when Lincoln was inaugurated, Buffalonians saluted him in absentia. Thirty-four light artillery guns from the 65th Regiment were wheeled into Niagara Square and boomed out a salute as the new President took the oath of office hundreds of miles away in Washington. The *Morning Express* had promoted that gesture of respect. Buffalo was rewarded for its Lincoln support by the appointment of lawyer James O. Putnam as consul to Le Havre. *Express* editor Almon Clapp was tapped as Buffalo's postmaster.

Above

The 65th Regiment, from Buffalo, was cited for gallant and meritorious service in many Civil War battles and campaigns. Organized in 1848 and composed of a number of crack militia companies, it saw service in the Canal Riots of 1849, the Draft Riots of 1863, the railroad strikes of 1877 and 1892, and during the Tonawanda lumbermen's strike of 1893. Mustered into the Volunteer Army in 1864, the regiment carried the dual designation of the 187th Regiment as well as the 65th. (BECHS)

A little more than a month after the Lincoln inauguration, Fort Sumter was bombarded and the long-delayed but inevitable Civil War was a melancholy fact. Buffalo and Erie County were quick to respond. Scarcely two weeks after the surrender of Fort Sumter, the first four of what would be many companies of volunteers departed in the direction of frightful casualties but "imperishable renown."

Throughout the war, Buffalo was able to fill nearly all its military quotas with volunteers. Only small deficiencies in the quotas had to be made up through the draft. As was the custom of the times, bounties were paid to woo the volunteers. Some Buffalo industrialists, Francis Root among them, paid the bounties out of their own pockets to encourage their employees to enlist. The Erie County Board of Supervisors, before the war was over, had budgeted nearly $2 million for bounties to volunteers, raising them from an early $100 to a maximum of $565 per man.

Though few had to be drafted to meet the quotas, the draft was a touchy subject in Buffalo and the *Courier* condemned it outright as unconstitutional. Buffalonians, including those responsible for enforcing the law, were highly sensitive to public remarks that might make necessary any more drafting than there was.

Above
The Buffalo City Guard was organized in 1837 as the result of the Patriots War of 1837-1838. During peacetime, social events broke up the ordinary routine of the militia. When the Civil War broke out, the militia could not join as regiment-existing organizations were not encouraged to do so, but its men volunteered until the organization was permitted to enter. (BECHS)

✝ JOHN

By the Grace of God, and the authority of the Holy See,
BISHOP OF BUFFALO.

To the Dearly Beloved Faithful Laity of the Diocese, Health and Benediction.

DEARLY BELOVED!---In the name of the God of Charity, and through that charity which He, who called us to be your Bishop, has given us for you; through that charity of Christ, in us, however unworthy, through which we would cheerfully give our life, if necessary, for each and every one of you; we beg of you, for Christ's sake, and for the sake of all that you love in heaven and on earth, to abstain from all resistance to law, from all riot, from all tumultuous gatherings, from all violence

In New York, many misguided men, yet very few we believe, of practical Catholics, have shed blood in the late riot; "and the voice of their brother's blood *cried to the Lord* from the earth." Some of the rioters have fallen, many more will, we fear, suffer much, many will, perhaps, be ruined; *all* will feel the painful sting of a guilty conscience, during the rest of life, and on their death-bed, (if indeed rioters who aid in murder could die otherwise than as it is written; "He that shall kill by the sword, must be killed by the sword." Apoc. XIII, 10;) they will either through God's mercy, sincerely repent for their participation in the riot; or be lost forever! Dearly beloved listen to the advice of a father who dearly loves you; submit to law and God will protect you. Should there be a draft, fewer will be drafted, than would, probably, be killed in an unholy struggle against law. And if any of you be drafted, we will try to protect and aid; friends will protect and aid; God will protect, aid, and bless, in more ways than we know or dare name.

Withdraw yourselves, then, we beg and exhort, from all who would excite to associations against the law of the land, or to violence, and mob-law. For God's sake; for the sake of your dear families; for the sake of your fathers and mothers, whether still pilgrims on earth, or mingling with the "blessed crowd of witnesses," who, from heaven, watch over your conduct on earth; we exhort you to *trust in God*, and not to lend yourselves to any exciter to mob or violence, which leads so often to murder. If you follow this advice of your Father in Christ, we confidently assure you that "Whosoever shall follow this rule, *peace will be unto him, and mercy;* and upon the Israel of God.---Gal. VI.

We require that this letter be read in every church on the Sunday after its reception.

Given at St. Joseph's Cathedral, Buffalo, on the Feast of Our Lady of Mount Carmel, A. D., MDCCCLXIII.

✝ JOHN, Bishop of Buffalo.

The Reverend Judson Benedict was one who created a stir when he preached in East Aurora that Christian tenets frowned upon the taking up of arms. He told members of his congregation of draft age that the choice was theirs to make, but he suggested that they "cheerfully submit" to any penalties that might be meted out as alternatives if they chose to stand firm against being drafted.

The Reverend Benedict soon found himself lodged in the Buffalo jail. An application for his release through a writ of habeas corpus was filed in State Supreme Court in Buffalo, and the writ was summarily denied. The application then was filed with Nathan Hall, by then the federal judge in Buffalo.

Judge Hall lost no time in granting the writ, ruling that only Congress could authorize a suspension of the privilege of habeas corpus and that Congress, even in those critical days, had not seen fit to do so. Judge Hall's release of the East Aurora minister was short-lived. No sooner had the Reverend Benedict walked out of the courtroom than he was rearrested and hustled into a waiting carriage that took him to the railroad station, from which he unwillingly departed to be ensconced again in a jail in Washington.

The grounds for the minister's original arrest were that his sermon might discourage

Above
As the Draft Riots raged in New York City in 1863, Bishop Timon issued this proclamation urging Buffalo's Catholics "to abstain from all resistance to law, from all riot, tumultuous gatherings, from all violence." (BECHS)

enlistments, the unsaid fear being that this would enhance the need for the dreaded draft. In fact the sermon seemed to have had no such effect. Nonetheless, those who volunteered were not without occasional vociferous complaints.

The Buffalo *Commercial Advertiser* found itself the target of a libel suit after it published a letter from a captain in a New York State regiment of volunteers complaining about the uniforms furnished his troops. The letter had harsh things to say about William Dorsheimer of Buffalo, New York State's treasurer at the time, whose duties included the securing of uniforms for the state regiment. Dorsheimer had ordered the uniforms from none other than the Brooks Brothers clothiers in New York City.

"A company clothed in them," complained the irate captain, "looks more like prison convicts than citizen soldiers." He described the uniforms as multicolored to the point of being piebald and so ill-fitting that they were "large enough for Falstaff's troops." He assailed the "home cowards" responsible for them and ended his letter: "If they don't follow us onto the field to steal the clothes from our dead bodies, it will be because they know they are not worth coming after."

The *Commercial Advertiser* not only published the letter but followed it with its own parting shot: "Do any of the state officers know anything about a check drawn by Brooks Brothers for $25,000 or $30,000? Did said check smell of bonus? We pause for a reply."

Brooks Brothers seems not to have been offended by the captain's complaints to the point of taking legal action. Dorsheimer was. He sued the *Commercial Advertiser* for $5,000 and costs. It is doubtful that the suit ever came to trial, but for awhile it provided a titillating diversion to the more somber war news in the pages of the *Commercial Advertiser.*

Buffalonians did themselves proud in the long and dreary war, not only in their numerical representation but in their heroic war record. By the time the war was over, Buffalo and Erie County had furnished more than 20,000 men to the Union cause and nearly one-quarter of them had spilt their blood at such far-from-home fields of battle as Rappahannock Station, Antietam, Fredericksburg, Bull Run, Chickahominy, Cedar Creek, Drury's Bluff, Fort Hudson, and Hatcher's Run.

Particularly those from the outlying towns in the county took easily to the saddle and

Above
The camp of the 100th Regiment N.Y.S. Volunteers in Virginia was called the "model camp" of the Army. This regiment was composed mainly of Buffalo-area volunteers. (BECHS)

Facing page
Members of the 21st Regiment New York Volunteers posed for the camera at Fort Runyon, Virginia, in July 1861. (BECHS)

were well represented as whole companies in nearly half a dozen cavalry and mounted-rifle regiments. One unusual Buffalo outfit was an artillery battery commanded by Colonel Michael Wiedrich. All of its officers and men were Buffalonians of German descent.

But, as always, most of the Buffalo-area volunteers were infantrymen. Sometimes they made up a company or two or several companies in a regiment. But five regiments—the 21st, the 49th, the 100th, the 116th, and the 184th—were "all Buffalo," or substantially so.

Two high-ranking Buffalo war heroes were General Daniel Davidson Bidwell and Colonel Edward P. Chapin. Young Chapin, a Buffalo lawyer, was slain in the fighting in Louisiana. Bidwell, astride his horse, took the bullet at Cedar Creek in the late days of the war. Bidwell was brought home for a civic funeral, first at City Hall and then beneath the dirgeful pealing bells of St. Paul's Church. Bidwell's name is remembered in one of Buffalo's residential avenues, Bidwell Parkway. Nearby Chapin Parkway is a double-barreled salute to the young lawyer-colonel, Edward Chapin, and the old doctor-colonel, Cyrenius Chapin.

But Buffalo did more than furnish men to the field of battle. It also furnished Elbridge Gerry Spaulding to the wartime United States Congress. Spaulding is credited with having been the financial genius whose "greenback" currency was indispensable to winning the war. He drafted the legislation that led to the issuance of legal-tender treasury notes, which circulated as paper currency known as "greenbacks."

Spaulding, a Buffalo lawyer who switched to banking, had been mayor of Buffalo in 1847, a state assemblyman, and a Congressman on numerous occasions. During the war, he earned a national reputation as "the father of the greenback," and his name became a household word. Ironically, his own hometown forsook him at the zenith of his popularity and national usefulness. Buffalo failed to reelect him to Congress in 1862, sending Democrat John Ganson to Washington in his stead.

Spaulding's defeat was part of a statewide tilt away from Republicanism in 1862, when Democrat Horatio Seymour was elected governor of New York State and Democrat William Fargo became mayor of Buffalo. These Democratic victories were an early warning of difficult times ahead in Buffalo for the Republicans.

Labor unrest had begun to surface. Machinists in the Buffalo foundries went on strike in 1862. Dockhands and stevedores on the Buffalo waterfront were unhappy with their lot, and there was talk of a general strike.

Employers balked at raising the wages of their restless employees. When strikes broke

Above
The artillery battery commanded by Colonel Michael Wiedrich, shown here during the battle at Cross Keys on June 8, 1862, consisted solely of Buffalonians of German descent. (BECHS)

out, they sought to break them by recruiting Negro labor. Striking workers who saw Negroes eased into their breadwinning jobs found it difficult to sympathize with the cause of blacks who still were slaves. Emancipation was not looked upon in Buffalo in a kindly way.

As the 1864 election approached, the labor scene in Buffalo was unsettled if not seething, the war was dragging on, and wartime casualties among Erie County's troops were mounting to what would be a total of 4,700 by the war's end. Yearnings for peace, fears of four more years of war, and resentment of onerous taxes were biting into Lincoln's Buffalo support.

The crowning blow came when Millard Fillmore, still packing political punch, came out with an endorsement of Lincoln's presidential adversary, General George B. McClellan. McClellan likewise was publicly favored by Mayor Fargo and by Dean Richmond, the powerful railroad builder. "I look upon the election of General McClellan as our last hope and this you can publish to the world," Fillmore told reporters.

Buffalo and Erie County, unlike most of the North, responded by giving their support, by the slimmest of margins, to McClellan. Lincoln was reelected, but in Erie County his 13,061 votes trailed McClellan's 13,368.

Less than six months later, the reelected President was felled by an assassin's bullet. Lincoln, who had come to Buffalo in triumph on a winter weekend in 1861, came back in death in the springtime of 1865. His westward funeral procession paused in Buffalo, where the late President lay in state in St. James Hall at Washington and Eagle streets.

Above
The funeral procession of President Lincoln passed through Buffalo on April 27, 1865. (BECHS)

CHAPTER VI

BUFFALO'S
BOOM TIMES

Buffalo's growth was not halted nor even much slowed during the Civil War. New industries, among them Farrar & Trefts, came onto the scene and opened up shop even in wartime. The city's population grew from 81,000 to 118,000 in the decade of the 1860s. But it was the end of the war that touched off an explosive growth that gathered glorious momentum through the rest of the 19th century and on into the 20th. Booming and raucously boisterous, Buffalo took its place among the leading cities of the nation.

It was Buffalo's Golden Age.

In the midst of what was to be its long Golden Age, Buffalo celebrated its golden anniversary—its 50th year as a city. Lawyer Eben Carleton Sprague was chosen to deliver the anniversary oration on the eve of the Fourth of July in 1882. After gamely trying to spell it all out in some detail, Sprague finally concluded that the statistical evidence of the city's growth not only was staggering, it was "simply unthinkable."

"The geographical position of Buffalo has but few rivals among the interior cities of the continent," the enthusiastic Sprague told his equally enthusiastic audience of anniversary celebrators. The city, he went on to say, was the beneficiary of pure water from "the Mediterranean Sea of America" and was abundantly lighted by gas—the price of which, he added

Facing page
Canal barges filled with cargo line the Erie Canal about 1870. Courtesy, Buffalo Savings Bank-Roy Nagle Collection. (BECHS)

jocularly (and more prophetically than he could have imagined), "provides an unfailing topic of denunciatory conversation."

In its 50th year as a city, Sprague noted, Buffalo had 1,137 manufacturing enterprises and a population of 170,000. (He had no way of knowing, of course, that the population would more than double to 352,000 by the time the century had wound down.) There were a total of 15 railroads in the city, he observed, adding that from the acres of tracks and the never-ending presence of so many railroad cars, "we might imagine that we are in the railroad center of the world."

After the anniversary gala, Buffalonians contentedly went back to their jobs, which were plentiful. Businessmen, all seemingly possessed of the Midas touch, went on with the business of drenching themselves in dollars. The expansion of their wealth, in fact, in due time became a matter of some concern to Eben Carleton Sprague. Less than two years after delivering his upbeat 50th-anniversary oration, Sprague issued this dire warning to a captive audience of Buffalo's wealthiest: "It was wealth without a conscience that sowed the seeds of the French Revolution and drove its possessors into exile and to the guillotine." Spread it around, he advised the Buffalo rich with the wherewithal to be philanthropic.

Above
The Buffalo Express Pictorial Year Book and Calendar for 1889 *contained this view of the Frontier Mills, Clinton Mills, and others located at Black Rock. From the Erie Canal Collection. (BECHS)*

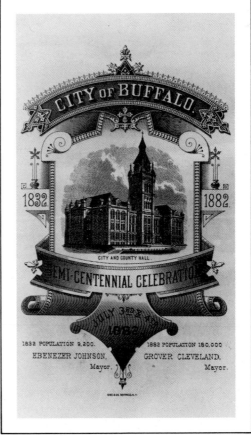

Top

Amos W. Sangster etched this view of Buffalo's harbor in 1886. It is one of a series of 153 Sangster etchings documenting the Niagara River. Dedicated to Grover Cleveland, the etchings appeared in an 1886 publication entitled the Niagara River and Falls from Lake Erie to Lake Ontario. *(BECHS)*

Bottom left

While editor of the Morning Express, *Samuel Clemens (center) posed with war correspondent George Townsend and Buffalo Courier editor David Gray, circa 1870. Courtesy, Library of Congress.*

Bottom, right

Buffalo's City and County Hall, which opened in 1876, embellishes this semi-centennial invitation. Grover Cleveland served as the city's mayor at the time. (BECHS)

Evidently Buffalo's 19th-century fat cats responded to his complete satisfaction, for some time later Sprague had occasion to remark, "Buffalo is not a snobbish city. There is no city where solid wealth is more sincerely respected."

Mark Twain visited Buffalo on the threshold of its Golden Age, and in 1869 he bought an interest in the *Buffalo Express* with the idea of settling down for good.

In Buffalo, he lived at 472 Delaware Avenue in a house bought for him as a wedding present by his new father-in-law. Not many months after the Twain wedding, his father-in-law died, a friend of his wife's died of typhoid while she was a houseguest, and then Twain's wife took ill after the premature birth of their first child. The rapid sequence of unhappy events was too much for Twain. He sold his interest in the newspaper at a loss and departed from Buffalo.

But others came in droves, and they stayed and prospered. When Sprague addressed the wealthiest of them at the dedication of the new Merchants Exchange on New Year's Day in 1884, the roster of brilliantly successful entrepreneurs was proliferating. There was not one among them who did not rightfully think of himself as a capitalist of the highest order and wear the trappings of capitalism with all the pride he could muster.

Above
An 1890 catalogue from the Sherman S. Jewett & Company offered heating and cooking stoves. The model with two eight-inch griddles sold for $10 and the model with two nine-inch griddles cost $11.50. (BECHS)

The Scatcherds, the Goodyears, and the Gratwicks made it big in lumber. The Klincks, the Bullymores, and the Dolds ruled the meat-packing industry. Sherman Jewett was in stoves but wore many hats comfortably, finding it not at all inconvenient to also serve as a bank president or take his turn as president of a railroad. There were the Hamlins, whose American Glucose Company supported not one but three fine houses on Delaware Avenue. There were the Glennys and their crockware, the Birges and their wallpaper empire, and the Carys whose abundant wealth sprang from Holland Land Company real estate.

The economically opulent and socially correct Rumseys were leather tanners, as were Jacob Schoellkopf, Myron Bush, Jesse Ketchum, and the Laubs. Schoellkopf, always a man of diverse interests, also found flour milling to his liking, a business that had been George Urban's first choice all along.

William Rogers and Frank Baird were collecting enviable reputations as iron-making tycoons. Colie & Son were off and running in "parlour furniture," predecessors of the modern-day Kittinger Company. The Wendt brothers, William and Henry, built their new Buffalo Forge Company plant right in the heart of the German neighborhood, the better to entice to their payrolls the hardworking German laborers.

Above
These men worked for the A. Ziegele Brewery, which was located at 835 Washington Street. By the 1890s, when this photograph was taken, Buffalo had 22 breweries. (BECHS)

The Buffalo landscape was dotted with breweries—22 of them by the 1890s. The kings of the brewing industry included Gerhard Lang and Magnus Beck. They had no worries about overproduction. There were 1,945 saloons to sop up their output.

Nearly as prolific as the brewers were the bicycle manufacturers. One of the best of the breed was the George N. Pierce Company, which would make the transition from two-wheelers to four-wheelers as the Pierce-Arrow Motor Car Company.

Coining money in soap were the Lautz brothers, R.W. Bell with his "Niagara" soap, and biggest of them all, John D. Larkin. Larkin had sort of an early-day "Avon Calling" soap business. He allowed into it as early partners Elbert Hubbard and Darwin Martin, imaginative young men who joined with Larkin in dreaming up innovative ideas to spur their mail-order soap sales with an endless variety of premium gifts.

Hubbard, when he abandoned the hectic business of merchandising soap, left with sufficient funds to establish the more peaceful Roycroft Institution in East Aurora where craftsmen, working at a more leisurely pace, printed books, tooled leather, and skillfully hammered away at artifacts of silver and bronze.

John Larkin, out of the Horatio Alger mold if anyone ever was, started with nearly nothing and built an empire in the world of soap that made the Larkin name a household word throughout the country. He was fond of propounding his theory that a bright boy, poor but with good ideas, had a better shot at success than did a boy merely born to the purple.

Larkin was one of Buffalo's major employers, and many of his employees were women. The unusual presence of so many "girls and young women" caught the eye of a *Buffalo Courier* reporter who visited the Larkin plant. He thought it worth noting that "to a marked degree, they seem happy and contented.

"A piano, which is in constant use during the noon hour, is an unusual feature of the Larkin plant," the reporter wrote. "To its strains, the young women dance and sing as the mood seizes them."

John J. Albright was another star in the crowded firmament who liked what he saw in Buffalo and chose to plant new roots there in 1882. The city had many reasons to be grateful that he did. In an era in which Buffalo did not lack for giants, Albright had few peers as a financier, industrialist, and patron of the arts and education.

Above
Designed by Edward B. Green of Green and Wicks, the Albright Art Gallery is an outstanding example of Classical Revival architecture. It is considered to be one of Buffalo's most distinguished buildings. (BECHS)

Facing page, top left
John D. Larkin sold his soap and other products with the use of a catalogue.

This cover for the 1913-1914 fall and winter Larkin catalogue was designed by Buffalo illustrator Alex O. Levy. (BECHS)

Facing page, top right
Created by Buffalo Pottery, Deldare Ware is art pottery characterized by a distinctive olive-green hue in contrast to the vividly colored design painted on its surface. Full production began in 1908

on the first series of Deldare Ware with a design adopted from various sources usually depicting old English lifeways, including Cecil Charles Windsor Aldins' Fallowfield Hunt paintings. (BECHS)

Facing page, bottom
Elbert Hubbard, who was involved in the soap-manufacturing business at one time, established the Roycroft Institution for craftsmen in East Aurora. (BECHS)

Dear Sister:-
We are at East
Aurora today and
are having a fine
time love to you a.
Skinny from

Will be home Violet
Saturday evening

Albright's clout as a respected financier helped bring to Buffalo the Lackawanna Steel Company (now Bethlehem Steel) and a new steel plant that was hailed as "the eighth wonder of the world."

Albright was a patron of the Nichols and Franklin private schools. His generosity as a patron of the arts gave Buffalo its pride and joy, the Albright Art Gallery. A generation or two after Albright, Seymour H. Knox, Jr., a latter-day multimillionaire, took the gallery under his beneficent wing. New York art critic John Russell has said of the gallery that now bears the names of both its principal sponsors, "Inch for inch and painting for painting, no museum in this country can better the Albright-Knox in Buffalo when it comes to art of the second half of this [the 20th] century."

Buffalo, when Albright came to it, was the focal point of most eastern railroads worthy of the name—among them, the main line of the New York Central, the Erie, the Lehigh Valley, the Delaware, Lackawanna & Western, the West Shore, the Buffalo, New York & Philadelphia (later part of the Pennsylvania), the Nickel Plate, the Lake Shore & Michigan Southern, the Michigan Central, and the Grand Trunk.

The railroads spawned or enriched such satellite industries as the Wagner sleeping-car works and General Edmund Hayes's Union Bridge Company. Buffalonians welcomed the city's role as a railroad center without compromising their affection for the old Erie Canal. In the midst of the railroad boom, Buffalonians spoke out for a reduction or even elimination of state-imposed tolls on the canal so that the venerable waterway could hold its head high in competition with the upstart railroads.

Meanwhile, traffic in and out of the Buffalo harbor was escalating by leaps and bounds, the Tonawandas were becoming one of the nation's busiest lumber-transfer points, the first telephone exchange began operations in 1879, and new buildings of architectural significance were changing the late-19th-century urban skyline.

The first public building with a price tag of more than $1 million was erected in the 1870s as the City and County Hall (now County Hall). It was designed by architect A.J. Warner of Rochester, and it cost nearly $1.5 million to build. When it officially opened on March 13, 1876, members of the bar in Buffalo ceremoniously marched from the old courthouse on Washington to the new hall on Franklin just below Eagle Street.

That night there was a gala dinner to celebrate the day and pay homage to the brand-new

Facing page, top
This 1890 photograph shows canal barges tied up below the Michigan Street Bridge on the Buffalo River. From the Erie Canal Collection. (BECHS)

Facing page, bottom
The George H. Notter boat yard was located at the foot of Virginia Street. Notter built "vessels, tugs, steamers, and canal boats." From the Erie Canal Collection. (BECHS)

GEORGE H. NOTTER,

H. L. BLISS, PHOTOGRAPHER, 379 MAIN ST.

Builder of Vessels, Tugs, Steamers and Canal Boats

Yard foot of Virginia Street,   (Near Round House,) on Erie Canal,   BUFFALO, N. Y.

City and County Hall. James O. Putnam, a senior member of the bar who had been Lincoln's envoy to Le Havre, spoke affectionately of "the four interesting females who stand as perpetual sentinels at the clock tower," henceforth to be forever "the guardian divinities of the city."

A hundred years later, Buffalonians would let loose a chorus of boos that effectively drowned out an ill-advised suggestion to remove the "perpetual sentinels." Putnam, protesting from the grave, had prevailed.

After the closing of the old courthouse at Washington and Clinton streets, a few public-spirited citizens, fearful that "the historic if not hallowed site" might fall into the hands of some devilishly motivated commercial user, bought it and made it available for a library.

Library facilities in Buffalo had been provided since 1836 by the Young Men's Association. A new Romanesque structure, designed by New York architect C.L.W. Eidlitz, was completed on the old courthouse site and opened in 1887 as the Buffalo Library. The fiercely independent Grosvenor Library, founded in 1870 and nearly as well endowed as the rich and reputable Young Men's Association had been, went its own scholarly way, putting up its own

Above
The Adam, Meldrum & Anderson Company occupied the American Block, seen in this 1886 photograph. Main Place Mall now occupies the site. (BECHS)

new building on Franklin Street. The Buffalo (Public) Library of 1887 stood until the early 1960s, when it was torn down to be replaced by the new Buffalo & Erie County Public Library, into which the Grosvenor had at last been merged.

Built at the same time as the new City and County Hall, and only a few blocks away, was Buffalo's first "high-rise" office building—the six-story, ultra-Victorian German Insurance Building on Main Street at Lafayette Square. A pleasant Sunday afternoon diversion for Buffalonians in 1875 and 1876 was to come downtown and examine the progress of the ornate, iron-laced structure in the making. Later known as the Buffalo Insurance Building, it stood until 1957, when a wrecker's ball demolished it to make way for a glass-faced office building of more contemporary design.

But there was much more going on than just the clatter of new construction. Downtown Buffalo was bursting at the seams as a bustling hub of retailing, and ambitious young merchants were boldly nurturing the roots of what would sprout as new department-store and specialty-store concepts.

William Hengerer, a German immigrant and Civil War veteran, came back after the war to

Above, left
This photograph of Buffalo's German Insurance Company building at the northwest corner of Lafayette Square was taken circa 1905. Courtesy, Buffalo Savings Bank-Roy Nagle Collection. (BECHS)

Above, right
This William Hengerer Company advertising card dates back to the time of the Pan-American Exposition in Buffalo in 1901. (BECHS)

work as a $6-a-week clerk for Barnes, Bancroft & Company, a dry-goods store with origins dating back to 1836. He became a partner in the business in 1874, and in 1895 the store took the "Wm. Hengerer" name.

Robert B. Adam emigrated from Scotland to Boston in 1857 as a merchandising apprentice. Ten years later, when he was ready to strike off on his own, he scanned the continent and chose Buffalo, establishing what would become the Adam, Meldrum & Anderson department store. Adam was so pleased with his choice that he urged his brother, James Noble Adam, to come over from Scotland. James Adam responded by opening the competing J.N. Adam dry-goods store. J.N. Adam not only made his mark as a merchant but got himself elected mayor of Buffalo.

Edward L. Kleinhans, off in Kentucky, viewed the retailing potential in Buffalo with the same enthusiasm as had Robert Adam. His Kleinhans men's store, opened in Buffalo in 1893, became one of the largest of its kind in the country. "I made my money in Buffalo and I want to leave it to Buffalo," said Kleinhans late in life. He kept his word. A generous bequest gave his adopted city its Saarinen-designed Kleinhans Music Hall, home of the Buffalo Philharmonic Orchestra.

Seymour H. Knox, Sr., five-and-dime-store pioneer, opened one of his early stores in Buffalo and in 1890 established his main office here. The Buffalo-based S.H. Knox chain of five-and-tens had more than 100 stores by the time Knox merged it with similar chains to form the F.W. Woolworth Company.

Like the new breed of merchants, young men with publishing careers ahead of them liked what they saw in Buffalo and started newspapers to compete with the *Commercial* (founded in 1835), the *Courier* (1834), and the *Express* (1846).

Edward H. Butler arrived in Buffalo from Le Roy at the age of 23. He started the *Sunday Morning News* in 1873, then added to the ranks of the daily newspapers in 1880 with his *Buffalo Evening News*. Norman Mack, who later became chairman of the Democratic National Committee, started the *Buffalo Sunday Times* in 1879 and made it the daily *Times* four years later.

Above
Lafayette Square had a parklike atmosphere in the 1890s. The Soldiers and Sailors Monument, a Civil War memorial, still stands at its center. Grover Cleveland delivered an address on the occasion of the laying of its cornerstone in 1882. (BECHS)

Top
Seymour H. Knox, at right, poses with employees of his store at 519 Main Street, circa 1894. This store was opened on December 18, 1893, four days after his first Buffalo store at 409 Main Street was completely destroyed in the Wonderland Building fire. In 1895 Knox moved his store to 395 Main Street. (BECHS)

Bottom, left
Norman E. Mack started the Buffalo Sunday Times in 1879 and four years later expanded it to the daily Times. Later he became a longtime member of the Democratic National Committee. (BECHS)

Bottom, right
Edward H. Butler began publishing the Sunday Morning News in 1873. Seven years later his daily Buffalo Evening News went to press. (BECHS)

The city was booming. Help-wanted signs were everywhere. It was as good a time as any and better than most for Buffalo to absorb a new wave of immigrants. This time it was the Poles and the Italians, most of them of peasant stock, who had to contend with the language barrier, housing shortages, and the difficulties of learning trades that would take them into something better than the hardest kind of unskilled labor.

Their coming enriched the city's ethnic mix, but the blending with the Irish and Germans was not easily accomplished. Their intrusion into traditionally Irish and German neighborhoods was at first resented by the feisty Irish and the intractable Germans. The Germans and the Irish were by now long and well entrenched, the Germans to the point of having seen a onetime German immigrant, Philip Becker, elected mayor of Buffalo in the 1870s, not once but again and again.

Few Italians had drifted into the city by then. Luigi Chiesa came in 1848, changed his name to Louis Church, and sold bird cages and mousetraps in a shop at Genesee and Elm streets. Louis Onetto came in 1868, opening an ice cream factory, a wholesale fruit business, and Buffalo's first macaroni factory. But it was in the 1880s and 1890s that the Italians began to come in substantial numbers. By 1892 there were 2,500 of them in Buffalo; by 1930 there were close to 20,000.

Martin Stephanowski, a 47-year-old laborer, and his family were the first Polish Catholics in Buffalo, arriving in 1864. But no more than 30 Polish families followed the Stephanowskis into Buffalo in the next decade. Most of the early Polish immigrants moved on to such Midwestern cities as Chicago, Detroit, and Milwaukee. Then the opening of St. Stanislaus Church in 1874, along with a Polish parochial school, made the Poles feel comfortable in Buffalo and helped trigger the biggest ethnic influx in the city's history. A total of 13,000 Poles came to Buffalo between 1875 and 1892. By the time they were into their fifth generation, there were 300,000 of them in the Buffalo area.

The city to which these new immigrants came was not only booming industrially and commercially but blooming academically and culturally.

A new State Normal School, ancestor of Buffalo State College, was authorized by the state legislature in 1867. It held its first classes in the fall of 1870 in a three-story building erected for the purpose on a site bounded by 13th, 14th, Jersey, and York streets. Such leading citizens as Judge Nathan Hall, lawyers Albert Tracy and Grover Cleveland, the *Courier's*

Above, left
Louis Onetto, seen here in front of his store at 129 Broadway in 1911, opened an ice cream factory, a wholesale fruit business, and a macaroni factory in Buffalo. Though Onetto came to the city in 1868, substantial numbers of Italian immigrants did not arrive until the 1880s and 1890s. (BECHS)

Above, right
The city's more affluent young women attended Buffalo Female Academy on Delaware Avenue at Johnson Park. Evergreen Cottage in the foreground was the former home of Ebenezer Johnson. (BECHS)

Joseph Warren, and industrialist Francis Root were on the first board of trustees.

The Jesuits in 1870 opened Canisius College next door to St. Michael's Church on Washington Street, naming it for the first German Jesuit theologian, St. Peter Canisius, and staffing it with German-born professors.

The University of Buffalo, though still centered primarily around the medical school, expanded into pharmacy in 1886, law in 1887, and dentistry in 1888. Dr. Roswell Park came from Chicago in 1883 to fill the university's chair of surgery and to become chief surgeon at Buffalo General Hospital. His study of malignant tumors led to the establishment of what is now the internationally renowned Roswell Park Memorial Institute for cancer treatment and research.

In 1885 the city built a new Central High School on Court Street at Niagara Square, a location that continued to serve its purpose well into the 20th century. On Delaware Avenue at Johnson Park was the Buffalo Female Academy, catering to socially proper, genteel young ladies. It was the forerunner of the Buffalo Seminary, which now has its academic home base on Bidwell Parkway.

Buffalo's theaters prospered, regularly headlining such superstars as Ellen Terry, Henry Irving, Edwin Booth, Julia Marlowe, E.A. Sothern, and Sarah Bernhardt. A new Music Hall was built in 1883, then rebuilt in 1887, along with the nearby St. Louis Church, after a spectacular fire in 1885 destroyed both buildings. The new Music Hall housed Buffalo's first symphony orchestra in 1887.

Building anything at all—be it a music hall, a church, an educational or charitable institution, a library, an art gallery, or a hospital—seemed to present not the slightest budgetary concern. There was an abundance of wealth waiting to be tapped, in fact eager to be tapped, for whatever monetary subscriptions were needed to serve the common good.

Those who possessed the wealth possessed enough of it to dispense it generously, not only for the common good but for their own well-being. They quickly learned the art of living well. Although they worked hard at their prospering businesses, they soon discovered that the good life did not consist of all work and no play.

The nouveaux riches were of sufficient numbers to carve out a separate and distinct class of "high society" in Buffalo's social structure. By the 1880s Buffalo could boast social registers

Above, left
Stone carvers take a break from their work on the rebuilt Music Hall about 1886. The building, which housed Buffalo's first symphony orchestra, later became the Teck Theatre. (BECHS)

Above, right
Ellen Terry toured the United States several times with Henry Irving's Lyceum Company. She is shown here, circa 1890, in her favorite role as Beatrice in Much Ado About Nothing. *Courtesy, Museum of the City of New York.*

and annual editions of the Blue Book of Society, along with the requisite cycle of charity balls, costume balls, and coming-out parties for debutantes.

Not all of those who qualified for the social register were vintage Anglo-Saxon or "old family." Many of them, as Buffalo historian John T. Horton has observed, had come as immigrants and managed the leap "from steerage to peerage in less than a generation." A memorable coming-out affair of the 1888-1889 social season introduced Helen Schoellkopf, daughter of Jacob Frederick Schoellkopf. She made her bow to society, "a picture in white tulle."

The well-to-do in their leisure hours took up golf, rode to the hounds, and even played polo. They traveled abroad in the summers or vacationed in the Adirondacks, at Saratoga, or at Newport. They built summer homes along the American and Canadian lakeshores.

The Carys, the Wadsworths, the Wilcoxes, the Scatcherds, and the Hamlins were among the first to ride to the hounds in the Genesee Valley hunts that dated from 1876. The Cary and the Rumsey boys dared to risk being ridiculed as dandies by publicly playing polo at the Hamlin Driving Park, better known as a trotting track that made Buffalo the harness-racing capital of the country.

Those in the upper echelons of business and society built elegant mansions up and down Delaware Avenue, mansions big enough to require household staffs of 10 or 20 servants. Domestic help was readily available and affordable. Immigrant couples jumped at the chance to be hired as servants at $20 a month, and they had never heard of the eight-hour day or the five-day week.

The rich also had their own exclusive private clubs. The Buffalo Club was founded in 1867, and the less straitlaced Saturn Club in 1885. There was a Yacht Club by the 1870s, and the Country Club of Buffalo came along in 1889.

The Buffalo Club was the preserve of those who formed the apex of Buffalo's late-19th-century power structure. Rexford Tugwell, one of Franklin Roosevelt's presidential "brain trusters," once described the Buffalo Club as "the resort of the wealthy, powerful, uncontaminated conservatives of the business community . . . a regional center of Capitalism at its time of most unlimited power." It is also the only club of its kind that can boast of having had two Presidents of the United States on its membership roster, Millard Fillmore and Grover Cleveland.

Above
Our Cottage at Idlewood *was taken of the Bartlett family on August 31, 1894. G.F.H. Bartlett, one of Buffalo's finest amateur photographers, created this exquisite document of a Buffalo family on a summer day. Courtesy, G.F.H. Bartlett Collection. (BECHS)*

The Buffalo Club, of course, was exclusively male as well as private. In 1877, when a reception at the club for the ladies was suggested, even the public press raised its editorial voice in dismay. "The ladies are entitled to their rights but men's clubs are not part of them," thundered the *Buffalo Express.*

Whether or not they were piqued, the ladies eventually opened their own private club, the Twentieth Century Club on Delaware Avenue. Its opening, in November 1896, received more prominently positioned coverage in the conservative Buffalo *Commercial* than did the first transmission of electric power from Niagara Falls a few days later. The Twentieth Century Club took a measure of pride in boasting that its Italianate clubhouse was the first of its kind to allow men on the premises as guests of its female members.

The icing on the cake for Buffalonians already dazzled by the glitter of their Golden Age was seeing the second Buffalo politico become President of the United States. Millard Fillmore had made it into the White House in 1850. Grover Cleveland did it in 1885—less than three years after he sat in City Hall as mayor of Buffalo.

Cleveland, a small-town boy from central New York, stopped off in Buffalo in 1855 on his way to Cleveland, Ohio, where he hoped some sort of magic from the similarity of their names would assure him a successful career in the law. His reason for stopping in Buffalo was to pay a courtesy call on his uncle, Lewis Allen, who lived on Niagara Street but was adding to his already considerable fortune by raising cattle on Grand Island.

Allen persuaded his nephew that if a law career was what he wanted, he need go no farther than Buffalo. He sent his 18-year-old nephew downtown to the law firm that handled his business, Bowen & Rogers. Cleveland presented himself at the law firm without bothering to mention his relationship with Allen. Unimpressed with his credentials, or lack of them, the lawyers informed Cleveland there were no job openings at the moment and dismissed him out of hand.

Infuriated when he heard how the job interview had gone, Allen stormed into the law office the next morning and told the surprised lawyers that if the services of his nephew weren't wanted, neither apparently was Allen's legal business. Allen was an important client and the law firm quickly reconsidered, taking Cleveland on as a lowly clerk.

Above, left
Grover Cleveland became assistant district attorney of Buffalo in 1863. This photo of him was taken one year later when the future President was 27 years old. From the Grover Cleveland Collection. (BECHS)

Above, right
A private women's organization, the Twentieth Century Club, met in this Italianate structure on Delaware Avenue. To the left is Temple Beth Zion. (BECHS)

The story goes that Cleveland made so little impression at first that once the lawyers forgot he was there and locked him in the office when they left for the day. "Someday I will be better remembered," the young Cleveland muttered to himself.

Cleveland passed the bar in 1857 and stayed on with the law firm until 1863, when he left to become assistant district attorney. That first faint brush with politics appealed to him, and he ran for district attorney in the next election. Defeated, he returned to the law. For the next 15 years, except when he took time out to be sheriff of Erie County, he practiced law with one after another of his lawyer friends as partners.

Cleveland was a jovial but somewhat pugnacious bachelor, a street-wise, colorful man about town. He enjoyed playing poker with his cronies, and he felt at home in the friendly ambiance of saloons and beer gardens. If there was one thing he liked better than German-American food, it was German-American beer. His preference for both in immoderate quantities caused him to take on an extra 100 pounds even when he still was a young man. His nieces and nephews snickered at his added weight and called him Uncle Jumbo.

Amiable enough unless pushed too far, Cleveland never was one to run from a street fight, even after he attained high office. Once when he was governor of New York, he came home from Albany for a night out with some of his old Buffalo pals. Grover was the first to leave the last saloon, and by the time his friends came out the door they saw two men rolling down the sidewalk, one of them choking the other. It turned out to be Cleveland who was doing the choking and an editor of a Buffalo newspaper who was being choked.

Prying the two apart, one of Cleveland's friends asked, "What's up, Grover?"

"I was just having it out with the son of a bitch," replied Cleveland, brushing off his coat.

Cleveland, like most knowledgeable citizens, knew that the price being paid for Buffalo's rampant growth was rampant corruption in City Hall. Municipal wickedness was growing nearly as fast as the city itself. Cleveland, who had absorbed Democratic politics in the Bowen & Rogers law office and who now had hankerings for political office, was persuaded to run as the Democratic candidate for mayor with a pledge to tackle the skulduggery.

Cleveland had enough political savvy to know how the city was being plundered, and by whom. The citizens had had all the plundering they could stand, and Cleveland was swept into office. He moved into City Hall in January 1882 and promptly kept his promise not to be

Above
When Cleveland was nominated for President in 1884, a grand demonstration was held in his honor in Buffalo. (BECHS)

a reformer but simply to run the city in a businesslike way.

His accomplishments in bringing order out of municipal chaos did not go unnoticed in Albany, where graft at the state level was becoming a way of life. The Democrats tapped Cleveland as their candidate for governor, and the voters in the state responded by promoting Cleveland from mayor to governor in 1883. In the fall of the following year Cleveland was promoted again. He was elected President of the United States.

A dozen years before, Cleveland had had more than a casual relationship with a young widow, Maria Crofts Halpin, who worked in the Flint & Kent department store and lived on Swan Street not far from Cleveland's apartment and law office at Main and Swan. Maria had numerous admirers, but it was to Cleveland that she chose to point the finger when she became pregnant.

Cleveland accepted all the financial responsibilities of fatherhood, but knowing he was only one of several possible fathers, he flatly refused to marry the girl. The child, a boy, was born on September 14, 1874. It took some doing on his part, but Cleveland arranged to have the boy adopted and given a new name. He grew up to become a prominent Buffalo physician.

Although Cleveland's role in the Maria Halpin affair was widely known, it caused no stir at all when he ran for mayor or for governor. But in the presidential campaign of 1884, the paternity issue finally became a political issue. The Republicans alluded to it, and not at all subtly, in a widely promoted campaign chant:

> Ma, Ma, where's my pa?
> Gone to the White House,
> Ha, ha, ha.

But Cleveland won the election anyway, and Buffalo Democrats soon had their own bit of doggerel to chant:

> Hoorah for Maria,
> Hoorah for the kid,
> I voted for Cleveland
> And I'm damned glad I did!

Above, left
An 1888 election poster offered Grover Cleveland and Allen G. Thurman as the Democratic nominees for President and Vice President. Though defeated in this election, Cleveland was reelected in 1892. From the Grover Cleveland Collection. (BECHS)

Above, right
Frances Folsom Cleveland was 22 years old when she became First Lady. She proved to be a thoughtful hostess with the necessary social grace. From the Grover Cleveland Collection. (BECHS)

When Cleveland was inaugurated as President in March 1885, one of Buffalo's most memorable and picturesque characters was lost to the city forever. Whatever other reasons he may have had for not coming back, he complained early in his Presidency that some of his old friends in Buffalo had expected too much from him in the way of favors.

During his first term, Cleveland gave the nation a White House wedding, taking as his bride Frances Folsom of Buffalo, daughter of his onetime bosom buddy and law partner, Oscar Folsom. Cleveland lost his bid for reelection in 1888. He tried again for the Presidency in 1892 and won. Between his two terms, Cleveland lived in New York. At the end of his second term, he retired from public life to Princeton, New Jersey.

In the last months of Cleveland's second term in the White House, there occurred in Buffalo an event of momentous significance that was to change the lifestyle of every business and household on the Niagara frontier. For the first time, electricity was transmitted to Buffalo from its inexhaustible source at Niagara Falls.

For an eon of geologic time, the falls had roared in magnificent, solitary splendor, bursting with potential energy but of no practical use even to a city as close as Buffalo. Only 20 miles from the falls and their awesome power, Buffalo might as well have been 2,000 miles away.

Electricity was available in Buffalo, but only in the most limited amounts, clumsily and primitively generated. Then, in the mid-1890s, scientists began to learn more about how to transmit electricity over long distances. When electricity was transmitted for the first time from Niagara Falls to Buffalo, at the stroke of midnight on November 15, 1896, the event created a new industrial revolution of sorts in Buffalo that, literally and figuratively, began lighting up the whole of the Niagara frontier.

"The power of the Falls will be transmitted to Buffalo as surely as the sun will shine," declared Nikola Tesla, the Yugoslav-born scientist whose work with alternating current was about to make it happen. And he was right.

Oddly enough, in a city accustomed to celebration, there was no celebrating in Buffalo as the first electric power surged in over the 20 miles of wire strung from Niagara Falls. Most Buffalonians went to bed without waiting for the midnight flipping of the switch that would

Above
Thousands gathered in Washington, D.C., for the inauguration of President Cleveland on March 4, 1885. From the Grover Cleveland Collection. (BECHS)

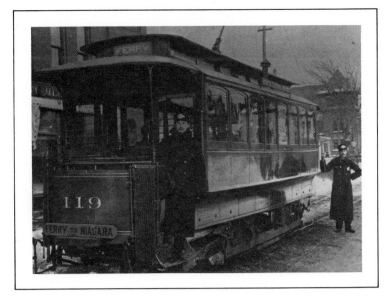

start the power flowing. It wasn't that they were jaded or indifferent. It was just that the significance of the accomplishment would take some time to sink in.

All of the initial block of Niagara power was assigned to the Buffalo Street Railway Company to run its streetcars. Only a dozen or so of those most intimately involved in the success or failure of the venture were on hand at Buffalo Street Railway's powerhouse on Niagara Street when the switch was pulled in Niagara Falls that started the flow of power to Buffalo. But somebody did think to fire the traditional cannon salute, and in doing so briefly roused the nearby citizens from their slumber.

It was 71 years since Augustus Porter, the old Black Rock patriarch, had first begged "Eastern Capitalists" to join him in a bold venture to harness the energy of Niagara. But his pleadings were ignored, and Porter died long before Niagara grudgingly began giving up its latent power.

The companies that finally succeeded in generating electricity and sending it to Buffalo had among their first "money subscribers" J. Pierpont Morgan, William K. Vanderbilt, Darius Ogden Mills, August Belmont, the Lehman brothers, and Lord Rothschild of London. Their board members included Mills, Nicholas Biddle, and John Jacob Astor. The names would have been unfamiliar to Porter, but the size of their bankrolls would have impressed him.

After Porter, three companies went through $1.5 million trying to build a canal that would tap into the Niagara above its rapids, move its waters through the village of Niagara Falls, and then drop it from the high bank above the Niagara Gorge. They were not thinking yet of electricity, but simply of waterpower.

The canal was nearly dug, but all three companies ran out of money before it became operative. The last of the three was being squeezed by its creditors, and on May 1, 1877, the power canal and its water rights went on the auction block.

One of the curious who went from Buffalo to watch the auction, and perhaps to bid if the price was right, was Jacob Frederick Schoellkopf.

The opening bid was $5,000; the second raised it to $20,000. The auctioneer implored the bidders to stop joking. At that point, Schoellkopf ventured a bid of $67,000. The auctioneer cried out Schoellkopf's bid again and again, as though to inspire a higher one. But no one had raised it by lunchtime.

Above
The Buffalo Street Railway received the first block of power to arrive in Buffalo from Niagara Falls in 1896. (BECHS)

After lunch, Schoellkopf's bid was topped by $100. There the bidding remained until 4:30 in the afternoon, when Schoellkopf upped his own bid to $71,000. "Going once, going twice, going three times," croaked the auctioneer at last. "And sold to Mr. Jacob Schoellkopf."

Schoellkopf, at the age of 57 a successful leather tanner and flour miller, returned to his Buffalo home at 486 Franklin Street the owner of a nonfunctioning power canal in Niagara Falls.

By the following year, Schoellkopf had formed his new Niagara Falls Hydraulic Power & Manufacturing Company. In it with Schoellkopf was George Matthews, his flour-milling partner. Schoellkopf's son Arthur took up residency in Niagara Falls to manage the new venture.

By 1882 Schoellkopf had built a small power station. Clustered around it, making use of its waterpower, were three flour mills (two of them Schoellkopf's), four pulp mills, a silver-plating shop, and the village waterworks. Its waterpower was also being used for the first time to generate a small amount of electricity that was made available to light a few stores and streets.

The tiny power facility was a forerunner of the later world-famous Schoellkopf hydro-electric station at Niagara Falls that delivered immense amounts of electric power until a rockslide at the Niagara Gorge demolished it on June 8, 1956.

It was Schoellkopf who blazed trails, who succeeded where others failed in latching onto the elusive power at Niagara Falls. Ironically, it was not Schoellkopf but those who meant to compete with him who managed the final breakthrough in learning how to move Niagara's power beyond the confines of Niagara Falls to larger consumer markets such as Buffalo.

Bringing Niagara's power to Buffalo was accomplished by two affiliated companies, Niagara Falls Power Company and the Cataract Construction Company. It was these Schoellkopf competitors who built the world's first super power station at Niagara Falls and then probed the world's best scientific and engineering minds in ambitious pursuit of a way to transmit their power to Buffalo.

Jacob Schoellkopf was celebrating his 77th birthday on the day Niagara Falls power first came to Buffalo. When he died, just short of two years later, his Hydraulic Power Company was carried on by his partner, Matthews, and by the Schoellkopf heirs.

Above
This June 7, 1956, photograph documents the first day of a series of rockfalls from the face of the Niagara Gorge and toward the upstream end of the multi-million-dollar Schoellkopf Station. Courtesy, Niagara Gazette.

The Schoellkopf company and the Niagara Falls Power Company went their separate ways for several years—the Schoellkopfs with their ever-expanding Schoellkopf hydroelectric station, and Niagara Falls Power with its great Edward Dean Adams station.

At last, in 1918, the two companies merged as a new Niagara Falls Power Company. The nature of the merger put the combined companies under the control and management of the heirs of Jacob Frederick Schoellkopf. The newly formed company evolved into what eventually became a key part of the modern-day Niagara Mohawk Power Corporation.

Much of the Schoellkopf stock in the power company reposed in the portfolio of the Niagara Share Corporation, a Schoellkopf-managed investment company in Buffalo. The 1956 rockslide that destroyed the Schoellkopf hydroelectric station naturally had an adverse effect on the price of the power company's stock. Once again, there surfaced the old legend of the Schoellkopf magic. The Niagara Share Corporation had sold the last of its shares only days before the rockslide. Grown and otherwise sophisticated men grumbled that the Schoellkopf-managed investment company must have known it was going to happen!

Above
Schoellkopf 3C is shown in this 1924 photograph during construction. The men are posed on a penstock constructed to carry water from the canal up above the power station to a water turbine. From the Niagara Mohawk Collection. (BECHS)

CHAPTER VII

THE PAN-AMERICAN EXPOSITION

In the same year that Buffalo received its first power from Niagara Falls, the city also got two new downtown office buildings of architectural significance. One was architect Louis Sullivan's vertical-lined high-rise that became known as the Prudential Building. The other was the massive Ellicott Square, designed in the style of the Italian Renaissance by Daniel Burnham.

Think big, architect Burnham begged the builders when he was retained to design the Ellicott Square. "Make no little plans," he told them. "They have no magic to stir men's blood."

The builders were easily persuaded, and Ellicott Square was for some time the world's largest office building. The extravagant dimensions of Ellicott Square were entirely appropriate, mirroring the expansive mood that prevailed in Buffalo in the Gay Nineties.

At the very moment when Sullivan's and Burnham's striking new office buildings were going up, big-thinking Buffalonians were contemplating a great Pan-American Exposition that would symbolize the image of a city on the move.

Above
Season passes were issued for various attractions at the Pan-American Exposition. (BECHS)

Facing page
President McKinley speaks from the Esplanade at the Pan-American Exposition on September 5, 1901. It was President's Day at the exposition. From the Pan-American Exposition Collection. (BECHS)

Word of such an exposition first leaked out in Atlanta, Georgia, at a Buffalo Day dinner held in connection with a Georgia exposition. But back in Buffalo, plans moved at a snail's pace and, in fact, were interrupted completely during the Spanish-American War.

Then, in early 1899, when it appeared that Detroit might snatch the Pan-American from Buffalo's grasp, influential Buffalonians moved fast. Enabling legislation that restructured a previous Pan-American Exposition Company was introduced in the state legislature on January 16, 1899, and passed three days later.

Lawyer John Milburn became president of the Pan-American, and lumber tycoon John Scatcherd was vice president. A finance committee headed by lawyer Franklin D. Locke took little more than an hour to draft a financing plan and then announced, "There will be no difficulty in raising all the money that will be needed."

A site was selected north of Delaware Park Lake between Elmwood and Delaware avenues, and leases were signed on September 5, 1899. All Buffalo awaited the coming exposition with eager anticipation—including the last of the ladies of the once-infamous Canal Street district, who hoped the Pan-American would bring back old times to their changing neighborhood.

The hometown girls found themselves momentarily threatened when their counterparts from New York City invaded the Canal Street district to share in the hoped-for renaissance. The Canal Street regulars rose to the challenge, and there ensued a grand hair-pulling battle that lasted for eight hours and was listed by the police as a riot.

The New York invaders were put on judicial notice to remove themselves from Buffalo within 24 hours. Their eviction was described by one Buffalo newspaper reporter as "a noteworthy victory for hometown industry."

In the meantime, however, there was a new century to be greeted. But when? It was a question that aroused a surprising amount of interest and controversy among Buffalonians, and indeed all Americans, during the early months of 1899. Editorials, letters to the editors, and occasional feature articles in Buffalo newspapers took sides on the question. Those holding the point of view that December 31, 1899, marked the end of the 19th century urged civic leaders to begin making plans for an appropriate celebration at midnight on that date. Proponents of the December 31, 1900, date were less demanding of swift civic action.

It was the latter point of view that ultimately won out. One logical argument—credited

Above
The illumination of the Pan-American Exposition was designed with the Electric Tower as the focal point. The tower was used as a searchlight, signaling at night. The signals were answered by an observation tower located miles away in Niagara Falls. From the G.F.H. Bartlett Collection. (BECHS)

to Dr. Albert Shaw, editor of the influential *Review of Reviews*—put it this way: "None of the people who have proposed to allow ninety-nine years to go for a century would suppose that a $1,900 debt had been fully met by a payment of $1,899." This argument must surely have appealed to the hardheaded businessmen of Buffalo, and local leaders planned to welcome the 20th century at the time when December 31, 1900, changed to January 1, 1901.

As daylight turned to darkness on the last day of the century, a crowd began to assemble in downtown Buffalo. Newspapers estimated it at "more than 100,000." A proportion of these thousands marched in a long parade that wound through the downtown streets to Lafayette Square. More thousands watched the parade, applauding the colorful units as they passed. All observers expressed admiration for the illuminated buildings to which softly falling snow gave added beauty.

The illumination of downtown Buffalo on this occasion was provided by a mixture of gas and electric lights. The City and County Hall (now Erie County Hall) glowed with 1,500 gas lamps. The front of the Iroquois Building featured a string of electric lights that formed "1901." On the Prudential Building, a bank of powerful electric lights flashed on to indicate the hour of midnight. As the new day, the new month, the new year, and the new century arrived, the crowd in downtown Buffalo went wild.

The Pan-American Exposition, a dazzling baroque city unto itself in which Spanish Renaissance was the dominant architectural theme, opened on an unseasonably cold May 1 in 1901. Its centerpiece was the Electric Tower, rising elegant and straight with a jewel-like pinnacle. A replica of it is the tower of Buffalo's Electric Building that remains an enduring and endeared downtown landmark to this day.

A popular gathering place at the exposition was the Temple of Music, where a great organ played and the bands of John Philip Sousa and the Royal Mexican Artillery entertained. All summer long, it seemed that nothing could mar the Pan-American's near perfection. In its fifth month, President William McKinley himself came to visit the Pan-American.

The presidential visit ominously got off on the wrong foot. McKinley's train, en route from his Canton, Ohio, home to the Amherst Street station nearest the exposition, slowed as it passed the downtown Exchange Street station. The usual cannoneers were waiting and, not

Above
This canal scene shows the northwest corner of the Electricity Building. Gliding under beautiful, arched bridges, a visitor could navigate the Grand Canal by either electric launch or gondola.

One could always walk, but a weary visitor could also travel around the exposition grounds by way of a miniature railway or by wheelchair. From the Pan-American Exposition Collection. (BECHS)

to be denied their simple pleasure, let loose a 21-gun salute. But the Coast Artillery gun crew had erred in placing the guns too close to the railroad tracks.

The windows of the train were shattered. The presidential entourage and luggage were hurled into the aisles of the cars. Drinks were spilled and glass was everywhere. The train, instead of merely slowing down, screeched to a hissing halt. Smelling salts were administered to the ailing Mrs. McKinley. A mystified but smiling President, meaning to restore calm, stepped to the observation platform and doffed his high silk hat.

The next day, September 5, was President's Day at the Pan-American. McKinley was in attendance, seemingly none the worse for his unexpectedly thunderous reception the previous afternoon. The following day, September 6, McKinley went to Niagara Falls but returned to the exposition in time for a 4:00 p.m. reception at the Temple of Music, where he would shake as many hands as could be clasped in an allotted time.

Toward the end of the line of handshakers was a rather handsome young man with a bandaged hand. His name, as the world would soon know, was Leon Czolgosz, and he had come from Ohio to Buffalo considerably in advance of the presidential visit to await the chance for what he was about to do.

As Czolgosz moved into close-range position for the presidential handshake, a shot was fired. It sounded like a muffled firecracker. McKinley rose on his toes, clutched at his chest, and pitched forward. Then came a second shot from the gun concealed in the bandaged hand. Blood stained the President's vest. Czolgosz was about to fire a third shot when he was viciously tackled, picked up and beaten about the skull, and sent sprawling again.

"Go easy on him, boys," said the injured President.

Outside were 100,000 visitors on the exposition grounds. Their shock exploded into anger as word of the shooting spread like wildfire. Shouts of "Kill the assassin!" and "Hang him!" echoed through the crowd. A carriage reeled and tottered, its horses urged to a dead run, as it sped Czolgosz away from the threatening mob and downtown to police headquarters. A police clerk took Czolgosz's only signed statement.

"I killed President McKinley because I done my duty. I didn't believe one man should have so much service and another man should have none."

But McKinley was not yet dead. Dr. Roswell Park, one of the most celebrated abdominal

Oct. 12, 1800.

surgeons in the country, was the obvious choice to attend the wounded President. But Park was in Niagara Falls performing surgery. When he learned of the shooting, he hurried back to Buffalo. By the time he arrived, an operation—undertaken, Dr. Park later charged, with "undue haste"—was already well underway. Dr. Matthew Mann, a gynecologist with no experience in treating gunshot wounds, was in charge. After the surgery, McKinley was removed to the home of John Milburn at 1168 Delaware Avenue.

Meanwhile, members of the President's Cabinet hurried to Buffalo, as did news correspondents. The press corps of 250 that came to follow the state of the President's health was the largest ever assembled. The newsmen occupied hastily improvised quarters in tents across Delaware Avenue from the Milburn home.

The President lingered on, and for awhile there seemed no reason to believe he wouldn't recover. But on September 13, he took a turn for the worse. By late afternoon, George Cortelyou of the White House staff gave the word that the press should be alerted.

"Tell the boys the President is dying," Cortelyou ordered. "They might as well know."

At 1:00 in the morning of September 14, the Buffalo *Commercial* jumped the gun and hit the streets with an extra. The headline announced, "He Is Dead." That was good enough for District Attorney Thomas Penney, who dispatched the coroner to the Milburn house.

As it turned out, the *Commercial* and the coroner were only slightly premature. The President was pronounced dead at 2:10 on the morning of September 14.

Vice President Theodore Roosevelt, thinking McKinley was out of danger, was off on a camping trip in the Adirondacks. When he finally was reached at his remote camping spot, his first reaction was: "I don't want to be President through a graveyard."

Roosevelt arrived at the Exchange Street station in Buffalo and was whisked off by carriage at such a fast clip that a cavalry escort had to gallop to keep up. At 3:30 on the afternoon of September 14, he took the oath of office in the library of the Ansley Wilcox mansion at 641 Delaware Avenue, wearing a gray frock coat and gray pin-striped trousers borrowed on the spot. John R. Hazel, United States District Judge in Buffalo, administered the presidential oath of office.

For Leon Czolgosz, the wheels of justice spun with furious speed. His trial began in Buffalo on September 23, and on the 24th, 10 days after McKinley's death, the jury returned a

Facing page, top left
Though photographs exist of McKinley prior to the assassination and of the interior of the Temple of Music after the tragic event, this artist's conception of the scene from Leslie's Illustrated Weekly provided Americans with a view of what the paper called "the foulest crime of the new century." From the McKinley Collection. (BECHS)

Facing page, top right
This photograph of the Wilcox House was made by Oscar Simon on the day Theodore Roosevelt was sworn in as President of the United States in the library there. Reporters are gathered on the lawn. (BECHS)

Facing page, bottom
President McKinley's remains were conveyed from City Hall to an awaiting train in Buffalo, New York. The funeral procession shown here is rounding the corner at Church and Main streets. St. Paul's Cathedral stands on this corner, with the Prudential (Guaranty) Building behind it. From the McKinley Collection. (BECHS)

LESLIE'S WEEKLY
ILLUSTRATED

Vol. XCIII—No. 2402   New York, September 21, 1901   PRICE 10 CENTS

THE FOULEST CRIME OF THE NEW CENTURY

verdict of guilty. The jury was out for only 34 minutes—and there were those who thought even that was unnecessarily long.

On October 28, 45 days after McKinley's death by assassination, Czolgosz was dead by electrocution at Auburn Prison.

The McKinley assassination had a chilling effect on the Pan-American, but the exposition went bravely on until November 2, 1901, by which time more than 8 million visitors had passed through its turnstiles. Most agreed that John Milburn had done a masterful job in presiding over the Pan-American both in its days of glory and in its hours of tragedy.

Milburn's presidency of the Pan-American, as it turned out, had an unexpected and enormously beneficial side effect. Indirectly, at least, it helped bring to Buffalo a new $60-million Lackawanna Steel plant which, expanded and modernized many times over, is the present-day Bethlehem Steel plant.

Lackawanna Iron & Steel was located in Scranton, Pennsylvania. In the last year of the 19th century, the company decided that being in Scranton worked to its disadvantage and settled on Buffalo as its first choice as a site for a new plant.

Walter Scranton, the company's president, came to Buffalo on March 23, 1899, with a letter of introduction to John Milburn. He outlined the company's plant-building plans and inquired of Milburn whether Buffalo had the men of vision and capital-raising capabilities to accommodate a venture of the scope he had in mind.

Milburn picked up his telephone and called John Albright. Albright, in turn, called William Rogers. Rogers was in Cleveland for the day, but he hurried home. By the following day, a deal to bring the steel plant to Buffalo was substantially agreed upon.

All were agreed that the perfect site for the plant was the shore of Lake Erie south of the city. Albright and Milburn, with the help of realtor Charles Gurney, then went about the delicate business of buying the lakeshore property without tipping their hand and driving up the price.

Because Milburn was president of the Pan-American Exposition Company and Albright was involved in it, the landowners assumed their land was being bought as the site for the still-to-come exposition—an impression that no one felt compelled to correct. "If the landowners had expected the land purchase was for a steel company," explained Albright many years later, "their price might have become prohibitive and the steel company would have gone elsewhere." As it was, the land was acquired at a reasonable price and plans for the steel plant proceeded on schedule.

The cold dollars-and-cents figures in the books of the Pan-American Company, however, showed that the exposition lost money. In addition to the financial loss, the exposition had been marred by the unspeakable tragedy of a presidential assassination. Yet for all that, Buffalonians in retrospect found the Pan-American to have been a splendid way to say goodbye to a 19th century that had been extremely good to them and to welcome a new 20th century toward which they entertained the most exuberant expectations.

Facing page, top
Deputy Sheriffs Brady and Haskell are in the foreground of this 1901 photograph showing 11 of the 12 jurors who convicted Leon Czolgosz of assassinating McKinley. A guilty verdict was returned on September 24th. A week earlier Judge Emery had been sent an anonymous and threatening note warning against this possible verdict. From the McKinley Collection. (BECHS)

Facing page, bottom
Even in the rain, crowds flocked to the exposition. From the Pan-American Exposition Collection. (BECHS)

Part II. Buffalo in the 20th Century, by Richard C. Brown

CHAPTER VIII

THE GOLDEN YEARS

The Pan-American Exposition revealed Buffalo to the nation and to the Western Hemisphere as "a city of enterprise, stability, and business energy." It now remained for Buffalo's leaders to build on this reputation.

There was a solid cadre of local leadership available to meet the challenge. Members of families with the names Adam, Albright, Allen, Baird, Desmond, Kellogg, Larkin, and on through the alphabet, joined with Schoellkopfs, Butlers, Knoxes, Goodyears, and others with vision, capital, and initiative. The sons and daughters of these leading families played significant roles in Buffalo's progress throughout the golden years of the first quarter of the 20th century.

The assassination of President McKinley brought to the White House a new kind of President, one with close ties to the second largest city in the Empire State. Buffalo shared many of the qualities—pride, energy, and optimism—of the youthful President Theodore Roosevelt, who was to become the prototype of the "strong" American Presidents of the 20th century.

Taking the oath of office in the Delaware Avenue home of his friend Ansley Wilcox marked only the latest of Theodore Roosevelt's visits to the City on the Lake. Prior to becom-

Facing page, top
A band concert added to the pleasure of canoeing on Delaware Park Lake, 1915. (BECHS)

Facing page, bottom
During the 19th century tennis was one of the few sports in which women participated. This photo by Harlow Boyce entitled After a Game of Tennis *was taken circa 1890. From the Boyce Collection. (BECHS)*

ing a nationally known figure, he had visited Buffalo a number of times to lecture on good citizenship before the members of the Liberal Club, a group interested in political reform. Heeding his lessons, by 1900 they had organized a Civil Service Reform Association that sought to fill municipal jobs through merit examinations rather than political patronage.

With TR in the White House, the reformers pressed on boldly for a "commission" form of city government, a plan favored by progressives of the time. They achieved their goal in 1916, when a new city charter put Buffalo's government into the hands of five commissioners elected from the city at large rather than from five districts or wards. One of the five commissioners acted as chairman or mayor.

The commission form of city government lasted only a little more than a decade in Buffalo. At the time of its inception, it was thought to be a progressive step in the direction of eliminating "bossism" from city government. Buffalo was the largest city ever to adopt the commission form of government, a fact that attracted much attention from progressives throughout the land.

Inhabited sections of the city grew outward from the river and the lake in the early decades of the new century. Homes of the wealthy occupied Delaware Avenue north of Niagara Square as well as Franklin, Elmwood, and some of the streets running between these thoroughfares. Other mansions were built along parkways intersecting the circles on Richmond and Delaware. The largest usually repeated the Queen Anne, Italianate, or Gothic styles popular in the 1880s and 1890s, though often with variations favored by individual owners and architects. The very rich had their palatial homes built of brick or stone, while the moderately well-to-do imitated the popular styles in wood with more modest dimensions—variations that came to bear the name Victorian. Still, these Victorian homes were large enough to accommodate a servant or two and perhaps a widowed or orphaned relative.

Around 1900 the prosperous Larkin enterprises—the Larkin Soap Company and its numerous affiliates—needed a new administration building in Buffalo. Frank Lloyd Wright, then in his early 30s and not yet internationally famous, was brought in from Chicago to design the new building. Wright came to Buffalo, a young rebel out of the West, to do the necessary site work before returning to his Oak Park studio to design the revolutionary Larkin Administration Building.

Above, left
Considered to be a masterpiece by architectural historians, Buffalo's Prudential Building was designed by Louis Sullivan of the Chicago firm of Adler and Sullivan. It has a steel-frame construction and a characteristic Sullivan facade which leads the eye upward to its cornice. Built originally as the Guaranty Building, this early office building was constructed between 1895 and 1898. (BECHS)

Above, right
The Ellicott Square Building was completed in 1896 at a cost of $3.5 million. Designed with Renaissance details by D.H. Burnham, it has a large central court with a glass roof. When it was built, it was the largest office building in the world. (BECHS)

In his autobiography, Wright referred to the Larkin Building as "the first emphatic outstanding protest against the tide of meaningless elaboration sweeping the United States." It had a plain exterior, a cliff of brick and stone, hermetically sealed against "the poisonous gases in the smoke from the New York Central trains that puffed along beside it." A central court provided interior light for the building. The top story was a conservatory and restaurant, while the roof was a recreation area paved with brick. Furniture of steel and magnesite—"probably the cement used by the Romans and good in Rome until today"—was fixed in place.

All who worked in the Larkin Administration Building appreciated it in practice, claimed Wright, but "it was all too severe for the Fundamentalist English taste of the Larkin family." The Larkins, complained the architect, never realized "the place their building took in the thought of the world—for they never hesitated to make senseless changes in it in after years." The building was finally torn down in 1950.

Frank Lloyd Wright had harsh words indeed for the architectural taste of the Larkins, describing them as "pall bearers for the remains of Thomas Jefferson." At the same time, he strongly approved of the architectural tastes of two Larkin executives, D.D. Martin and W.R. Heath, for whom he designed residences. Low-slung horizontal lines and broad eaves made these and two other "Prairie Houses," all designed in 1903 and 1904, startlingly different from anything else in Buffalo at the time. These four homes have survived and remain today among Buffalo's best-known structures.

Of course, most Buffalo residents during the golden years were neither rich nor poor, but somewhere in between. This large middle class lived in single-family homes or flats outside the areas of more pretentious homes. Bungalows, a new style of middle-class house, began to appear in Buffalo near the time of World War I. At first the newly built bungalows confined their occupants to one floor. As time passed, however, attics under the moderately sloping roofs of the bungalows might be converted into additional living space, either for members of the family or to be rented out. In the latter case, they became known as "income bungalows," recognized as adaptations of the original style.

More typical of Buffalo's rental housing was the two-family flat, which made its first appearance in the 1920s. These resembled two single-story houses, one on top of the other. A living room, dining room, and kitchen made up the front part of each, with a bathroom and three or four bedrooms "down the hall." Each had a front porch, with the roof of the lower

Above
The Darwin Martin residence was part of a complex of buildings located at 123 Jewett Parkway in Buffalo. Scholars consider the Martin development to be Frank Lloyd Wright's most important Prairie School residential complex. This front view of the Martin Home was made in 1907, three years after it was built. (BECHS)

porch serving as the floor of the upper one. Thrifty Buffalo home buyers could live in one unit and rent the other until both were paid for. Today these two-family flats can be seen in most parts of the city, but especially in north Buffalo along both sides of Colvin and adjacent streets.

Apartments, as we know them today, were relatively late coming to Buffalo. One reason was that apartments bore a connotation of "French-style" living, thought by conservative Buffalonians to be slightly scandalous. Nevertheless, the Lexington Apartments were occupied early in the 20th century by substantial citizens and other apartment complexes were built as far north as Amherst, between Delaware and Elmwood, by the 1920s.

What kinds of activities engaged Buffalonians during the first quarter of the 20th century? To begin with, making a living took a considerable part of each adult male's waking hours, whether that male slept at night in a Queen Anne mansion, a Victorian house, a bungalow, or a two-family flat. Sons of the well-to-do tended to follow their fathers into business, banking, or the professions, or perhaps into industrial leadership. Sons of the less prosperous tended to follow their fathers into what have become known as blue-collar occupations. Of 100 workers employed in 1920 in Buffalo's five leading industries, 42 were engaged in foundry and machine-shop work, 20 in flour and grain milling, 16 in the iron and steel industry, 16 in printing establishments, and the remaining 6 in the growing manufacture of motor vehicles and parts. Added to these would be Buffalo's share of the 543,000 persons employed nationally in railroading, a share larger than most cities' as Buffalo was then the nation's second largest rail center.

Buffalo women working outside their homes made up only 19 percent of the city's labor force in 1920. Mainly they held poorly paid white-collar jobs as elementary-school teachers, salesclerks, typists, and telephone switchboard operators.

Within their leisure hours, Buffalonians of both sexes and all ages had ample opportunities for outdoor enjoyment in the city's magnificent park system. "The Park," planned by Frederick Law Olmsted in the 1870s, had become Delaware Park by 1900. "The Parade" had been renamed Humboldt Park. Riverside, South, and Cazenovia parks had also been established. These five plus 20 minor parks and parkways added up to more than 1,000 acres free

Above
Members of the 19th-century baseball team of Buffalo posed for a studio photograph, circa 1900. Buffalo was one of America's first cities with its own professional baseball team. (BECHS)

and open to the public. Moreover, city parks were becoming places to do things rather than areas to be looked at only. Bicycle paths, baseball diamonds, wading pools, bowling greens, and small lakes for rowing and canoeing were replacing flower gardens and "Keep Off the Grass" signs.

Baseball was unquestionably the leading spectator sport. Buffalo in the 19th century was one of the first American cities to have a professional baseball team. After that the city had at one time or another professional teams in a variety of minor leagues and, for one year, in the old Federal League, a rival to the two major leagues of the time. Thousands watched the professionals play. Additional thousands themselves played baseball for Buffalo's many amateur teams, which also attracted crowds of spectators to their games.

Golf and tennis were yet to become the popular mass sports they are for spectators and participants today. Still, Delaware Park contained a public golf course by 1912, and there was talk of building tennis courts in the same area. Professional football and basketball were still embryos by the early 1920s, though both games had been played by amateur high-school and college teams in the Buffalo area since the turn of the century.

A few women of the time played golf or tennis, but only these few engaged in active sports, with the exception of bicycling. The "safety bicycle" took the country by storm in the 1890s, and its widespread use for exercise and for transportation lasted well into the 20th century. The "safety," unlike earlier bicycles, had two wheels of the same size with the seat or saddle placed above and between them. When pneumatic tires—invented half a century before but now achieving their first practical use—were added to its wheels, the popularity of the safety bicycle was amazingly enhanced. Such a machine could be modified to enable ladies to ride it with little change in attire.

The first woman in the United States credited with riding a safety bicycle was Buffalo-born Mrs. William F. Smith, whose husband built the first lady's bicycle in America. Bicycle clubs were prominent in Buffalo for decades, with members of both sexes joining for excursions, races, and other activities. Physicians endorsed this form of ladylike exercise. "No other invention for 200 years," declared one practitioner, "has, from a physical point of view, done so much for the human family."

Amateur and professional bicycle races were popular for a time, with some of the speediest riders in the country calling Buffalo home. Outdoor road races were less frequent

Above
Members of the Ramblers' Bicycle Club pose at the Sheridan Drive boathouse in 1912. From the Buffalo Savings Bank-Roy Nagle Collection. (BECHS)

after 1900, but six-day bicycle races for professionals were held indoors in Buffalo's sports arenas for many years into the 20th century.

Then, as now, Buffalo used its waterways for work and for play. Major industries, including those known then or later as Socony Mobil Oil Company, Republic Steel Corporation, Donner-Hanna Coke Corporation, and two divisions of Allied Chemical, concentrated their activities along the Buffalo River. The Erie and the Bennett grain elevators stood on the bank of the hardworking stream that as late as World War I served as a dumping place for Buffalo's sewers. In the years immediately following that war, Buffalo harbor stood at the height of its first 100 years' existence. From the lighthouse at its entrance, an observer could watch the *State of Ohio* pass by on its way from Buffalo to Cleveland—that is, until the boat was destroyed by fire in 1924.

Other sights in and around the harbor might include busy little tugs such as the *John M. Truby* shepherding lake boats into berths along the Buffalo River and the Lake Erie Basin, or the freighter *W.H. Stevens*, which carried a few passengers along with its cargo between Buffalo and other cities on the Great Lakes. Canal boats could be seen emerging from the Black Rock Channel and the Evans Ship Canal.

Buffalonians seeking entertainment on the water might take a steamer trip to Erie Beach with its elaborate casino on the Canadian shore. Another time they might enjoy a day at Canada's Crystal Beach, reached by means of the paddle-wheeled *Pearl*, or board an excursion boat to Grand Island from a dock at the foot of Amherst Street. Members of the Buffalo Yacht Club could go for a pleasant sail on Lake Erie or the upper Niagara River, then return to their clubhouse at the foot of Porter Avenue. More strenuous entertainment was available to members of the West Side Rowing Club from their base near the quiet waters of the Black Rock Canal.

The Erie Canal, the waterway responsible for much of Buffalo's 19th-century prosperity, underwent a change in the early decades of the 20th. For years canal traffic had declined because the mule-drawn boats were too slow and too small to compete with the railroads. Widening, deepening, and straightening the old canal at points between Albany and Buffalo would provide a channel that could be used by barges and other motor-driven vessels. Work on this project began in the 1890s. When it was completed in 1918, the new waterway was re-christened the New York State Barge Canal.

Above
The Erie Beach Casino on Lake Erie was built in the 1880s and closed in 1930. From the Buffalo Savings Bank-Roy Nagle Collection. (BECHS)

Facing page, clockwise from top left
The invention of the safety bicycle greatly popularized the sport of bicycling. These turn-of-the-century women were among the many ladies who enjoyed the sport. (BECHS)

Between 1892 and 1899 the Corona made excursions to Woodlawn Beach, south of the city. (BECHS)

Legislation to permit the city to pursue plans for a park system was passed in 1869. Frederick Law Olmsted's innovative concept provided Buffalo with a system of large and small park spaces

connected by wide, green, and forested parkways. (BECHS)

The entrance to the Buffalo River and Harbor is seen in the distance of this photograph, circa 1910, with the coal trestle, the Bennett Elevator, and the China of Erie. (BECHS)

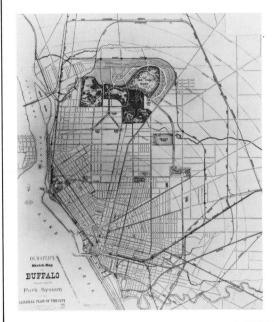

By this time Buffalo's rough, tough Canal Street or "towpath" section had begun to show signs of old age, though it continued to offer its dubious charms until it finally succumbed to bulldozers and wrecking cranes in the 1940s and 1950s, making room for the Dante Place Apartments (later renamed the Marine Drive Apartments). In the earlier part of the century, however, canal and lake sailors continued to seek out this wild and wicked section during their layovers between trips.

Some years before the Prohibition Amendment, the Buffalo Board of Fire Underwriters reported on a survey of 80 buildings lining two of the towpath section's principal streets, Canal and Commercial. Of the 80 buildings, 58 were saloons, five were noted as "Special," and one was marked "refused to allow survey." Probably Water, Evans, State, River, and Le Couteulx, the dark alleylike streets that intersected Commercial and Canal, had an equally high ratio of saloons to total buildings. The thirsty sailor or incautious visitor who wandered there might find more danger than he had bargained for. Bodies had a way of turning up in the murky waters of the canal that gave the towpath section its name.

There were, of course, quieter and more decent drinking places in early 20th-century Buffalo. Workingmen could enjoy a game of cards, a glass of wine, a mug of beer, and plenty of conversation in their neighborhood tavern—the poor man's club. Families found food, drink, and music to their taste in a number of outdoor beer gardens that moved their tables indoors during unseasonable weather. Theater bars, such as that at the Gayety, offered theatergoers a chance for refreshment between acts as well as before and after performances.

Buffalo's beer-drinking tradition, well established by its early residents, was reinforced by waves of 19th-century immigrants from Germany. Buffalo's brewers of the early 20th century could draw upon the immense store of barley held in the city's grain elevators—at times amounting to a third of the nation's total supply—using the barley to produce malt that was either turned into beer locally or marketed elsewhere for the same purpose. As the 20th century began, brewing was a significant industry in the City by the Lake, with a total of 18 breweries and 16 malt shops in Buffalo in 1900. Twenty years later Prohibition put an end to this industry, at least temporarily.

Whether going to work, to a tavern, to church, or to a park, thousands of Buffalonians daily made use of public transportation. What might be called the city's first mass-transportation system was a branch of the New York Central Railroad known as the Belt Line. This 15-mile loop was originally constructed to transport passengers around the outskirts of the city.

Above
Buffalo's impressive theaters staged vaudeville and burlesque, as well as legitimate drama. Theaters like the Gayety offered a bar so that theatergoers could partake of refreshment close to the stage. From Buffalo Savings Bank-Roy Nagle Collection. (BECHS)

It proved so useful, however, that industries developed alongside its tracks, while residential areas soon extended far beyond the Belt Line.

Two trains an hour ran around the Belt Line each way, starting from the New York Central's Exchange Street depot. The route went west along the Niagara River, paralleling the Erie Canal, through Black Rock, across the northern part of the city, and back through the great area of railway tracks, factories, and working-class homes known as the East Side. The trip took 45 minutes and included 20 stops.

Within the city, horse-drawn vehicles first appeared as public conveyances in 1860, when four "horsecars" offered transportation from the Buffalo River to Genesee Street. Horses pulled these cars on tracks that were gradually extended to all the major streets of the city. But horsecars were slow, and their motive power dirtied the streets. By the 1890s, in Buffalo as elsewhere, cleaner, faster, and more efficient electrified "trolleys" had become the favored form of public transportation.

Buffalo's first trolleys entered service in 1892, with their electric power generated locally. The "Milburn agreement" between the city and the company receiving the franchise to operate electrified street railways provided for a five-cent fare that could be changed only by mutual agreement between the street railway company and the city. Buffalonians enjoyed this low fare for more than three decades.

When alternating-current electric power reached Buffalo from Niagara Falls in 1896, the street railway was the first beneficiary. Public transportation expanded more rapidly in Buffalo than in most other cities, to the profit of streetcar riders and company alike. Extension of the trolley lines made possible the development of Kenmore, Buffalo's first true suburb, and the beginnings of other suburban communities.

Electrified cars also ran to Lockport, Tonawanda, and smaller cities in an interurban system that reached its heyday around 1920. After that the interurbans began a gradual decline that ended in their virtual demise during the Great Depression. In effect, the interurbans served as a transitional step from an almost total reliance on steam railroads to an equally complete dependence on automobiles for transportation between cities.

Buffalo trolleys met the same fate as the interurbans, though less rapidly and for somewhat different reasons. Strikes by operating personnel before, during, and after World War I interrupted service for greater or lesser periods of time. Regardless of the justice of the

Above
The high-speed Lockport-Olcott suburban electric trolley, seen here in 1906, was destined to make its last trip October 31, 1939. From the Buffalo Savings Bank-Roy Nagle Collection. (BECHS)

strikers' cause, there can be little doubt that the strikes and the violence that accompanied them drove customers away. Beginning in 1923, electric buses using the overhead trolley wires but not the tracks were introduced. Nonetheless, some tracks remained in use until the late 1940s, when the last of them were finally paved over. By then gasoline-powered automobiles and buses had completely replaced the electric trolleys.

Buffalonians had reason for satisfaction on August 7, 1927, when dedication of the Peace Bridge opened the way for direct automobile traffic between their city and Canada. Buffalo was a center for world news on that day, as the Prince of Wales shared the spotlight with Vice President Charles G. Dawes, Secretary of State Frank B. Kellogg, Prime Ministers Stanley Baldwin of Great Britain and W.L. Mackenzie King of Canada, and Governor Alfred E. Smith of New York. Through the magic of radio, an estimated 50 million people heard the congratulatory words and the snip of the ribbon-cutting ceremony, as Secretary of State Kellogg, advancing from the American side, and Prime Minister Baldwin, from the Canadian side, met in the center of the bridge. "There," wrote a Buffalo journalist on the scene, "in the center of a span across the frontier unequalled in the nation's history—a border over which no sword has crossed in more than a century—were spoken the salutations of officers and diplomatic representatives of the two great peace-loving English-speaking nations."

During the half-century following the dedication of the Peace Bridge, Buffalonians suffered through the Great Depression, fought another world war and two lesser ones, experienced the social unrest of the 1960s, and tried to adjust to economic dislocations brought on by the St. Lawrence Seaway. Small wonder, then, that from the perspective of the 1980s the early decades of the 20th century seemed to be their golden years.

Above
Throngs jam the sidewalks in the Broadway-Fillmore area to observe passage of the last streetcars in Buffalo on July 1, 1950. Note the celebrating riders. Courtesy, Schweikard Studio. (BECHS)

Facing page
Amos W. Sangster, a local artist known for his etchings of the Niagara River, paints a romantic harbor scene in Tow Leaving Buffalo Harbor, circa 1884. (BECHS)

Top
Established in 1878, Buffalo Forge Co. specialized in the manufacture of portable forges and blowers. By 1883 more of them were in use than all other makes combined, and they were distributed to every state in the Union. (BECHS)

Above
This political cartoon of November 12, 1887, bears the title, The Political Game of Euchre and the subtitle, Now that the Autumn Elections Are Over, a Little Game Will be Played for the Democratic Presidential Nomination. (BECHS)

Facing page
The railroad is closely identified with the growth and prosperity of Buffalo. By 1887, Buffalo was the terminal point of 11 trunk line railroads that radiated north, east, and south. (BECHS)

THE MAIL CARRIER OF 100 YEARS AGO.

The FLIGHT of the FAST MAIL on the
LAKE SHORE AND MICHIGAN SOUTHERN. RY.

THE POPULAR PASSENGER ROUTE BETWEEN THE EAST AND WEST, UNION DEPOTS, NO FERRY TRANSFERS, NO DELAYS.

COPYRIGHT 1875 BY J. A. BURCH, BUFFALO, N.Y.

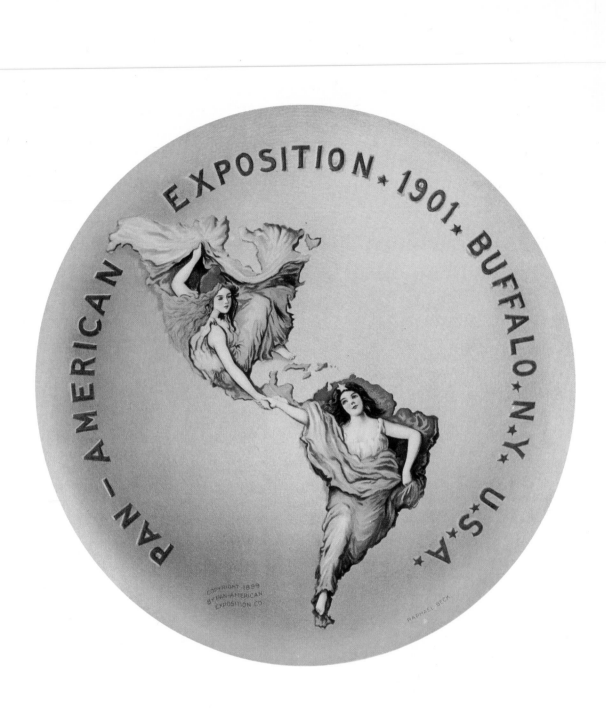

Above

Western New York artist Raphael Beck designed the official seal for the Pan-American Exposition. The emblem was reproduced on souvenirs, and its graceful composition remains a memorable image today. Chromolithograph by Niagara Lithograph Company of Buffalo. (BECHS)

Facing page

Evelyn Rumsey Cary's painting, The Spirit of Niagara, served as the basis for the official poster of the 1901 Pan-American Exposition, Niagara. The Art Nouveau design illustrates a legend attributed to local Native Americans. (BECHS)

Top
John Key captures the colorful Exposition Midway in his painting of the North Midway, a street of ballyhoo, barkers, and spielers, circa 1901. (BECHS)

Above
The Board of Architects, elected to insure the architectural harmony of the Pan-American Exposition, collectively decided on a formal, symmetrical ground plan. The result of this careful planning was the Rainbow City. (BECHS)

Top left
The boundaries of the Pan-American Exposition grounds, shown in this map, correspond to Delaware and Elmwood avenues on the east and west; the railroad tracks north of Great Arrow, where a railroad station was located, on the north; and Delaware Park on the south. From the Pan-American Exposition Collection. (BECHS)

Top right
This Evelyn Rumsey Cary design was used on countless exposition souvenirs. (BECHS)

Bottom
The Temple of Music, designed by Buffalo architects Esenwein and Johnson, was the center for concerts and recitals at the Pan-American Exposition. (BECHS)

Top
Future of Air Travel *was painted by H.H. Green in 1917. (BECHS)*

Above
Glenn Hammond Curtiss alights in the water at Hammondsport, New York, after having hit a dummy battleship with a bomb from a height of 900 feet. (BECHS)

CHAPTER IX

WHISTLES, WHEELS, AND WINGS

When the first gasoline-powered automobile crossed the Peace Bridge in 1927, Buffalo was at its height as a railroad center, second in the United States only to Chicago. Powerful railroad enterprises were the city's leading employers, providing 20,000 jobs. And railroads were munificent sources of municipal revenue through the taxes they paid on $90 million worth of property within the city.

Early on, the Lake City had seemed a natural terminus for rail lines connecting it with important markets in the United States and Canada. Railroads had long since surpassed the Erie and the New York State Barge Canal as carriers of heavy freight, and they had yet to feel the competition of long-haul trucks. Likewise, competition for passengers from private automobiles, buses, and airplanes was still years in the future. Little wonder, then, as one railroad historian declared, "No American city during the late nineteenth and early twentieth century owed more to railroads than did Buffalo."

Buffalo's railroad history began in 1834 with horse-drawn cars. Two years later the Buffalo and Niagara Falls was the first chartered steam railroad. In 1843 a railroad to Attica connected Buffalo with Albany through a chain of small lines. By the 1850s Buffalo and New York City were linked through what eventually became the New York Central system. During the same

decade steam trains first crossed the Niagara into Canada above the Whirlpool Rapids on a suspension bridge designed by John A. Roebling. Sir Casimer S. Gzowski, a noted Polish-Canadian engineer, designed a later railroad bridge across the Niagara. Known as the International, it connected Buffalo at Niagara and Bridge streets with the Canadian Grand Trunk Railroad downriver from Fort Erie, Ontario.

In the latter half of the 19th century, railroad entrepreneurs consolidated old lines and built new ones linking Buffalo with the north, south, east, and west in a rail network that looked on a map like a giant spiderweb. A total of 13 trunk lines served the city, including the New York Central, the Erie, the Lackawanna, the Pennsylvania, the Nickel Plate, and the Lehigh Valley, as well as several smaller lines. Added to the thousands of miles of rail lines connecting Buffalo with other communities were 700 miles within the city used for storage, switching, and making up trains.

One of the city's ubiquitous railroads was the Lackawanna, which ran from Buffalo to New York by way of northeastern Pennsylvania, where the line had an interest in anthracite (hard coal) mines. Out of this combination came one of the best-known personalities of her day—Phoebe Snow.

That Phoebe Snow was imaginary detracted little from her fame. Dressed always in immaculate white, she was created in 1900 to advertise the cleanliness of travel on the Lackawanna Railroad. Since Lackawanna locomotives burned hard coal rather than the usual soft, smoky, bituminous coal, the line was presumably the cleanest in the country. It was this virtue that Phoebe Snow was created to symbolize. As one of the many advertisements in which she appeared declared:

> I won my fame and wide acclaim
> For Lackawanna's splendid name
> By keeping bright and snowy white
> Upon the Road of Anthracite.

Phoebe Snow was as much a casualty of World War I as any soldier killed in France. In 1917 the federal government issued an order compelling all American railroads to burn soft coal, and Phoebe disappeared from public notice. In the 1950s, her name was resurrected and given to Lackawanna's No. 3, a deluxe, ultramodern streamliner making the daily run between New York and Buffalo. But alas, the Phoebe Snow of the 1950s was pulled by a diesel locomotive rather than by one burning hard, clean, nearly smokeless, anthracite coal.

Above
The International Bridge was built to link U.S.-Canadian railroad traffic. Completed in 1873, the superstructure (shown here circa 1890) was strengthened at the turn of the century to accommodate the heavier locomotives making increased trips across the Niagara River. (BECHS)

Facing page
This World War I poster attests to Buffalo's railroad might with a call for citizens to fill 2,000 freight cars with provisions for victims of the war. (BECHS)

Most Buffalonians knew their railroads through the stations or depots where passenger trains arrived and departed. Though all the railroads offering passenger service had ticket offices on Exchange Street, the New York Central was the first to build an actual station there. Known as the Exchange Street Station, it was enlarged several times between 1870 and 1907 as other lines besides the New York Central began to use it.

In 1917 the Delaware, Lackawanna and Western opened a station near Buffalo Creek where Main Street and South Park Avenue join. Two years later the Lehigh Valley Railroad constructed a handsome station at the corner of Main and Scott streets. In 1929 the New York Central constructed a new terminal on Buffalo's east side. Standing 15 stories tall, this huge terminal was designed to service 200 passenger trains every 24 hours. It contained a giant concourse and waiting room, shops, restaurants, offices, and space for ticket sales. A huge buffalo stood at one end of the concourse to remind passengers of the city they were arriving at or departing from.

The fate of Buffalo's railroad stations reflects the decline of passenger service. The Lehigh Valley Station closed in 1952 and was subsequently demolished to make way for the General Donovan State Office Building. The old Lackawanna Station, known as the Erie-Lackawanna Station after the merger of the two lines in 1950, closed in 1962 and stood abandoned for nearly 20 years. In the end, even the best efforts of the Landmark Society of the Niagara Frontier could not save it as an architectural reminder of the great days of railroad travel. The huge Central Terminal (or Penn-Central Union Station, so named after the merger of these two great eastern lines) has lost nearly all of its original functions, turning into a burdensome piece of real estate whose ultimate fate remains in doubt.

Buffalo's decline as a rail center occurred over a period of half a century, not in one sudden, gigantic collapse. What happened here was not much different from the experience of other cities—except that Buffalo, being near the top, had farther to fall. Certainly the Great Depression had its effect, in Buffalo as elsewhere. The financially troubled Erie abandoned its locomotive and car shops in Buffalo in 1932, with a consequent loss of jobs and payroll. This cutback only postponed further declines in revenue for the Erie, however, and the system was forced into bankruptcy in 1938. Nevertheless, a reorganized Erie survived, as did other trunk lines, to serve city, state, and nation well during World War II. But wear and tear on existing equipment and roadbed inevitably brought on a decline in service during the immediate postwar years.

Above
Pictured is the waiting room of the Lehigh Valley Railroad Station which was located at Main and Scott streets. (BECHS)

Facing page, top
Wilbur Porterfield, photographer for the Courier Express, captured these steam locomotives on film. Buffalo left behind a great railroad era with their disappearance in the mid-1950s. From the Porterfield Collection. (BECHS)

Facing page, bottom
Crowds await Thomas E. Dewey, the Republican candidate for President, at the New York Central Terminal in October 1948. Courtesy, Buffalo Evening News/William Dyviniak. (BECHS)

To better meet competition from other kinds of transportation, eastern railroads engaged in a series of mergers in the quarter-century following the end of World War II. Among those affecting Buffalo, the Erie and the Delaware, Lackawanna and Western merged to become the Erie-Lackawanna. In 1961 the Pennsylvania bought control of the Lehigh Valley, in effect constituting a merger. Seven years later the Pennsylvania and the New York Central joined to become the Penn-Central, avoiding a federal antitrust suit by promising better service and greater efficiency to the area formerly served by the two separate systems.

Improvements in efficiency and service during the postwar decades were far more noticeable in the hauling of freight than in the carrying of passengers. Operating on the principle, "If you can't whip them, join them," railroads initiated "piggyback" service, carrying loaded truck trailers on railroad flatcars to their ultimate destination, where they could then be handled by local truckers. Similarly, the railroads developed three-level rack cars to haul automobiles from assembly factories to distribution points. In 1965 the New York Central ran a daily "auto-train" from Detroit to Buffalo with a capacity of carrying 1,800 automobiles. Computers, standard containers, new machinery, and increasing mechanization resulted in further improvements. Switching yards, such as Penn-Central's Frontier Yard in east Buffalo,

Above
David W. Sowers is shown at the steering handle of his Columbia Electric Stanhope on Linwood Avenue during February 1900. This was a real snow test for the vehicle, which was number two of the first lot of 10 built for resale. (BECHS)

became marvels of mechanization, sorting out and reassembling thousands of freight cars daily, all of it done almost "untouched by human hands" by a single operator in a central tower equipped with a computer.

In the meantime, however, passenger service declined. Never again would thousands of travelers crowd stations to board trains pulled by snorting, hissing, whistling steam locomotives. Buffalo's railroads, like others throughout the country, turned to diesel locomotives in the 1950s, and diesels honked horns instead of blowing whistles. The sound of the last steam whistle on a locomotive in Buffalo can be dated precisely at 7:05 p.m. Eastern Standard Time on Saturday, October 15, 1955, when Baltimore & Ohio train number 252-521 arrived at the Erie-Lackawanna Station from Pittsburgh, Pennsylvania. For many, the silencing of the steam whistle ended the great, romantic age of railroads.

Protest mounted as railroads throughout the country curtailed their less profitable passenger lines or abandoned them completely. The federal government responded in 1971 by chartering the National Railroad Passenger Corporation, popularly known as Amtrak, charged with responsibility for keeping at least a skeletal passenger service going. Abandonment of unprofitable and unnecessary routes was permitted, however, and within a few months Buffalo lost its western trains to Chicago. In recent years, under Amtrak, there has been a modest growth of passenger service to and from Buffalo. The Buffalo-Chicago route, however, is limited to one train that departs at 3 a.m.

It may well be that increased costs of gasoline will combine with other factors to bring passengers back to the railroads. It may be, too, that steam locomotives will make a comeback as the cost of diesel fuel increases and coal returns to fashion. If such developments should take place, railroads might find themselves in a situation similar to the early days of automobiles, when steam, electricity, and fossil fuels competed as motive power for the "new-fangled" vehicles.

Such competition was very much in evidence in Buffalo in the late 19th and early 20th centuries. Henry R. Bird built four cars named for himself in Buffalo between 1895 and 1897. One of these, a friction-drive, kerosene-fueled vehicle, was entered in the *Chicago Times-Herald* race of November 1895, but it failed even to reach the starting point. Automobile en-

Above
This charming photograph taken circa 1910 shows a group of electric vehicles gathered at the fountain in front of the Albright Art Gallery. Courtesy, Automobile Club of Western New York. (BECHS)

NEW YORK TO PARIS.   *Thomas Car fording a stream (Siberi*

cyclopedias also list a car called the Arrow Locomotor, built by Adolph Moesch and Company of Buffalo in 1896. Dr. Truman J. Martin, among the earliest automobile owners in Buffalo, drove a Stanhope Electric down Delaware Avenue in 1897. He had bought it in Hartford, Connecticut, where it was built by the Pope Manufacturing Company, and had it shipped to Buffalo by railroad, as there were no cross-country highways at the time. Even had there been suitable highways, Dr. Martin's journey would have been a slow one because the Stanhope Electric's batteries had to be recharged every 50 miles.

Other early automobile owners in Buffalo included Edward H. Butler, Ellicott Evans, George S. Gatchell, Spencer Kellogg, H.A. Meldrum, Dr. V. Mott Pierce, E.R. Thomas, and Burt Wright. Some owned electrics; others had steam-propelled cars; but eventually all drove automobiles with internal-combustion gasoline engines. Like Dr. Martin, these Buffalonians usually bought their first cars from manufacturers in other parts of the country. Soon, however, it became possible for Buffalonians who so desired to buy cars built in their own local factories.

More than 30 different makes of automobiles were manufactured in Buffalo during the first half of the 20th century, most of them in the early decades of the century. Included among these were the Brunn and Babcock electrics, the Brooks Steamer, and the Kensington. The last-named began as the product of the Kensington Bicycle Company, then became an electric and later a steamer made by the Kensington Automobile Company, and still later became a gasoline-engine car—all this in the five years of the Kensington's existence, 1899-1904.

Other Buffalo-made cars included the Austin-Lyman, manufactured by a company of that name in 1909; the Warren Noble, built by Warren Noble in 1933; the Eagle, produced by the Eagle Automobile Company in 1904-1905; and the Ess-Eff, a product of the Ess-Eff Silent Motor Company. The Ripper ceased production in 1903 when V.E. Ripper, owner of the company, disappeared with the firm's cash and some of its machinery.

One of the best-known names is the Thomas Flyer. This automobile achieved much of its renown by entering a New York-to-Paris "around the world" race in 1908. Starting from New York on Lincoln's Birthday, the Flyer covered 13,341 miles, reaching Paris on July 30—only to find that Protos, the entry from Germany, had arrived four days before. The judges nevertheless declared the American car the winner because it had been driven by way of Alaska, thereby traveling a little more than 3,000 miles farther than the German car. Buffalo cele-

Above
A series of picture postcards was produced in Buffalo, with around-the-world shots of the race that the Thomas-Flyer made and won in 1908. This photo taken in Siberia is entitled Thomas Car Fording a Stream. *(BECHS)*

Facing page, top left
The New York Central included this advertisement in a 1932 timetable. It stresses the luxurious comfort of air-conditioned dining cars: "Dust, soot, smoke and heat are locked out." (BECHS)

Facing page, top right
In 1908 the Thomas-Flyer automobile became famous by winning the New York-to-Paris "around the world" race. This advertisement for the 1907 Thomas-Flyer contains clever devices meant to catch the eye. (BECHS)

Facing page, bottom
The Thomas Motor Bicycle, advertised here for $200 circa 1900, was one of several E.R. Thomas Co. products. (BECHS)

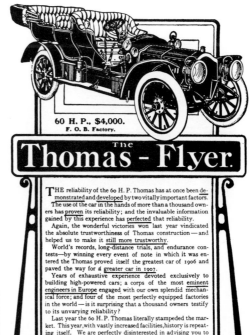

brated the return of the Thomas Flyer with a grand parade. Escorted by the 74th Regiment Band, the internationally famous car led a line of automobiles a mile long as the parade wound from the city line to Lafayette Square.

In the long run, the Thomas Flyer's international reputation did little to improve its sales. At first the Thomas factory at 1200 Niagara Street boomed, turning out taxis and fire engines as well as passenger cars. But later models of the Flyer were poorly designed, causing trouble to their owners. The company compounded its problems by making false claims concerning its automobile's durability, declaring that during the race the car was "never in the repair shop, none of the valves ground or changed; not a sparkplug was changed; nor were the crankshaft bearings changed or adjusted."

Without doubt the best-known and most successful automobile manufactured in Buffalo was the Pierce-Arrow.

The Pierce-Arrow evolved in a number of steps. In fact, the company organized by

Above
These stripers at work at the Pierce-Arrow Plant in the 1920s were typical of the skilled workmen that were employed there. A striper had to be adept at using a mink brush and a palette in applying designs to these luxurious automobiles. (BECHS)

The *PIERCE-ARROW* differs from other cars in three ways—in its engine, in its body and in the way the two are combined to make the most thoroughly artistic, comfortable, and dependable car ever built.—The Pierce-Arrow Motor Car Co. Buffalo

George N. Pierce first made tricycles and then bicycles before turning to the manufacture of automobiles at the beginning of the 20th century. The firm sold 25 of its first model, the Pierce Motorette, in 1901. Three years later the company's featured model was called the Great Arrow, a name later attached to the street running along the south edge of the company's new manufacturing complex, built in 1906 at 1685 Elmwood Avenue. George N. Pierce left the firm a few months after its name was changed to the Pierce-Arrow Motor Car Company in 1908. For the next 30 years, the Pierce-Arrow plant was one of the greatest manufacturing companies ever developed in Buffalo, employing as many as 10,000 persons at its peak.

For most of those 30 years, the Pierce-Arrow automobiles were built entirely in the Elmwood Avenue establishment and largely by hand. George N. Pierce and his successors took little interest in a production race, preferring instead to make a fine luxury car. For a time the Pierce-Arrow Motor Car Company made a dependable truck that won a solid reputation during World War I, but this product was subsequently sacrificed to turning out the classic Pierce-Arrows of the 1920s. Never once did the Pierce-Arrow make the annual list of the 15 largest-selling cars in the United States. It won its fame through quality, not quantity.

Above, left
This 1912 advertisement, with its illustration of the good life, appeared in Country Life in America. Until its later years the company maintained the standard of the hand-built car. Courtesy, Pierce-Arrow Society. (BECHS)

Top right
This Pierce Motorette, owned by the Buffalo and Erie County Historical Society, was one of 25 first-year models sold in 1901, the year that Pierce first produced automobiles. (BECHS)

Above, right
Edward G. Felthauser owned the first Pierce automobile that came off the line at the Pierce-Arrow Company's Elmwood Avenue plant. Here it is, pictured circa 1906, near Holland, New York, in the midst of a road trip. (BECHS)

The Pierce-Arrow Motor Car Company was uniquely a Buffalo concern. All the parts for its automobiles were made and assembled in its local plants, at first on Hanover Street and then at the complex on Elmwood Avenue. The complex included several buildings—a machinery plant, a manufacturing plant, and an assembly plant, as well as an office building, body shops, a laboratory, and a hospital—and, when completed, contained 1.5 million square feet. Among the executives who led the company during its most successful years, playing significant roles in community affairs in addition to their business activities, were George K. Birge, Colonel Charles Clifton, and Henry May.

George K. Birge, member of a wealthy Buffalo family that had developed a wallpaper firm known throughout the world for its quality products, served as president of the Pierce-Arrow Motor Car Company from 1908 until 1916. Colonel Charles Clifton, first treasurer of the company under George N. Pierce, then became president and chairman of the board, serving also as president of the National Automobile Manufacturers Association from 1912 to 1927. Henry May, vice president under Pierce, was the production head—solid, efficient, and described as the "sheet anchor of the business."

This trio led so well that the Pierce-Arrow Motor Car Company made a profit of $5 million in 1916. At this point George Birge called on a New York banking house to assist in recapitalizing the company, exchanging the old stock for a larger number of new shares, and listing the new securities on the New York Stock Exchange. Birge, who owned 7,000 shares of the original 15,000, sold his stock at $1,000 a share and, having realized a total of $7 million, left the company.

Great things were expected of the Pierce-Arrow Motor Car Company with its ownership more widely distributed, but such was not to be the case. The new board of directors hired an outside firm, headed by George W. Goethals of Panama Canal fame, to manage the company. Goethals' management experts fired a number of Pierce-Arrow's engineers and superintendents of the manufacturing operation, disrupting the family-type relationship that had been largely responsible for the company's success. All of this was too much for Henry May, who left and never came back.

May had begun working for George N. Pierce in 1873, when he got himself hired as an errand boy at $1.50 a week for the firm of Heinz, Pierce, and Munschauer—an operation, May later recalled, that turned out "bird cages, tinware, toilet seats, bath tubs, water filters, and washing machines." The hardworking lad with the German accent made a favorable impres-

Above
In December of 1933, Pierce-Arrow Master Salesmen were photographed while on an Atlantic cruise. From the Buffalo Savings Bank-Roy Nagle Collection. (BECHS)

sion, and Pierce brought him along when he formed his new company making children's tricycles, and then bicycles. When the company turned to making automobiles, it was reorganized with Pierce as president, May as vice president, and Clifton as treasurer.

Henry May stayed on with the automobile company after George N. Pierce left. A blunt, taciturn, direct man, he was respected by his colleagues and the workers in the plant. According to William H. Gardner, a member of the Pierce-Arrow board of directors, "The whole company revolved around Henry May. . . . He was the brains of the Pierce-Arrow factory." There is considerable evidence to show that he was largely responsible for the smoothness of Pierce-Arrow's manufacturing operations in the years before World War I. Certainly he was sorely missed in later years.

In 1921 the company lost $8 million. Had it not been for Colonel Clifton, Buffalo probably would have lost the Pierce-Arrow car at that time. Under Clifton's guidance, there were a few good years in the 1920s. Still, the company found it hard to compete against the growing giants of the automobile industry. Merger seemed to be a solution, and in 1928 Pierce-Arrow joined with the Studebaker Corporation. Backed by Studebaker, the company continued to turn out fine cars, reaching its peak production in 1929 by manufacturing 8,422 cars and 494 trucks. The previous year, Pierce-Arrow had ceased making 6-cylinder cars, preferring to concentrate on the company's new "straight 8's." In 1930 Pierce-Arrow came out with a magnificent V-12 to compete with the 16-cylinder top-of-the-line Cadillac.

Such optional features as toilets, writing desks, and a choice of interior color schemes were available for Pierce-Arrow purchasers. So, too, were custom-designed cars. One of these, built for an Asiatic potentate, had a gold-plated radiator and a gold radiator cap encrusted with jewels.

Pierce-Arrows were occasionally used in ways unforeseen by their producers and designers. As these speedy automobiles could outrun anything generally available to law-enforcement officers, they were often the car preferred by bootleggers and other malefactors on the Niagara frontier and elsewhere.

One bootlegger engaged in smuggling liquor from Canada to Buffalo during Prohibition days devised a particularly ingenious way of using the Pierce-Arrow V-12—one presumably undreamed of by the designers of this powerful engine. Since the 12-cylinder model could run on only four cylinders, the enterprising bootlegger drove his car across the Niagara River

Above
The Pierce-Arrow Motor Car Company's office building was located on Elmwood Avenue. This manufacturing complex was built in 1906. Note the arrows incorporated into the brick facade. From the Buffalo Savings Bank-Roy Nagle Collection. (BECHS)

bridges, past unsuspecting U.S. customs officials, with the eight inactive cylinders serving as containers for whiskey.

Studebaker Corporation became a victim of the Great Depression, being plunged into receivership in 1933. At that time a group of Buffalo businessmen bought control of Pierce-Arrow from Studebaker for $1 million—an indication of how the value of the company had plummeted. Sales continued to shrink, from 2,152 in 1933 to 875 in 1935. Still, the company persisted until 1938, when it became insolvent and liquidation of its assets was ordered.

Critics have maintained that the Pierce-Arrow died of self-satisfaction because its makers could not or would not keep up with current demands. Probably the company's failure was inevitable in time, as it was a pygmy among giants. But there is something heroic about the Pierce-Arrow Motor Car Company as one that died rather than compromise its standards or disappear as a division of some larger entity. Buffalonians still point with pride to the Elmwood Avenue complex where one of the nation's finest cars was once produced. Subdivided today into offices and small businesses, it still bears the name "Pierce-Arrow" on its front.

The car itself lives on, thanks to the Pierce-Arrow Society, whose members publish a quarterly journal and lovingly preserve old models of the greatest car ever made in Buffalo— possibly the greatest ever made in the United States.

Though the Pierce-Arrow has drifted into a nostalgic part of Buffalo's past, Buffalonians today can take pride in their continuing contributions to the automobile industry.

History has it that Buffalo bankers rebuffed Henry Ford at the beginning of his career, but there is little evidence that the automobile tycoon held this against the city. Around 1910 the Ford Motor Company took over the John R. Keim Mills at Buffalo from which it had been buying various automobile parts. This brought to Ford the services of William S. Knudsen, a Danish immigrant who had already demonstrated his production skills as assistant superintendent of the Keim shop. Knudsen rose in the Ford hierarchy until he left to join General Motors as general manager of Chevrolet in 1922. Later Knudsen became president of General Motors. His son Semon Emil Knudsen, born in Buffalo in 1912, reversed his father's progression, working his way up to executive vice president of General Motors in 1959 and then transferring his talents to become president of the Ford Motor Company in 1968.

Above
The Ford Motor Company began manufacturing in 1910, using the J.R. Klein steel plant. The Ford Fuhrmann Boulevard assembly plant opened in 1938. This Ford, complete with the newest features, was manufactured about 1929. Courtesy, Buffalo Courier Express. (BECHS)

Thomas A. Murphy, president and board chairman of General Motors in the 1970s, was born in the Western New York town of Hornell. He spent several of his early years in Buffalo before moving with his family to Chicago. The Knudsens, Murphy, and other fine administrators associated with Buffalo show that this city has been a fertile source of executive talent for the upper levels of the motor world.

Of even greater significance to the motor world have been the contributions of tens of thousands of anonymous workers in the automobile plants of Western New York. When the elder Knudsen joined Chevrolet in 1922, he selected a site on East Delavan Avenue as a body and assembly plant for that General Motors car. The East Delavan plant has expanded since that time, shifting its products in the process until today it is mainly concerned with providing axles for General Motors cars. Chevrolet's River Road plant was constructed in 1937 with automobile engines as its chief product. It, too, has expanded and may become the only plant in the General Motors empire to manufacture the popular, gasoline-efficient, 4-cylinder engines. The number of workers in these two plants has increased to the point that Chevrolet is now the largest industrial employer in the Buffalo area.

Ford has run Chevrolet a close second as a producer and employer in this region, in some years even pulling into first place. In fact, the Ford Motor Company was here first, beginning manufacturing in the old Keim plant in 1910 with William S. Knudsen as director. Soon this became an assembly plant, and with increased demand, Ford built another at Main and Rodney—a building now occupied by the Trico Products Corporation. Ford's Fuhrmann Boulevard assembly plant, opened in 1938, closed in 1950 after turning out nearly 2 million cars.

In the same year Ford opened its Buffalo Stamping Plant, which makes hoods, doors, floors, and other sheet-metal parts for Ford cars. Ford's Buffalo Stamping Plant was one of the first especially designed to make extensive use of automation, somewhat to the concern of the United Auto Workers union. Workers declined in numbers, becoming chiefly inspectors, as stamped parts, often large and bulky, passed for considerable distances from machine to machine, being loaded, unloaded, and transferred mechanically. Production at the Buffalo Stamping Plant clearly showed the benefits of automation, with output substantially higher than at the older, nonautomated Dearborn Stamping Plant.

A number of other Buffalo manufacturers—Trico Products Corporation (windshield wipers), Dunlop Tire & Rubber Corp., and Harrison Radiator (a division of General Motors)—employ thousands of persons in activities closely related to the automobile industry. If the

Above

The Pierce-Arrow Society's International Meet was held in Western New York in 1978. Here, with the Historical Museum in the background, Buffalonians had the opportunity to inspect the classics. Courtesy, Buffalo Evening News/Ronald J. Colleran. (BECHS)

payrolls and production of these firms are added to those of Ford and Chevrolet, the continuing significance of Western New York to the automobile industry is clear. Equally clear is the impact of that industry on the economic health of Buffalo and vicinity. In fact, this mutual relationship today far surpasses that of the Pierce-Arrow Motor Car Company in the early decades of the 20th century.

While the manufacture of automobile parts remains a pillar of the Buffalo economy, the production of airplanes, at times a major industry here, has dwindled to practically nothing.

The mass production of airplanes in Buffalo began through the conjunction of an aviation genius, Glenn Howard Curtiss, and a historic event, the coming of World War I. Thanks largely to Curtiss's talent, Hammondsport, the Central New York village of his birth, soared to an impressive array of aerial firsts in the years between 1908 and 1914. It was the first major manufacturing site for airplanes. It had the first large training school for pilots and also the first for aircraft designers. And on nearby Lake Keuka, Curtiss perfected the world's first hydroplane.

Above
In 1907 headlines proclaimed aviation genius Glenn Hammond Curtiss to be "The Fastest Man in the World." (BECHS)

When war broke out in 1914, the European powers were quick to realize the value of powered aircraft for observation of the enemy's maneuvers. Soon Curtiss was receiving requests from the Allied powers for the various training planes he had developed. As the orders increased, he realized he would have to move to an area with a much larger labor force than was available at Hammondsport. Buffalo could provide the labor needed and had the advantage of proximity to Canada. Planes for the Allies could easily be shipped through Canada without serious violation of President Woodrow Wilson's injunction for Americans "to be neutral in thought as well as in deed" during the first years of the great European struggle.

Late in 1915 Glenn Curtiss moved his entire manufacturing operation from Hammondsport to rented space formerly occupied by the Thomas Flyer Automobile Manufacturing Company on Niagara Street in Buffalo. There he and his associates developed the plane popularly known as the "Jennie," the name derived from the plane's model number, JN-4. In October 1917 the War Department announced the letting of contracts for the construction of 20,000 airplanes, 5,000 to be built abroad and 15,000 in the United States. Of these, 5,000 were Jennies built at Buffalo by the Glenn Curtiss Corporation, which moved from Niagara Street to a new plant on Churchill Street and eventually to a huge factory at 2050 Elmwood Avenue, north of Hertel.

Top
Both the Pierce-Arrow automobile and the Curtiss JN-4 were indigenous to Buffalo. (BECHS)

Above
This Curtiss JN-4 was also known as a "Jennie." Of 15,000 U.S. airplanes contracted by the War Department in 1917, over 6,700 planes were Curtiss "Jennies" built in Buffalo. From the Hauser Bob Collection. (BECHS)

Early in 1917 Curtiss proposed building a giant "flying boat" capable of crossing the Atlantic under its own power in the air, thereby avoiding the menacing German submarines that took such a toll of surface ships. Once in Europe the big planes were to be used as bombers. The ambitious plan got under way in December, when several Navy engineers were sent to the Curtiss plant in Buffalo to participate. However, severe winter weather caused the experimental project to be moved to Long Island. From this project came the NC-4, the first airplane to make the transatlantic flight, doing so in a series of hops, May 8-May 27, 1919.

Curtiss closed his Buffalo factories when the Armistice ended the need for warplanes. During the 1920s his company continued to operate hangars and flight facilities at an airport near where Niagara Falls Boulevard, Sheridan Drive, and Eggert Road intersect today. Glenn Howard Curtiss himself had the misfortune to die in 1930 following an appendicitis operation at Buffalo General Hospital. His name lived on, however, as half the Curtiss-Wright Corporation, which built planes in Buffalo and the town of Tonawanda before and during World War II.

In 1924 Major Reuben H. Fleet formed Consolidated Aircraft in Buffalo, occupying rented space in the old Curtiss plant on Elmwood Avenue. Consolidated introduced another great name in Buffalo's aircraft history, that of Lawrence D. Bell. When Bell came to Buffalo in 1928 to join the Consolidated Aircraft Corporation, he had already worked for 16 years in the aircraft business though he was only 34 years of age. Under his direction Consolidated continued to develop flying boats as its main product. When the company moved to San Diego in 1935 to permit year-round flight testing, Lawrence Bell decided to stay in Buffalo and form his own company. He incorporated Bell Aircraft Corporation on July 10, 1935, with himself as president and general manager. Bell continued as general manager until 1954 and as president and then chairman of the company until his death two years later at the age of 62.

Two years after its incorporation, Bell Aircraft's "plant" consisted of 40,000 square feet of leased floor space in one corner of the sprawling Consolidated Aircraft building on Elmwood Avenue. Its work force numbered about 100. But the fledgling company had managed to develop the first all-Bell plane—the Airacuda, a new type of long-range fighter plane that made its initial flight in 1937.

Within a year the Airacuda was superseded by the famous P-39 Airacobra, a smaller, faster, cannon-bearing Bell fighter that saw wide use on the battlefronts of World War II. Wartime production of the P-39 and other planes pushed up employment figures rapidly. By 1944 Bell Aircraft had more than 55,000 workers at five plants, two of which were located at Buffalo and Niagara Falls. During the war years these two plants produced nearly 13,000 completed aircraft plus enough spare parts to raise the total to an equivalent of more than 16,000.

Lawrence D. Bell and his company scored as many impressive firsts as had Glenn H. Curtiss half a century before. Among Bell's significant aviation achievements were the nation's first jet-propelled airplane, the world's first commercial helicopter, the world's first supersonic airplane, the world's fastest and highest flying airplane, and the first jet-propelled vertical takeoff and landing airplane.

By the time of Bell's death in 1956, the company was actively engaged in space-age research and manufacturing. In 1960 Textron, Inc., bought Bell's entire defense business. The company is now known as Bell Aerospace Textron, a name more nearly reflecting its present orientation and ownership, and has its headquarters on Niagara Falls Boulevard in the town of Wheatfield.

The Curtiss and Bell plants were by no means the only firms to manufacture aircraft and related products in and around Buffalo. The Irving Airchute Company began making parachutes here as early as 1919. Consolidated Aircraft was a large Buffalo concern before it moved to California, eventually becoming part of General Dynamics. Scott Aviation, Wendt Aircraft, Gwinn Aircar Company, and the Argonaut Aircraft Company, though smaller than the giant concerns, were active in Buffalo at one time or another between 1920 and 1940.

Why has Buffalo played such a prominent role in the development of transportation, from the great railroad age of the 19th century to the modern world of wheels and wings? Part of the answer lies in the city's location in the industrial northeast with so many of the American and Canadian population centers within a few hundred miles. But certainly another part lies in the characteristics of the people. They came, as the poet Carl Sandburg wrote, "from six continents, seven seas, and several archipelagoes," and they brought with them or learned here skills that made them productive, hardworking contributors to the success of a thousand different enterprises.

Top
Workers at a Buffalo plant manufacture airplane wings. Working conditions changed when the Armistice ended the need for warplanes. (BECHS)

Above, left
Lawrence D. Bell began working in the aircraft industry at the age of 18. He joined Consolidated Aircraft Corporation 16 years later, and remained in Buffalo to form Bell Aircraft Corporation

in 1935. He is pictured here with Harry S. Truman, then U.S. Vice President, as they examine an early development model of a helicopter. Courtesy, Bell Aerospace Textron. (BECHS)

Above, right
Bell Aircraft Corporation built 10 aircraft in the famous "X-series," known as "flying laboratories," which broke all previous world records for altitude and speed. Bell's X-1A flew 1,650 miles per

hour on December 12, 1953, and six months later attained a height of 90,000 feet. Lawrence Bell (in suit), founder of the aircraft company which bears his name, gives his blessing to the Bell X-1A and to pilot Major Charles E. Yeager who was nicknamed "The Fastest Man Alive." All X-series aircraft were built at Bell's Niagara Frontier plant. Courtesy, Bell Aerospace Textron.

CHAPTER X

BUFFALO'S ETHNIC NEIGHBORHOODS

Ellis Island opened with some ceremony on January 1, 1892, as the first federal receiving depot for immigrants to the United States. In keeping with the formality of the occasion, United States Commissioner of Immigration John B. Weber welcomed Annie Moore, an Irish girl from County Cork, as the first immigrant to step ashore at Ellis Island and presented her with a $10 gold piece.

John Weber, himself the son of an immigrant from Alsace, was born in Lackawanna but enlisted from Buffalo's Seventh Ward as a member of the prestigious Ellsworth Regiment at the beginning of the Civil War. Resigning with the rank of colonel at the end of that war, he returned to Buffalo to begin an active career as a Republican politician and officeholder. In 1870 Grover Cleveland, a rising star in Democratic ranks, defeated Weber for the office of sheriff of Erie County by a mere 300 votes. Four years later Weber ran for the office again and was elected by a wide margin.

In 1889 President Benjamin Harrison appointed Weber commissioner of immigration. It was Weber who recommended the narrow strip of land known as Ellis Island as the site for a new federal receiving center. He set up the rules and processes followed during Ellis Island's early years and presided over its official opening in 1892.

Facing page
In July of 1910 children dressed for rainy weather stand at the intersection of Louisiana and South streets in Buffalo's First Ward. Photo by Frank Fisher. (BECHS)

During his term as commissioner of immigration, John Weber headed a five-member committee appointed by President Harrison to tour Europe to investigate the reasons for increasingly heavy immigration to the United States. As part of the same tour, they were charged with investigating and reporting on alleged cruelty to Jews in Russia. Weber's report, printed in both English and French, was widely distributed in the United States and western Europe, but not in Russia.

In 1893 Grover Cleveland replaced Benjamin Harrison in the White House, as Harrison had replaced Cleveland in 1889. Though Weber and Cleveland were fellow Buffalonians and personal friends, Weber knew the Democratic President would have relatively little sympathy for a Republican commissioner of immigration. Weber resigned and returned to Buffalo, where he held a series of quasi-governmental positions. He died in 1926 after more than a half-century of public service, interspersed with travel on three continents, during which he retained his lively interest in questions of immigration.

Whatever happened to Annie Moore? No one knows. Possibly she came to Buffalo, like so many Irish before her, by way of the Erie Canal or by railroad. Following her one brief moment of public recognition, she lapsed into the anonymity of the other millions who entered the United States with the intention of becoming permanent residents.

Western New York in general and Buffalo in particular have attracted immigrants since the early days. Each generation has seen one or another ethnic group predominating in numbers, arranged vertically like layers in a multitiered cake and horizontally across the city in ethnic neighborhoods like patches in a quilt. Like layers of a cake and patches in a quilt, these ethnic neighborhoods brought variety, sustenance, and color to the city.

At first, of course, Buffalo was an Indian "neighborhood," numbering about 700 Senecas in 1817, when Buffalo was still a village. Thirty years later they had moved to the Cattaraugus Reservation, though an occasional Seneca could still be seen on the city streets. By this time Buffalo was pretty much a "Yankee neighborhood," populated by people descended from New England families rather than by immigrants coming directly from some foreign land. English, Welsh, and Scottish blood predominated among most but not all early Buffalonians. A total of 58 black people lived in Buffalo in 1828. By the 1820s, 30 or so German families had

Above
The Most Reverend Edward D. Head, current bishop of the Roman Catholic diocese of Buffalo, is pictured on May 12, 1976 (when St. Joseph's New Cathedral was razed), examining the contents of the copper box that had been placed in the two-ton cornerstone of the New Cathedral in June 1912. Courtesy, Buffalo Evening News/Robert E. Stoddard. (BECHS)

settled in or near the city. And in 1815 Patrick O'Rourke brought his family here, the first Irish Catholics to make their home in Buffalo.

The Irish who followed the O'Rourkes established the first true ethnic neighborhood in Buffalo. It is generally said they settled here in large numbers after building the Erie Canal. Although this was certainly true in some cases, most came to service the canal and its related industries after the waterway was already completed.

Large numbers of Irish settled first in the "Flats" near their main source of work—hard, poorly paid, manual labor associated with loading and unloading lake and canal boats. Many of them worked as "scoopers," shoveling grain from the holds of lake boats that carried wheat and rye from western farms. Eventually many of the Irish settled in South Buffalo, where they dominated the old First Ward. Even then, however, they continued to be active as scoopers. As late as 1940, when most of the "scooping" was done mechanically rather than by hand, nine of every ten members of the local Grain Shovelers' Union were South Buffalo Irishmen.

Thus the Irish founded the first ethnic neighborhoods in Buffalo before spreading throughout the city and its suburbs, setting the pattern that would later be followed by other immigrant groups. Also like the later immigrant groups, the Irish started at the bottom layer of the cake. The Irish were the first substantial group of Roman Catholics to arrive in the United States, and for them the Church became a means of social mobility. At one time nearly every Irish family in Buffalo numbered a priest or a nun, or both, among its members. As the ranks of Roman Catholics swelled with the arrival of later immigrant groups, Irishmen rose to fill higher places in the religious hierarchy. In 1847 John Timon became the first bishop of the Roman Catholic Diocese of Buffalo—the first in an unbroken string of 10 consecutive Irish-American bishops that has extended down to the present.

The presence of so many Irish-Americans in politics, in Buffalo and other cities, has been explained on the grounds of traditional Irish conviviality. Another possible explanation lies in the fact that Irishmen spoke English, though at first with a brogue, and could therefore act as intermediaries between the dominant Anglo-Saxon groups and later non-English-speaking immigrants swarming into the cities. Whatever the reasons, the Irish have been prominent in Buffalo politics for a century or more. Such familiar names as Sheehan, Conners, Fitzpatrick, Doyle, Mahoney, Crotty, Crangle, and Griffin suggest the extent of Irish influence not only in city politics, but up through the state to the national level, from the 1880s to the 1980s.

Above
Wilbur Porterfield's photograph entitled Dusty Work, Buffalo Harbor, *turns the dangerous, backbreaking work performed by laborers in the grain elevators into a romantic picture of a bygone era. The Irish have been traditionally associated with this aspect of Buffalo's history. From the Porterfield Collection. (BECHS)*

More than a century ago, immigrants from the German states began to surpass those from Ireland in numbers. By the 1840s German-Americans made up one-third of Buffalo's population and were the largest foreign-born group in the city.

Unlike the Irish, German immigrants to Buffalo settled inland from the waterfront in an East Side area known as the "Fruit Belt" because of its street names. And while the Irish immigrants were almost universally Roman Catholics, their German counterparts embraced a variety of religious faiths. German Catholics in 1832 built St. Louis Church, originally a log structure, at Main and Edward, where its cathedral-like successor stands today. Three years later German Protestants built themselves a place of worship on Hickory Street.

Along with the other religious groups from Germany came a number of well-educated Jews. These German Jews settled along North, Franklin, and Tupper streets. In 1850 they organized an Orthodox congregation, Beth Zion, at Ellicott and Clinton streets. Later, as most German Jews in the United States joined the Reform movement, Beth Zion (now located on Delaware Avenue) became a Reform congregation.

German-Americans organized for political purposes, as most ethnic groups have. All in all, eight German-Americans have served as mayors of Buffalo, from Philip Becker, Buffalo's first foreign-born mayor, in the 1870s, to George Zimmerman in the 1930s. But German names became known in other activities besides politics. Louis Fuhrmann (for whom Fuhrmann Boulevard was named) not only was elected mayor of Buffalo but was a leading meatpacker, as were such other prominent German-Americans as Christian Klinck and Jacob Dold.

As the number of German-Americans in Buffalo increased, they spread from the Fruit Belt part of the Fourth Ward into the Fifth and Seventh wards. This entire area took on the flavor of German culture, making German food, German beer, and German music available to all Buffalonians, whether German or not. Annual German-American Day picnics attracted thousands until recently.

German immigration tapered off in the early 20th century, as Chancellor Otto von Bismarck promoted programs to keep young Germans satisfied at home, and German-American influence in Buffalo began to be diluted. Anti-German feeling during World War I also played a significant part, leading to changes in a number of street names. Though it may not have lessened the bank's influence, the directors of the German-American Bank, chartered in

Above
Temple Beth Zion, on 43 Niagara Street between West Eagle and Franklin streets, was dedicated in 1865. The congregation remained there for over 20 years. Earlier, when the structure had a steeple, it had served as the Niagara Street Methodist Episcopal Church. (BECHS)

1882, decided to change its name to the Liberty Bank. After the war, the national-origins quota system of the 1920s cut down on all immigration from Europe, and German-American influence was further reduced as descendants of the old German wards in Buffalo moved elsewhere.

The largest numbers of immigrants from Ireland and Germany had arrived in the United States before the opening of Ellis Island. If New York was their port of entry, they came through Castle Garden, an immigrant receiving station operated by the state. By the time Ellis Island began operations, the sources of immigration had largely shifted from northern and western Europe to the southern and eastern regions of that continent. Immigration from northern and western Europe by no means ceased; Annie Moore was evidence to the contrary. Nevertheless, in the period after 1892, she was the exception—not only because she was Irish, but because she was female. Three males passed through Ellis Island for every female that entered during the same period.

Between 1892 and 1920, the majority of people coming to the United States were of Italian or Polish descent. Both groups were well represented in Buffalo.

Polish people began settling in Buffalo more than 20 years before Ellis Island opened. In 1873 John Pitass, then a young Polish seminarian from Rome, arrived in Buffalo to find no more than 30 Polish families living here. Father Pitass established St. Stanislaus Church at Townsend and Peckham streets, opened Buffalo's first Polish parochial school, and organized Buffalo's first Polish-language newspaper. He became known as the "Patriarch of Polonia."

By the time Annie Moore stepped off the landing barge at Ellis Island, as many as 13,000 Poles were making their homes in Buffalo. The original Polish neighborhood still clustered around St. Stanislaus Church, but by this time a second Polish community was thriving in the Black Rock section of the city, while a third was centered in the area bounded by Clinton Street, Snow Street, and Buffalo Creek.

Polish men, newly arrived, headed for these neighborhoods, attracted by boarding-houses operated by couples who spoke their language and cooked familiar foods. These boardinghouses, the Polish churches (by 1929 Buffalo had 14 Roman Catholic churches with largely Polish-American congregations), and organizations such as Dom Polski and the Polish

Above
Campaign buttons depict German-Americans who held the office of mayor. To this date there have been eight German-American mayors of Buffalo. (BECHS)

Alliance cemented the growth of Polonia, as the Polish community as a whole was called. By 1960, of 324,300 foreign-born persons living in Erie County, 82,249 were Polish—representing slightly more than 25 percent of the total and the largest single group among the foreign-born. In 1969 and again in 1976, Karol Wojtyla visited the Polish Catholic community of Buffalo; in 1978 he became Pope John Paul II.

A state census taken in 1892, the year Ellis Island opened, put the number of Italians living in Buffalo at about 2,500. Eighteen years later the Italian-American population in the city had grown to 11,399, and by 1920 Italian-Americans had become the third largest ethnic group in Buffalo, surpassed in numbers only by those of German and Polish descent. By 1940 the Italians had overtaken the Germans to become the city's second largest ethnic group.

If Father John Pitass could be called the "Patriarch of Polonia," then Louis Onetto deserves a similar title for Buffalo's Italian-American west side. An early member of that community, he arrived as an 18-year-old in 1868, a generation before the heaviest immigration from Italy to the United States. He lived until 1943, only seven years shy of his 100th birthday.

Louis Onetto's beginnings were modest, as were those of most immigrants. But he suc-

Above
Buffalo's German-American Bank at Main and Court streets changed its name to Liberty Bank after World War I created much anti-German sentiment. As a result of such changes, along with the limitations imposed on immigration, German visibility was lessened. Courtesy, Buffalo Savings Bank-Roy Nagle Collection. (BECHS)

ceeded far above the level of the majority. His businesses were different from the grain, steel, and chemical industries that dominated Buffalo's economy at the time. Small things—ice cream, peanuts, popcorn, and macaroni—were the products that Onetto's enterprises provided for hungry customers.

By 1892 Onetto was well known throughout Buffalo, and he was chosen to portray Christopher Columbus in the city's parade honoring the 400th anniversary of the discovery of America.

A religious man, Louis Onetto helped in the building of St. Anthony of Padua, the first Roman Catholic Church in Buffalo with a congregation made up largely of Italian-Americans. He was also instrumental in launching *Il Corriere Italiano*, the first Italian-language newspaper in the city.

It has been said that immigrants from Italy only learned they were Italians in the United States. It is true that most Italian immigrants identified with the village or province they came from, rather than with the nation as a whole. Immigrants from the island of Sicily settled mainly on Buffalo's lower west side, an area that soon became known as "Little Italy." Im-

Above
Shops and busy people at Broadway near Fillmore make up the heart of Buffalo's Polonia in this photograph taken circa 1929. (BECHS)

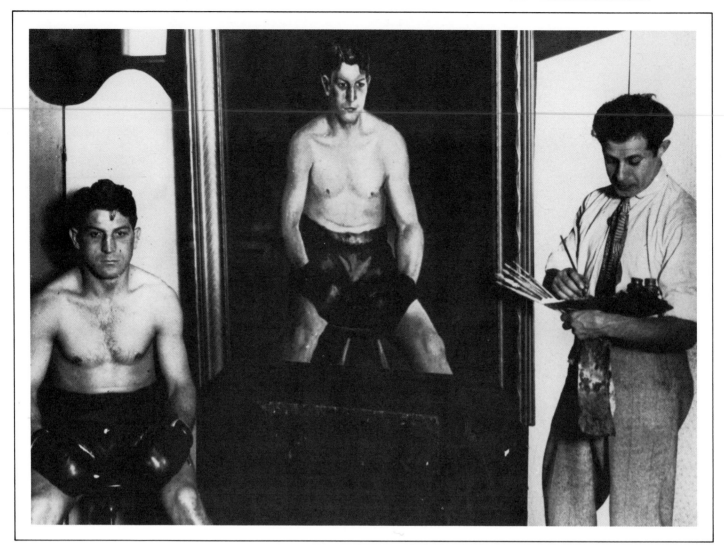

migrants from Abruzzi clustered along East Delavan Avenue; Calabrians came to South Buffalo and Hopkins streets; and Neapolitans occupied homes on a few blocks of Swan and Seneca streets.

Italian-Americans seem to have done less with their political power than the Irish, the Germans, and the Poles. Only one Italian-American, Frank A. Sedita, has been elected mayor of Buffalo, but he served three terms between 1958 and 1973. Numerous descendants of immigrants from Italy have represented Buffalo in the state legislature, while others have occupied important city and county offices.

In addition to the "Big Four"—Irish, Germans, Poles, and Italians—a number of other ethnic and religious groups have made Buffalo their home. From Poland and Russia have come thousands of East European Jews—so many that they soon outnumbered the earlier German Jews. What might be called the first Jewish community in Buffalo clustered along North, Franklin, and Tupper streets. With the arrival of the East European Jews, however, the

Above
Boxer/artist Tony Sisti painted this portrait of champion Lou Scozza. From the Scozza Collection. (BECHS)

William Street area became the heart of a new Jewish community. Later this heart shifted north and west to the Hertel-Colvin area. Jews coming to Buffalo after World War II have generally settled there or in the suburbs.

Two nonimmigrant groups have established identifiable ethnic neighborhoods in Buffalo. By far the older of these two groups is the black community. Though many blacks now living in Buffalo are comparative newcomers to the city, their ancestors in most cases arrived in America before there was a United States.

Buffalo in 1870 had only a small black community, numbering about 700. The community expanded slowly, reaching only about 1,000 in 1892. By 1920, however, there were five times as many blacks living here, most of the increase coming through migration brought on by the economic boom during World War I. The Second World War had a similar effect, drawing blacks to Buffalo from the South directly or from such northern cities as Detroit, Chicago, Philadelphia, and New York. By 1960 there were slightly more than 74,000 blacks in Buffalo, second only to Poles as an ethnic group. The 1980 census will undoubtedly show that black Americans have become the city's most numerous ethnic group, constituting about one-third of Buffalo's population.

Above
Mayor Frank A. Sedita served longer than any previous Buffalo mayor. He is shown campaigning on Court Street in September 1968. City Hall is in the background. Courtesy, Buffalo Evening News/Barney Kerr. (BECHS)

Blacks have displaced people of German and other European descent in the Fruit Belt and in other East Side areas. Similarly, Puerto Rican Americans, the second largest non-immigrant ethnic group in the city, now occupy the former "Little Italy" on Buffalo's lower west side.

Because Puerto Ricans have been citizens of the United States since 1919, they need no passports or visas to cross the water that separates their island from the mainland. Only a few actually made the trip before World War II, however, and Puerto Rican migration has been largely a postwar phenomenon carried on through the air—making Puerto Ricans now living on the mainland the first airborne migrants in history. One estimate places the total number of Puerto Ricans in Buffalo at about 30,000. Probably a minority of these came directly from the island, as an increasing proportion of these Spanish-speaking Americans are mainland-born. Their community centers on Swan Street, where other persons of Hispanic descent join Puerto Ricans in various activities.

In addition to these groups that have identifiable ethnic neighborhoods, more than 100 nations or would-be nations have furnished immigrants to our city. Generally those coming from any one nation have been too few in number to form an authentic "neighborhood," although Ukrainians to a total of perhaps 12,000 have settled in and around Buffalo. Refugees from the 1956 uprising have noticeably augmented the number of Hungarian-Americans in the city. Czechs, Slovaks, Austrians, and Rumanians; Spanish and Portuguese; people from the three Scandinavian countries; French-speaking people from Europe and Canada; Greeks and Turks; Moslems from Yemen—all these and more can be found among Buffalo residents of the past and present.

Immigrants from Asia have been relative latecomers to the Buffalo scene. National immigration policy barred permanent residents from China between the 1880s and the 1940s, while citizens of Japan were shut out by exclusionary agreements and laws for 50 years of this century. Since the liberalization of quotas in the 1950s, however, immigrants from China and Japan, along with Indians, Pakistanis, and Koreans, have come to Buffalo in search of homes, education, and jobs.

Least noticeable among newcomers to Buffalo have been the English-speaking immigrants from England, Scotland, Wales, and Northern Ireland, who have merged with the dominant culture so quickly and easily as to earn the name "the silent immigration." Also included among these "silent" immigrants should be the English-speaking Canadians. The 1960

Above
The Little Harlem Hotel was a popular entertainment spot. It was declared a landmark by the Buffalo Landmark and Preservation Board, which deemed it important to Buffalo's black history. Courtesy, Paul Woodson/Little Harlem Hotel.

Facing page, top left
This menu for the Little Harlem Hotel advertises "the gayest spot in Buffalo" on Michigan Avenue. Famous entertainers played to standing-room-only crowds. Courtesy, Paul Woodson/Little Harlem Hotel.

Facing page, top right
Mary Talbert was a leader in Buffalo's educational and cultural life during the early 20th century. (BECHS)

Facing page, bottom
Proud Buffalo youths march in the cold to honor Martin Luther King in January 1972. Courtesy, Buffalo Evening News/Richard Roeller. (BECHS)

census found nearly 67,000 Canadian-born persons living in and around Buffalo, and no doubt their numbers have increased during the past two decades.

Annual reports of the International Institute of Buffalo furnish evidence of the almost incredible variety of national and ethnic backgrounds among residents of the Buffalo area. From its headquarters on Delaware Avenue, the International Institute offers a wide range of services to the foreign-born and their families, whether they have come to this area recently or more than a generation ago, permanently or temporarily. The institute's 1979 report shows that it served 5,560 families from one or another of 112 nations, and that 51 different languages were used in dealing with their problems.

Recently the International Institute has established suboffices to assist those who, because of work schedules, lack of transportation, or physical handicaps, are unable to avail themselves of services offered at the institute's headquarters. The locations of these "outreach centers" point to the continuing existence of ethnic neighborhoods in the Buffalo area. Thus, for example, there are outreach centers in the Polish Union Hall, 761 Fillmore Avenue, and the Polish Community Center, 1081 Broadway; two at 261 Swan Street and 254 Virginia Street, serving Buffalo's Spanish-speaking residents; and one connected with the Yemenite Association at 109 Ridge Road, serving the city's Arab community.

Observers of the American scene during the past three decades have recorded a significant rise of ethnicity—that is, a greater consciousness of and interest in one's own ethnic origins. This development has been especially marked among black Americans, among second- and third-generation descendants of immigrants from central and southern Europe, and most recently, among persons of Hispanic descent. Manifestations of this phenomenon range all the way from bumper stickers proclaiming "I'm proud I'm Polish," through Alex Haley's *Roots* as a book and television blockbuster, to a serious and scholarly reconsideration of the "melting pot" theory as an explanation for immigrant assimilation in America.

The Niagara Frontier Folk Art Council, Inc., is one manifestation of the rise of ethnicity in the Buffalo area. This council is the outgrowth of a series of programs presented in the auditorium of the Buffalo and Erie County Historical Society beginning in December 1963. Nine ethnic groups took part the first year, with each group presenting one Sunday afternoon pro-

Above
Peter Gust Economou was a Greek immigrant who began as a busboy in Buffalo and rose to prominence as an internationally renowned restauranteur. (BECHS)

gram over a period of three months. Within a few years, interest in these programs had outgrown the resources of the Historical Society and the capacity of its auditorium, and a number of prominent ethnic-group leaders formed the Niagara Frontier Folk Art Council, Inc.

The council was founded as a nonprofit educational and cultural organization with the avowed purpose of promoting better understanding, friendship, and Americanization among the various ethnic groups of this region. Major financial support for its activities is provided by Erie County. Its principal activity continues to be the coordination of a series of ethnic programs, most recently presented in the auditorium of the Learning Center on the Buffalo State University College campus. The number of programs has grown to the point that they now take place on both Sunday afternoons and evenings. Thus, an "Italian-American Afternoon" may be followed by an "Irish-American Evening" one Sunday, while an "Afro-American Afternoon" is followed by a "Greek-American Evening" a week later. As many as two dozen ethnic programs are presented each year, culminating in February with the presentation of a six-hour program to which each participating group contributes a 10-minute segment. Called the United Folk Festival, this mammoth program attracts attentive and appreciative audiences each year to the auditorium of Bennett High School.

Historians tell us that Irish immigrants originated the first public festivals associated with a specific ethnic group. Being too numerous for private dinners, the Irish paraded on St. Patrick's Day in Boston, New York, and Philadelphia early in the history of the United States. In Buffalo an annual St. Patrick's Day parade has become an established tradition, though sometimes curtailed, postponed, or canceled completely because of the city's treacherous March weather. No doubt the customary parade has lost some of its significance as a purely Irish celebration, since nearly everyone claims a degree of "Irishness" on St. Patrick's Day.

Similarly, German-American Day has lost much of its former significance in Buffalo. This loss is due in part to the antipathy engendered toward all things German by two world wars in which Germany was an enemy of the United States. But it is due in even larger measure to the diffusion of Buffalo's German community. No longer is there a neighborhood within which German-American culture flourishes. Even the Turnverein, the German athletic and social club, has moved to North Tonawanda from its former home in Buffalo.

Ethnic festivals continue to be popular among groups that have taken up residence in Buffalo more recently than the Irish and the Germans. The celebration and elevation of Polish culture is almost a year-round affair in the Broadway-Fillmore area of east Buffalo and its near-

Above, left
Mama Judie, the "Doll Lady" of Buffalo, was recognized by Mayor James D. Griffin when he proclaimed December 2, 1979, as Mama Judie Day. The mayor pronounced that Judie McDonald had kept her black heritage alive through her creations of needlework, wall hangings, and dolls (some of which are pictured here). Courtesy, Patricia Brazill. (BECHS)

Above, right
Laszlo Szabo, shown here in 1958 with his painting The Old Philosopher, *was born in Budapest, Hungary, and came to Buffalo in 1924. He became one of the city's most successful portraitists. Courtesy, Buffalo Evening News. (BECHS)*

by suburbs. Some Polish-Americans have advocated special celebrations on Kosciuszko Day, in honor of the Polish patriot who helped the United States win freedom in our War of Independence. At Easter time the Broadway Market emphasizes traditional Polish foods and artifacts associated with the religious occasion. And Dingus Day, celebrated the day after Easter, provides a fun-filled release after the long Lenten season.

For several years past, black Buffalonians have made Jefferson Avenue the locale for their "June'teenth" celebration, marking the date that slaves in Texas learned of their freedom. Two different groups of Italian-Americans have held Connecticut Street festivals in honor of their culture. Columbus Day in October has traditionally been a time for Italian-American parades and festivals, but increasingly it is becoming a Hispanic-American holiday in Buffalo and in other cities with large Spanish-speaking populations.

Probably the most successful and best-attended ethnic festival in recent years has been the one held in May at the Hellenic Orthodox Church of the Annunciation on the corner of Delaware Avenue and West Utica Street. Greek immigrants to Buffalo have never been numerous enough to form an ethnic neighborhood, and they and their descendants are scattered around the city and its suburbs. But they have remained loyal to their church, which has become a center for the preservation of Greek traditions in their new homeland. In each of the past three years, more than 100,000 Buffalonians have enjoyed Greek food, Greek music, and other aspects of Hellenic culture at the annual festival.

Buffalo's downtown Convention Center has become home for an annual multiethnic festival. Those in attendance can, for a price, partake of food and drink dispensed from booths sponsored by various ethnic groups of the city. Music and dance associated with the sponsoring groups are presented as entertainment. In this and in other cases, ethnic festivals have become commercial ventures, somewhat overshadowing their original functions in preserving and transmitting native cultures brought to the United States by immigrants.

Nevertheless, ethnic festivals, the United Folk Festival, and the work of the International Institute serve as useful reminders that only a century ago 42 percent of Buffalo's residents were foreign-born. Today the figure is less than 9 percent, but ethnic traditions are still strong, adding strength, color, and variety to life in the City of Good Neighbors. Inevitable conflicts have occurred and periods of adjustment have been required, but Buffalo has benefited in many ways from those who have lived for a time in ethnic neighborhoods—and from their descendants who have found new homes for themselves in other parts of the city and its suburbs.

Above
Puerto Rican folk dancers proudly display ethnic costumes and youthful charm as they perform at the M&T Plaza in the summer of 1981. Photo by Edward W. Chester. Courtesy, Carmita Rodriguez.

Above
This 1905 photograph of members of Buffalo's German Turnverein marks an age of German-American culture. (BECHS)

CHAPTER XI

NOT BY BREAD ALONE

John Joseph Albright was one of the moving forces behind the Pan-American Exposition that brought Buffalo fame at the beginning of the 20th century. A successful industrialist, Albright helped form the Lackawanna Steel Company, interested himself in the New York Central Railroad system, participated in banks leading later to the Marine Midland complex, and assisted in harnessing the power of Niagara Falls by means of the Niagara, Lockport, and Ontario Power Company. But Albright was more than an industrialist. Knowing that humans need more than material sustenance to survive, he became a civic benefactor and patron of the arts in Buffalo. A member of the Buffalo Fine Arts Academy for many years, Albright served as its president from 1895 to 1897.

The Buffalo Fine Arts Academy is one of the city's oldest cultural organizations and the fountainhead of significant art activities in the area. Founded in 1862, the academy occupied a number of downtown sites until 1887, when it obtained permanent galleries in the old Buffalo Public Library building on Lafayette Square. Then in 1900 came the news that John J. Albright would donate money to build a separate home for the academy. Albright had meant to have the new gallery built in connection with the Pan-American Exposition, but unforeseen difficulties postponed until 1905 the dedication of what was to become known as the Albright Art Gallery.

Facing Page

The 1981 Allentown Art Festival was filled with crowds of people from all over the continent. Since its founding in 1957, the festival has grown to be possibly the largest of its kind in America, with hundreds of thousands attending annually. Courtesy, Buffalo Evening News/Smith. (BECHS)

Standing on a happily chosen site in Delaware Park overlooking the lake, the new gallery was a magnificent structure 250 feet long by 150 deep. Architect Edward B. Green designed it in the classical Greek style popular at the time. Buffalo's social and intellectual elite attended the official dedication on May 31, rightly realizing this was an outstanding event in the city's cultural history. Catalogs at the opening described the holdings as comprising about 50 casts of Greek and Roman sculpture; several marble busts; more than 200 oil paintings by American and foreign artists; and a strong collection of more than 200 prints by Dürer, Rembrandt, Turner, Millet, and Whistler. It mattered little to Buffalonians that critics of the collections wrote that the American painting section was "spotty," the European "academic and weak."

Whatever the strengths and weaknesses of its collections, the Albright Art Gallery gained three distinctions during its early years. Following the death of its first director, Dr. Charles M. Kurtz, in March 1909, his assistant, Cornelia Bentley Sage, succeeded him. A Buffalonian by birth, Miss Sage was only 26 at the time she became permanent director in 1910, the first woman in the United States to become director of a major art museum. She remained in this position until 1925. Her purchases and transient exhibitions gave somewhat more attention to sculpture than was customary for art museums in the United States, thereby giving the Albright a second distinction. As a third, powerful electric lights, unique at the time, created the illusion of daylight as interior illumination for the gallery.

The board of directors in 1925 chose William M. Hekking to take the place formerly occupied by the first (and only) female director of the Albright Art Gallery. During Hekking's tenure the gallery assembled a contemporary sculpture collection recognized as the finest in America. Director Hekking was no admirer of the modern or contemporary in any art form, and the collection owed less to him than to A. Conger Goodyear, vice president of the Buffalo Fine Arts Academy, and Anna Glenny Dunbar, honorary curator of sculpture for the gallery. In fact, William Hekking resigned as director in 1931 because of his opposition to trends in art at the time. He remained in Buffalo, becoming art critic for the *Buffalo Evening News* and a leader of those who tried in vain to curtail the purchase and exhibition of contemporary art by his successor, Gordon Bailey Washburn.

Schism between admirers of the old and the new in art harmed the gallery's reputation in the 1930s and 1940s. Tight budgets during this time, under a series of directors, also restricted purchases and other activities.

At about the time the Albright was celebrating its 50th anniversary, Gordon MacIntosh

Above
The handsome architecture of the Albright Art Gallery is viewed from the west side of the structure. From the Porterfield Collection. (BECHS)

Above
Augustus Saint-Gaudens' Caryatids, supporting the Albright Art Gallery structure built in 1905, stand alongside the 1962 building in this view of the Albright-Knox Art Gallery's striking contrast of styles. Courtesy, Albright-Knox Art Gallery.

Smith came as its new director. During Smith's regime the gallery doubled in size, exploded in terms of attendance at special exhibitions, and gained stature as the home of a contemporary art collection rated among the two or three best in the country. This reputation has been maintained and enhanced under the current director, Robert T. Buck.

Such benefactors as A. Conger Goodyear and Seymour H. Knox aided greatly in achieving these results. Making use of wealth earned originally through his father's partnership with Frank W. Woolworth in a chain of five-and-ten stores, and augmented through other enterprises, Knox's gifts to the gallery by 1970 totaled at least 213 paintings, 106 sculptures, and 25 prints. Though Goodyear's contributions were fewer in quantity, they were no less in quality. Seymour H. Knox was also the principal contributor to the fund that permitted the addition of a new building to the original gallery. When this addition was opened with appropriate ceremonies on January 19, 1962, the entire structure was renamed the Albright-Knox Art Gallery.

Special exhibitions of Knox's and Goodyear's gifts were held during the 1960s. But the exhibitions that drew the greatest crowds were "Paintings and Drawings by Vincent Van Gogh" and "The Works of Andrew Wyeth," both held in 1962, and "Pop Art" in 1963. It is safe to say that nearly all Buffalonians in attendance at the three liked and understood the Van Goghs and the Wyeths more than the pop art. Nevertheless, the Albright-Knox remained dedicated to the contemporary in art, beginning with abstract expressionism, and proceeding through pop art, op art, kinetic art, constructivism, shaped painting, and the latest of current styles, all of which have been represented at the Albright-Knox either in special exhibitions or as part of the permanent collection.

This is not to say that artistic affairs in Buffalo went on without controversy. Certainly the Albright-Knox's addiction to the contemporary aroused continuous comment and criticism among local artists and critics. Likewise, controversy arose over plans for structural additions to the original gallery. The first architect hired favored adding two wings on the lower side of the building, the side facing Delaware Park. When revealed to the public, his plan aroused almost universal condemnation as a desecration of one of Buffalo's most beautiful buildings. A second architect proposed a two-story glass building of contemporary style to sit beside the main building but separated from it visually by an open sculpture court. This plan, too, aroused opposition as an improbable and undesirable marriage of disparate styles. Nevertheless, the plan was adopted, and the result has turned out to be surprisingly harmonious.

Above
The Albright Art Gallery launched a fund drive in 1960 toward the construction of an additional building. Gordon Bunshaft (left), designer of the new structure, proposed a modern design as a counterpoint to the already standing classical building. Largely funded by Seymour Knox (right), the addition led to the Albright-Knox Art Gallery that Buffalonians enjoy today. Posed to the right of Bunshaft are Manly Fleischmann and David Rockefeller. Courtesy, Buffalo Evening News/Hinkson. (BECHS)

In 1965 Buffalo put itself on the international culture map with its "Festival of the Arts Today," a cooperative venture that surprised connoisseurs as well as thousands of ordinary Buffalonians. The Albright-Knox played host to the festival with the cooperation of the New York Council on the Arts, the State University of New York at Buffalo, the State University College, and the Buffalo Philharmonic Orchestra.

"Can This Be Buffalo?" was the title of an illustrated article that appeared in *Life* magazine a month after the festival closed on March 8. Yes, it can be and is, the *Life* correspondent reported. "Buffalo last month exploded in a two-week avant-garde festival that was bigger and happier than anything ever held in Paris or New York." Police had to be called one Sunday to handle a traffic jam on Elmwood Avenue as 66,500 art lovers tried to get into the Albright-Knox Art Gallery, which finally had to be closed against the oncoming crowds.

According to the *Life* correspondent, the "far out" Festival of the Arts Today was as full of "come-ons" as a country fair. The most sensational attraction was a pair of dancers. "Nude except for a coating of mineral oil and locked in an embrace, they moved slowly across the stage for eight minutes while a Verdi aria and the sound of falling rocks blared from a tape recording." Other attractions included orchestral works with unusual sound effects such as popping paper bags; four bizarre plays by Eugene Ionesco; and kinetic art that often looked like "pinball machines on a jag." Still, the *Life* article concluded, "Buffalo took it all—the hokum and shocks included—with healthy curiosity and good-humored appreciation."

Another observer at the festival noted that Lukas Foss, conductor of the Buffalo Philharmonic Orchestra, had to caution his musicians to keep a straight face as they fired noise-makers and popped balloons in a Concerto for Piano and Orchestra by John Cage.

Lukas Foss followed Joseph Krips, who in turn had succeeded William Steinberg, in a series of distinguished conductors beginning in the 1940s and extending to the present. Foss was succeeded by Michael Tilson Thomas of the Boston Symphony, and then by Julius Rudel of the New York City Opera, the present conductor of the Buffalo Philharmonic.

The orchestra itself could be considered the grandchild of forebears that performed from the 1880s to the early 1920s. It was reborn in January 1932 as the Buffalo Symphony Orchestra and was supported by the Federal Works Progress Administration (WPA) from 1936 to 1939. When this support ended, a combination of private donors, annual fund drives, and tax revenues from local governments kept the orchestra alive.

Above
This early photograph shows the Buffalo
Symphony Orchestra at Saratoga Springs
in 1896. (BECHS)

Art Today

In 1940 the Buffalo Philharmonic Orchestra gained a permanent home in the Kleinhans Music Hall, a gift of the Kleinhans family whose name graces the largest men's clothing store in Buffalo. Recognized as one of the finest music halls in the world, it was designed by Eliel Saarinen and stands near the southern end of Richmond Avenue in an arterial configuration appropriately known as Symphony Circle.

Buoyed by the success of their first festival, leaders of Buffalo's major cultural organizations decided to hold another in 1968. The Studio Arena Theatre joined the list of sponsors for the second festival, which bore the cryptic name "Plus X Minus: Today's Half-Century." Nearly as cryptic was Studio Arena's contribution to the festival—a world premiere of *Box-Mao-Box* by Edward Albee. Opinions of the new play were perhaps best summed up in the *Saturday Review*, whose account was titled "Woman Overbored. . . ." But the coup of presenting an Albee premiere showed that the Studio Arena Theatre had indeed become a shining star in Buffalo's cultural firmament.

That star first started to glisten in 1927, when the Studio Theatre opened in a second floor hall at the corner of Elmwood Avenue and Anderson Place. Jane Keeler, dramatics teacher at the State Normal School in Buffalo (now the State University College), served as director of the theater and its companion school for 32 years. Under her direction, the Studio Theatre and Theatre School moved from place to place before finding a permanent facility in a converted Universalist Church at the corner of Hoyt Street and Lafayette Avenue. Middle-of-the-road plays and musicals were presented there for nearly three decades with casts made up mostly of amateurs.

In 1965 the Studio Theatre's board of directors made the decision to go professional, with Neal DuBrock as executive director. In support of the new goal, friends of the theater raised money for a down payment to purchase the Town Casino, a storied but abandoned nightclub on Main Street between Tupper and Chippewa streets. Craftsmen converted the former nightclub into an arena-type theater with room for audiences of 500. Hence the new name—the Studio Arena Theatre—when the remodeled facility opened on October 7, 1965, with a presentation of Eugene O'Neill's *A Moon for the Misbegotten*, starring Colleen Dewhurst and James Daly.

Neal DuBrock, an accomplished screenwriter, had served his directorial apprenticeship at the Circle in the Square in New York. After coming to Buffalo, he had directed plays at the Statler-Hilton Hotel and at the Albright-Knox Art Gallery. He continued to direct in the early

Above
The Albright-Knox Gallery's installation, "Art Today," is seen through the Sculpture Court Entrance. Kinetic and optic art were featured during the highly publicized "Festival of the Arts Today" in 1965. The sensational two-week exhibition inspired comparisons of Buffalo with Paris and New York. Courtesy, Albright-Knox Art Gallery.

Facing page, top left
Executive producer Neal DuBrock made the Studio Arena Theatre into a first class regional playhouse. Courtesy, Studio Arena Theatre. (BECHS)

Facing page, top right
Jane Keeler directed the Studio Theatre and Theatre School. Courtesy, Studio Arena Theatre/Charlena Smith Studio.

Facing page, bottom
The Studio Arena's premier production, A Moon for the Misbegotten, starred James Daly and Colleen Dewhurst. Courtesy, Studio Arena Theatre. (BECHS)

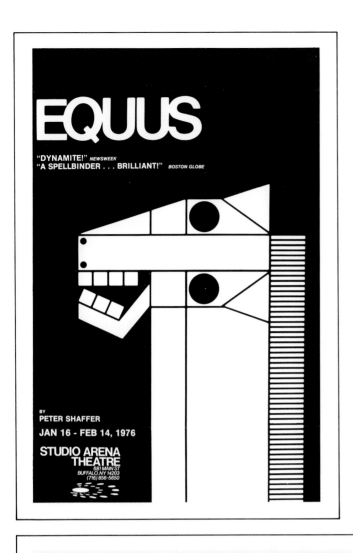

EQUUS

"DYNAMITE!" NEWSWEEK
"A SPELLBINDER . . . BRILLIANT!" BOSTON GLOBE

BY
PETER SHAFFER
JAN 16 - FEB 14, 1976

**STUDIO ARENA
THEATRE**
681 MAIN ST
BUFFALO, NY 14203
(716) 856-5650

A MOON FOR THE MISBEGOTTEN – October 198

STUDIO **arena** THEATRE

PRESENTS

james
daly

AND

colleen
dewhurst

IN

eugene o'neill's

A MOON FOR THE MISBEGOTTEN

WITH JOHN O'SHAUGHNESSY

DIRECTED BY

josé quintero

Set Designer
ROBERT MOTLEY

Lighting Designer
DAVID ZIERK

Costume Co-ordinator
DUANE ANDERSEN

Production Stage Manager
JIM WAY

years of his new position, but increasingly his time was taken up with scheduling, casting, and the myriad details involved in making the Studio Arena Theatre into a first-class regional playhouse. Most persons familiar with his work during the years before he resigned in 1979 would agree that he had succeeded in reaching that goal. David Frank, a young Englishman, succeeded DuBrock as artistic director.

So successful was the Studio Arena Theatre that it outgrew its original facilities. In the late 1970s it moved to the west side of Main Street, almost directly opposite its previous location. There it took over the Palace Theatre, built as a showcase for burlesque at about the time that traditional form of entertainment was grinding to a halt in Buffalo. The move gave the Studio Arena Theatre more audience space; additional room for sets, dressing rooms, and refreshment facilities; and larger accommodations for the theater school. At the Studio Arena Theatre Buffalonians have seen in person a myriad of well-known performers—Pat Hinkle, Bonnie Franklin, Jo Van Fleet, Celeste Holm, Jon Voight, Van Johnson, and Betsy Palmer, to name only a few. Professional graduates of the theater school include Buffalo-born Michael Bennett, dancer, choreographer, and creator of *A Chorus Line*, and Nancy Marchand, the newspaper owner in the long-running television series *Lou Grant*.

The Albright-Knox Art Gallery, the Buffalo Philharmonic based in Kleinhans Music Hall, and the Studio Arena Theatre are among the brightest stars in Buffalo's cultural firmament, but they are by no means the only ones. Ethnic theater has always been lively in Buffalo—including a Yiddish theater on William Street active in the early 20th century; the African Cultural Center, established in the 1950s; and the Jewish Center Little Theater. Numerous ethnic groups have formed cultural organizations that perform music, display arts and crafts, and present dances, both folk and artistic. During the 1960s there were at least five active classical ballet schools in Buffalo.

Buffalo is blessed with a number of colleges and universities, each of which adds cultural gloss to the city in one way or another. Three of these are more than a century old—the University of Buffalo, now a major unit in the State University of New York, being the oldest of all. A first attempt to establish a university here failed in 1836, only four years after the state issued Buffalo its charter as a city; but a second effort succeeded, and on May 11, 1846, the New York State Legislature incorporated the "University of Buffalo."

For 40 years the "university" was nothing more than a medical college. Then a college of pharmacy, a law school, and a dental school were added. A college of arts and sciences was finally established in 1920, in a building on Niagara Square owned for many years by the Women's Educational and Industrial Union of Buffalo. The Knox family aided in the purchase and maintenance of this building. In 1922 Dr. Samuel Paul Capen became the University of Buffalo's first full-time chancellor, a position he held until 1950. Dr. Capen invigorated the college of arts and sciences, but only when the State University assumed control were there sufficient resources to make the former University of Buffalo a major force in the city's cultural life.

In 1954 Dr. Clifford C. Furnas became the ninth chancellor of the University of Buffalo. For the next eight years, he led the university on an extensive building program that strained its financial resources. After two years of negotiation, the state of New York assumed the major share of the university's financing; at the same time, the University of Buffalo Foundation,

Inc., was chartered to receive and administer private funds in support of the new state institution. On September 1, 1962, the old University of Buffalo became the new State University of New York at Buffalo, eventually to become the largest unit of the state university founded in 1948.

Under its new name, the university augmented existing cultural programs and inaugurated new ones. Its music department had already achieved excellence under the leadership of Cameron Baird, donor of Baird Hall on the university's Main Street campus. But after 1962 the university was able to add the distinguished Budapest String Quartet to its campus attractions. In the same year a $200,000 grant from the Rockefeller Foundation established the Center for Creative and Performing Arts, bringing creative avant-garde composers and performers from all over the world to the Buffalo campus. These musicians gave concerts at the Albright-Knox Art Gallery and at Baird Hall, winning loyal audiences and sympathetic press reviews.

In 1970 construction began on a new campus for the university, outside the city of Buffalo in the town of Amherst. The new campus was to be seven times the size of the Main Street campus, which was to become a center for the health sciences. Work on the Amherst campus dragged on throughout the 1970s, in part because of various disagreements and in part because of budget restraints. It finally became clear that skyrocketing costs and revised enrollment projections would force curtailment of the original ambitious plans, despite the strenuous efforts of Dr. Robert L. Ketter, president of the university since 1971. As Buffalo approached its sesquicentennial, it became equally plain that the major focus of the State University of New York at Buffalo was shifting from the city to the northern suburbs.

Canisius College opened its doors for the first time on September 5, 1870, making it the second oldest institution of higher education in the city of Buffalo. Named for the famous post-Reformation German Jesuit, St. Peter Canisius, it had German-born Jesuits as its first six presidents, and its first three American-born presidents were of German extraction. The German influence no doubt accounted for especially strong music departments at Canisius well into the 20th century. Musical skill is probably no longer a requirement for appointment to the presidency of Canisius, although Father James M. Demske, president since 1966, does play the trombone.

Father Michael J. Ahern, president of Canisius between 1919 and 1923, had an interesting idea that, if successful, could have made Buffalo an American Oberammergau. A sumptuous outdoor theater with seats for 4,000 spectators was built behind Old Main Hall on the Canisius campus of that time. Two passion-play summer spectacles were presented there, the first during the summer of 1920 and a second in 1923.

Father Ahern's project required an electrician from New York's Theatre Guild to operate the elaborate light panel. A former stage manager for Sir Beerbohm-Tree was brought from England, and camels for the Nativity tableau were also imported. In spite of audiences totaling upwards of 100,000 for each of the two summers, the spectacles created enormous deficits. Consequently, the grand conception ended when workmen tore down the outdoor theater in the fall of 1923. The electrician went back to New York; the stage manager presumably went back to England; and the camels, after grazing on campus grass from May to September, became permanent residents of the Buffalo Zoo. In the words of Charles A. Brady, professor of English and historian of Canisius College's first 100 years, "The great adventure was but a memory." Had it succeeded, Father Ahern would have initiated a unique cultural attraction for Buffalo.

State University College at Buffalo is only a year younger than Canisius. Originally known as State Normal School, and located on Normal Avenue, it owed its existence in large part to Jesse Ketchum; Ketchum Hall, on the Elmwood Avenue campus to which the college moved in 1931, is named in his honor. Another building, as well as the main entrance road to the campus, is named in honor of Dr. Harry Rockwell, who served as president of the college from 1915 to 1951. He was succeeded by Dr. Harvey M. Rice, who resigned in 1958 to become president of Macalester College in St. Paul, Minnesota. Dr. Paul G. Bulger arrived in 1959 to become president of the college by then known familiarly as "Buffalo State."

Under Presidents Rice and Bulger, Buffalo State grew explosively in size, enrollment, and diversity of programs. Dr. Bulger in particular had an intense interest in the arts. During his administration the college invited Charles Burchfield to the campus and established the Burchfield Center as a gallery and library for showing and studying the work of this outstanding American artist. In 1967 Buffalo State's new president, Dr. E.K. Fretwell, Jr., announced his intention of dedicating the college to its role within the city of Buffalo, developing programs designed to help in the solution of urban problems. Under his leadership, and that of Dr. D. Bruce Johnstone who succeeded him as president in 1979, the college has played this role, not only in seeking solutions to the city's problems but also in maintaining and enhancing the college's place in the cultural life of Buffalo.

Always strong in art education, in the 1960s and 1970s Buffalo State added prize-winning artists to its staff—artists who continued to win awards in local, regional, and national exhibits. Members of the performing-arts and design departments work closely with the Studio Arena Theatre. On campus, interested faculty and students have carried on the strong dramatics program begun by Jane Keeler decades ago. Meanwhile, the Burchfield Center has extended its influence and interests with the hope of becoming a little brother to the Albright-Knox Art Gallery.

D'Youville and Medaille colleges, located within the city limits, along with Daemen and Villa Maria colleges in nearby suburbs, are smaller and younger institutions of higher education. They, too, help to light up the cultural firmament, shining brighter with each special exhibit, play, recital, concert, or dance performance. No doubt the same will hold true when the downtown campus of Erie Community College opens in the renovated Old Post Office, a massive Gothic edifice originally dedicated in 1901.

Above
Canisius College played against St. Bonaventure University in this 1979 basketball game. Courtesy, Harry M. Hadaway.

Two other major cultural attractions in the city are the Buffalo and Erie County Historical Society, on Nottingham Court, and the Buffalo Museum of Science, at the east end of Humboldt Parkway.

The Historical Society, originally founded in 1862 with Millard Fillmore as its first president, now occupies the only building remaining from the Pan-American Exposition, deeded to Buffalo by New York State in 1902, enlarged with funds provided by the city during the 1920s. In more than three-quarters of a century, the society has had only five persons directing its multitude of activities: Dr. Frank H. Severance, executive secretary, 1902-1931; Robert W. Bingham, engaged as curator in 1922, becoming director in 1934; Dr. Wilbur H. Glover, 1952; Dr. Walter S. Dunn, Jr., 1963; and in 1980, the current director, Robert L. Damm. These five men have supervised temporary and permanent exhibits, collections of manuscripts, artifacts, and art objects, educational functions, and publishing ventures so ably that the Buffalo and Erie County Historical Society is recognized as one of the leading organizations of its type in the country. Visitors to its museum galleries are both entertained and instructed by the exhibits, while scholars from far and near come to avail themselves of the historical resources collected and maintained by the society's library and manuscript divisions.

Visitors to the Buffalo Museum of Science enter a building finished in 1929 at a total cost of more than $1 million, and renovated with additional funds a number of times since. Originally the museum held 11 halls, branching from a single large entrance hall and arranged so as to present an orderly sequence from the Hall of Primitive Races to the Hall of Physics and Chemistry. Chauncey Hamlin was its principal benefactor, and gifts from other prominent local families—Knoxes, Goodyears, and Schoellkopfs, among others—enabled the staff to install exhibits of high quality. On the roof of the museum is the Kellogg Observatory, donated by Mrs. Spencer Kellogg as a memorial to her husband. An auditorium, a library, and additional exhibit space make up the remainder of the Buffalo Museum of Science.

The museum is more than a repository of knowledge. It attempts to add to that knowledge through research in various areas, and it dispenses knowledge through its exhibits and through educational activities ranging from those designed for young children to a lively adult-education program. At times it has offered programs in music and art in addition to its major focus on the physical sciences. In the late 1970s, thanks to a massive public fund drive, a thorough renovation brought the museum's exhibits and physical facilities up to a modern standard.

Above
Dr. Clifford C. Furnas (second from left), the ninth chancellor of the University of Buffalo, became the first president of the State University of New York at Buffalo. He is seated with Averell Harriman, Seymour Knox, and Karr Parker in this circa 1957 photograph. (BECHS)

Two important libraries served Buffalo during the century before they merged under the sponsorship of Erie County. One was the Grosvenor Library, named for Seth Grosvenor, a merchant and financier who at his death in 1857 bequeathed the money to build a free reference library and to purchase books for it. Eventually established in its own building on Franklin Street, the Grosvenor developed along unique lines with specialized collections in its medical department, its local history and genealogy sections, and its business and labor department. In addition, through large and small gifts, the Grosvenor developed a collection of sheet music and popular records that brought it great distinction. George Nathan Newman was a principal benefactor of the Grosvenor Library, donating books, records, and money to expand its usefulness.

The Buffalo Public Library of necessity developed along different lines from the Grosvenor, which was essentially a reference library. Broader, more general collections, distributed among the main and seven branch libraries, marked the Buffalo Public's efforts. Both the Buffalo Public and the Grosvenor received tax money from the city, an uneconomical system that brought acute financial problems by the middle of the 20th century. One obvious solution was merger, but this was easier to suggest than to accomplish. Both were old, proud,

Above
The first executive secretary of the Buffalo Historical Society was Dr. Frank H. Severance, who held the position from 1902-1931. (BECHS)

established institutions with conflicting philosophies and competitive services difficult to adjust. The merger was finally achieved after nearly a decade of negotiations. The two libraries became one—the Buffalo and Erie County Public Library—and their collections are now housed in a new and larger building on Lafayette Square, site of the old Buffalo Public Library.

Dr. Joseph B. Rounds directed the merging of the two libraries and the methods whereby surrounding towns could join the Erie County system. This work has continued under the present director of the county library system, Paul M. Rooney. Severe budget cutbacks in the early 1970s caused almost fatal losses in library services. Nonetheless, Erie County's assumption of major financial responsibility for the library system has proved beneficial on the whole. Indeed, the Albright-Knox Art Gallery, the Studio Arena Theatre, the Museum of Science, and the Buffalo and Erie County Historical Society, as well as numerous other cultural organizations in the Buffalo area, have all come to rely on a combination of private funds and public tax money. Not only wealthy and public-spirited Buffalo families have realized that man does not live by bread alone—local governments in the area have come to the same realization.

Above
This 1956 photograph shows bird watchers in Forest Lawn Cemetery. The Buffalo Museum of Science currently offers a telephone service, Dial-a-Bird, which gives the latest sightings. Courtesy, Buffalo Courier Express/Simmons. (BECHS)

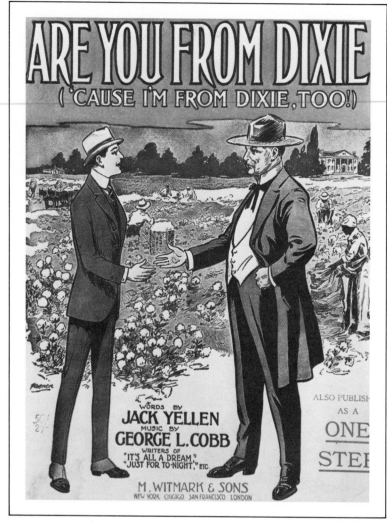

Buffalo has contributed individuals as well as institutions to the cultural life of the nation—among them, songwriter Jack Yellen, historian and writer Paul Horgan, artist Charles Ephraim Burchfield, and novelist Taylor Caldwell.

"Happy Days Are Here Again!" Franklin D. Roosevelt made it his campaign theme song in 1932. So did subsequent Democratic presidential candidates, including Harry Truman, John F. Kennedy, and Lyndon Johnson. By 1980 it had become a bipartisan tune—the theme song for the nomination, election, and inauguration of Republican President Ronald Reagan.

Though all Americans are familiar with the tune, few know it was the product of songwriting team Yellen and Ager—the front half of which was a native of Buffalo. A graduate of the old Central High School on Niagara Square, Jack Yellen was a behind-the-scenes showbusiness figure from the Dixieland era until the time of Elvis Presley. He was a versatile participant in American popular culture for nearly 50 years—an independent songwriter and music publisher; a contributor of songs and comedy skits to *George White's Scandals* and other Broadway shows; a writer for Sophie Tucker ("Last of the Red Hot Mamas"), Van and Schenck, and other famous vaudeville teams; and a scriptwriter for Metro-Goldwyn-Mayer and other giant Hollywood studios of the time.

Above
Buffalo songwriter Jack Yellen made a big hit with the song "Are You from Dixie?" for which he was paid only $1,000. Courtesy, Buffalo and Erie County Public Library Music Department.

Jack Yellen's first big hit was a song called "Are You from Dixie?" ("Yes, I'se from Dixie / Well, I'se from Dixie, too!") With the $1,000 a music firm paid him for it, Yellen made the down payment on a house for his parents on Cedar Street in Buffalo. Had he held out for royalties, he could have bought them a mansion.

"Down by the O-hi-o," "Hard-Hearted Hannah," "I'm Waiting for Ships That Never Come In," and "I Wonder What's Become of Sally" were other Yellen hits, although none of the hundreds of popular songs he had a part in ever returned him more in royalties than "Happy Days Are Here Again." It always amused Yellen that the song was written in 30 minutes for an obscure little movie called *Chasing Rainbows*, released by Metro-Goldwyn-Mayer only a few months before the stock-market crash of October 1929 ushered in the Great Depression. Somehow the song seemed to catch the chin-up spirit of Americans determined to sing and dance their way through economic hardship. When FDR coupled it to his successful campaigns, "Happy Days Are Here Again" was on its way to becoming an American classic.

Even before the Beatles arrived with a new style of music, Jack Yellen had retired to "Melody Meadows," his name for the farm he had bought in the Springville hills, near enough to his beloved Buffalo for him to "come to town" to visit with old friends. A copy of

Above
"Happy Days Are Here Again" became one of America's favorite tunes. Few people know that it was written by Buffalonian Jack Yellen for an obscure musical called Chasing Rainbows *which opened a few months before the stock market crashed. Courtesy, Buffalo and Erie County Public Library Music Department.*

the sheet music for "Happy Days Are Here Again," autographed by Franklin D. Roosevelt, occupied a prominent place in Yellen's memory room at Melody Meadows.

Paul Horgan, winner of two Pulitzer prizes in history, was also born in Buffalo. His prize-winning works, however, are set in the American Southwest, where the family moved in pursuit of the dry climate needed to combat his father's tuberculosis.

In his younger years, Paul Horgan lived at 228 Lexington, where he was born in 1903; in a house on Middlesex that has since been torn down; and for six years at 133 St. James Place. His father, Edward Daniel Horgan, was at one time assistant manager of the Germania Life Insurance Company with offices in the Ellicott Square. His mother, born Rose Marie Rohr, was the daughter of Matthias Rohr for whom Rohr Street in Buffalo was named. During his elementary school years, young Paul attended Nardin Academy.

Great River: The Rio Grande in North American History was awarded the Pulitzer prize in 1954, and *Lamy of Santa Fe: His Life and Times* in 1975. Horgan has written 40 books in all—among them a novel called *Things As They Are*. He wrote in its foreword, "Even if backgrounds and places suggest the real . . . these pages are not to be taken as fragments of an autobiography of my early self." In spite of this disclaimer, the house described in *Things As They Are* is clearly the house at 133 St. James Place where the Horgans lived, and the school the youngster in the book attends is clearly Nardin.

Charles Ephraim Burchfield was not born in Buffalo but came here in 1921 at the age of 28. A graduate of the Cleveland School of Art, not yet able to earn a living solely as an independent artist, he came to Buffalo as assistant designer and later head of the design department for the world-famous wallpaper company, M.H. Birge and Sons.

During his years in Western New York, Charles Burchfield's painting went through two distinct phases. Between 1921 and 1943 he depicted urban scenes, many of them interpretations of Buffalo sites. He painted the houses, the harbor, bridges, and machinery. "Black Iron," "Freight Cars Under a Bridge," and "Old Houses in Winter" are among his many watercolors dating from this period. At first glance they seem somber and grimly realistic. And yet there is a lyric quality shining through that was to become more pronounced in Burchfield's later work.

In 1929 the Rehn Galleries in New York took over his work, guaranteeing enough sales to support Burchfield, his wife, and their five children. With some hesitation but much relief, Burchfield left his job with Birge and became a full-time artist. Four years earlier he had moved his family from Buffalo to a home at 3574 Clinton Street in suburban Gardenville.

It was not until 1943, however, that Burchfield shifted from urban scenes to nature and the seasons as the major focus of his painting. "I'm going to give you more sounds and dreams, and—yes, I'm going to make people smell what I want them to, and with visual means," he wrote to his New York representative in 1944. From that time on, Burchfield's watercolors dealt with subtle, ever-changing aspects of the seasons. These lyrical, dreamlike paintings earned him a reputation, as one critic put it, as "a poet of light and weather."

A shy man, Charles Burchfield avoided teaching until 1949, but during the next three years he taught at the Art Institute of Buffalo, the University of Buffalo, and the Buffalo Fine Arts Academy. In November 1952 he had a violent, crippling attack of lumbago which caused him to forego teaching. Still, with the aid of a rigid back brace, he was able to carry his painting apparatus into the field, continuing his work there and in his Gardenville studio until his death in 1967.

Facing page
Born in Buffalo in 1903, Paul Horgan became a Pulitzer prizewinning author for two of his 40 books, Great River: The Rio Grande in North American History *and* Lamy of Santa Fe: His Life and Times, *in 1954 and 1975 respectively.*

Today hundreds of homes and galleries display Burchfield's work, either in the original or in reproduction. Probably the best-known 20th-century artist to be associated with Buffalo, his name and reputation are perpetuated through the Burchfield Center on the campus of the State University College.

Taylor Caldwell, born in England but a resident of the Buffalo area for much of her life, has become one of America's most productive novelists. She has averaged better than a book every two years since her first, *Dynasty of Death*, was published in 1938. All her work has sold widely, and some of her novels have been transformed into movies and television spectaculars. Taylor Caldwell could best be described as a romantic historical novelist, with stories that range in time and setting from ancient Rome to modern America—though none has Western New York as its locale.

In March of 1941, the French writer and critic known as André Maurois arrived to teach a course in French literature at the University of Buffalo. In a fragment of autobiographical writing, he later recalled that friends in New York had told him, "You won't like Buffalo." They warned him about the climate, calling it "very tough," with only two seasons, "winter and the month of August." They described Buffalo as "primarily industrial," and undoubtedly grim to anyone with his cultivated tastes.

After a few months' residence in Buffalo, Maurois found his friends' condemnation of the city to be wide of the mark. No city in the world possessed finer trees, he wrote, especially as he saw them leafing out in the spring and in full splendor during the summer. "The seas of

Above
The description of Buffalo's tree-lined streets and avenues as remarkable "seas of verdure" seems appropriate to this view of Chapin Parkway circa 1912. (BECHS)

verdure which I saw from the window of my room in the Hotel Lenox reminded me of my house at Neuilly and the green waves of the Bois de Boulogne." It was not only the city that pleased Maurois. "Among its inhabitants I found friends who suited my heart and my temperament."

If Maurois returned to Buffalo 40 years later, he would look in vain for most of the trees he admired. Most of the older ones have been replaced by younger trees or have vanished completely, victims of the dreaded elm disease that devastated the leafy bowers along Delaware and Richmond avenues. But he still could find friends to suit his heart and temperament. He would find some among the staff members and students of Buffalo's colleges and universities. He would find others among those who guide the work of Buffalo's art galleries, museums, theaters, and music halls, and among those who visit these cultural attractions. No doubt he would be asked to address the Twentieth Century Club or the Scriptores, and there is no doubt he would find kindred spirits among their members.

Probably André Maurois could find friends among the thousands—indeed, hundreds of thousands—who annually visit the mid-June outdoor exhibit originated in 1957 by the Allentown Village Society. Each year since then, the Allentown Art Festival has attracted to Buffalo hundreds of artists and crafts people from all over the eastern United States and Canada. The controversies arising over the basic purpose of the festival have done nothing to diminish the throngs of visitors to the area between West Tupper and North on Delaware and Franklin. It is Buffalo's biggest artistic extravaganza and probably one of the largest of its kind in the entire United States. And it is one more piece of evidence to show that if Buffalo was ever "primarily industrial," it has never been exclusively so—certainly not in the 20th century.

Above
Delaware Avenue, seen here in 1917, was only one of many streets lined with numerous trees, many of which were replaced or destroyed by elm disease. (BECHS)

Home of the Buffalo and Erie County Historical Society. (BECHS)

In 1836 the Young Men's Association formed a library in Buffalo. Shortly afterwards, its members formed standing committees interested in relics, artwork, scientific specimens, and historical materials. Today, four of Buffalo's most respected cultural centers directly trace their common heritage to these YMA committees. One of them is the Buffalo and Erie County Historical Society.

The Buffalo Historical Society was founded in 1862 by 14 men in the community. Elected first president of the new society, former U.S. President Millard Fillmore guided the organization through its first five years. From 1865-73 the Society had space in the YMA building, then on the third floor of the Western Savings Bank, and later at the Buffalo Library. By 1879 the Society had published the first of its 40 hardcover volumes of its *Publications.* The library of the Society already had 9,360 books, 7,570 pamphlets, 689 maps and charts, 118 manuscripts, and 23 manuscript volumes by 1887, when 10,500 volumes of the Rev. Dr. John C. Lord Library were added.

The Society campaigned successfully in the 1880s for a suitable Forest Lawn Cemetery monument to the Indian orator Red Jacket. Later, the Society received the original Red Jacket medal given to him by George Washington in 1792. The Red Jacket Award, now given annually by the Society to an outstanding leader, is a replica of this symbol of friendship between American and Indian nations.

The War of 1812 burial grounds in Williamsville were restored and placed under the Society's care in 1898.

In 1901, after the Spanish-American War, the Pan-American Exposition was held in Buffalo. A white-marble, Doric-style building was built as the New York State building at the Exposition. Partially funded by the City of Buffalo and the Historical Society, it was deeded to the Society the following year. At the dedication ceremonies, other donors presented the Lincoln statue now on the Portico.

Regional histories and hardcover volumes continued to be published, and lectures and school tours were given in the new building. After 1922, four dioramas and nine murals were added to the exhibit galleries. The Apostolic Clock, the museum's most popular feature, was donated in 1923.

Space became a problem by the 1920s. George Cary, the building's original architect, was commissioned to design library and auditorium additions. As part of Buffalo's 100th anniversary in 1932, the Society unveiled a plaster-relief exhibit showing the village of Buffalo as it looked in 1813.

In the early 1930s the Society staff began giving radio talks and later historical dramas. WPA artists painted the five lunettes on the upper floor of the museum in the 1940s, and an authentic Indian log house was reassembled on the edge of Mirror Lake.

In 1952 the Society began publication of its *Niagara Frontier* quarterly, its newsletters for social studies teachers, and its *Adventures in Western New York History* essay series for young people. The first definitive biography of Millard Fillmore was published in 1959.

Local history exhibits were introduced at the Erie County Fair; they were the forerunners to the highly competitive exhibits by local historical societies in the Historical Building at the annual County Fair today. The Congress of Local Historical Societies and the Erie County Historical Federation were formed with Society support. The annual Junior Historians Conventions were inaugurated for seventh-grade students to compete for prizes. Special assistance was given to the restoration projects at Fort Niagara.

Partial Erie County funding was obtained in 1956, and in 1960 the name of the Society was changed to the Buffalo and Erie County Historical Society. A historic markers program was well under way, the annual Red Jacket Awards for distinguished civic service were initiated, and three Society chapters were organized to assist the Society in specific historical programs.

A major exhibit, the 1870 Street, sponsored by the Junior League of Buffalo, opened in 1962. In the years that followed, there was a gradual modernization of the museum galleries that included an ethnic exhibit, People of our City and County; Canal Town, Military Heritage on the Niagara Frontier; Business, Industry and Transportation; and three successive Iroquois Indian galleries. The pioneer exhibits were updated, and the Glassware and Pilot House exhibits were installed in new galleries underneath the Portico. An extremely successful series of 12-15 ethnic evenings per year was inaugurated—the beginnings of the Niagara Frontier Folk Art Festivals held today.

Successful campaigns were waged to save the Buffalo Lighthouse, now the symbol of the Society, and the Wilcox House, where Theodore Roosevelt took his oath of office in 1901. The House is now the Roosevelt Inaugural National Historic Site. Special assistance was given to local historical societies setting up their own museums in Erie and Cattaraugus counties. Historical movies were shown, loan kits of replicas and duplicate museum items were made to schools, and cooperative museum courses began with the University of Buffalo and the State University College at Buffalo. A large number of federally funded work-study students and New York State Council on the Arts interns were employed by the Society. Later, federally funded CETA staff members and CETA projects aided departments during the 1970s and early 1980s.

By 1905, the American Historical Association had already ranked the Society in size and scope with state historical agencies. Two Awards of Merit have been received from the American Association for State and Local History for unique contributions made by its *Adventures* series and for its ethnic programs.

The microfilm editions of the papers of Peter B. Porter and Millard Fillmore were made possible through state and federal grants, as were the inventories of special collections and the construction and research for temporary and long-term exhibits. During Erie County's 1971 Sesquicentennial the Society published its *History of Erie County: 1870-1970* volume, and it has recently inaugurated a new exhibit catalog series with Glassware, Ironworks, and Buffalo Works as the first three.

Space problems have taken first priority in the current Society operations. Shortly, the Exposition Building will be returned to its original use as an exhibition hall. Research and developmental activities will be moved to nearby quarters along with the extensive collections in storage.

The Society's founders set about to "discover, procure, and preserve whatever may relate to the History of Western New York, in general, and the City of Buffalo, in particular." Today, its historical materials are widely used for study, publication, and exhibition. *Buffalo: Lake City in Niagara Land*, sponsored by the Society for the City's 1982 Sesquicentennial, will serve as a lasting account in the tradition set forth by those founders.

CHAPTER XII

WINTER— AND THEN SPRING

Buffalo's storm of the century began about 11:00 in the morning of Friday, January 28, 1977. For hours the temperature hovered below 10 degrees Fahrenheit, while snow blown by winds gusting to 70 miles an hour reduced visibility to zero. By Friday night hundreds of people were stranded in office buildings, schools, police stations, fire halls, factories, and bars. "It was like New Year's Eve," reported some of those who took refuge in these drinking places, not yet realizing the seriousness of the situation.

The Buffalo downtown YMCA opened its rooms and showers to women for the first time ever during the storm. Kitchen workers at Millard Fillmore Hospital in Buffalo provided free meals for 1,400 persons other than patients between 4:00 and 7:00 on the afternoon of the storm. Drifting snow made most streets and highways impassable, blocked railroad lines, and closed Buffalo International Airport.

On Saturday, January 29, President Carter issued a "declaration of emergency" for four Western New York counties, thus permitting governmental agencies to move in and help with rescue efforts under the authority of the Federal Disaster Assistance Administration. Later three more western counties and two in the northern part of the state were added to what the President on Saturday, February 5, 1977, designated a "major disaster area," the first

Facing page
Pedestrians took to the streets due to the ban on motoring after the 1977 blizzard. Memories of the storm and its aftermath remained alive in the minds of Buffalo residents for years to come. Courtesy, Buffalo Courier Express/Ron Schifferie.

such ever for a snow emergency.

The disaster focused national attention on Western New York. Television networks broadcast pictures and commentary concerning the storm and efforts at cleanup for 11 consecutive nights in late January and early February—all of them datelined "Buffalo." When there was time for counting, a total of 23 storm-related deaths was recorded. Of these 18 were in Erie County, including 11 in the city of Buffalo. In money terms, the Buffalo Chamber of Commerce put the estimated cost of the "Great Blizzard of '77" for Erie and Niagara counties at $297,870,000.

Long-time residents of Buffalo and Western New York took the disaster in good spirits—indeed, with a sort of grim satisfaction at having endured. Survival T-shirts, snowflake and snow-shovel pendants, and anniversary parties kept alive the memory of those winter days and nights. But underneath all the good humor, and interspersed among the stories of "what we did during the blizzard," was the realization that nature had struck Buffalo a stunning body blow.

By the time of Buffalo's Great Blizzard, American cities of the Northeast and upper Midwest lay in an "arc of economic crisis." The arc began at Baltimore, ran north and west as far as Minneapolis, and then turned south to St. Louis. Buffalo stood nearly at the center of this arc, suffering from many of the same factors that had brought on economic crisis for its sister cities. All these cities suffered to some extent from the severe winter of 1976-77. But, as *Newsweek* reported in a July follow-up article, "No American city was hurt as much as Buffalo by the winter weather."

Although city authorities were criticized for lack of preparation and for inexcusable confusion in cleaning up the storm's damage, most people realized that little could be done to avoid winter storms in the eastern lake region. Likewise, it seemed that little could be done to halt the decline in Buffalo's grain trade.

For a century or more, the grain trade had been a pillar of Buffalo's economy. Throughout the 19th century, this trade consisted mainly of transshipment of grain with relatively little being milled in Buffalo itself. Lake boats and railroad cars carried grain from the lower Midwest to Buffalo, where it was unloaded and stored in huge elevators until it was reloaded and shipped on to another destination. The grain elevators stood along the harbor rim and on or near the banks of the Buffalo and Niagara rivers. Some of the elevators rose more than 300 feet tall. All together they had a capacity for storing millions of bushels of grain. At the turn of the century, elevators in Buffalo charged 5/8¢ for raising, weighing, and discharging one bushel of grain. The charge for storing one bushel of grain for 10 days was 1/4¢. Though these charges were small, multiplied by millions of bushels they brought considerable sums into the Buffalo economy.

After 1900 shipment of western grain from Buffalo grew less common, as the city developed its own flour-milling and animal-feed industries. Inexpensive electric power was a major encouragement to grain processing here, so much so that by the 1930s Buffalo stood as the first city in the United States in flour milling and in production of animal foods from grain. During these years most grain reached Buffalo by lake rather than by railroad, carried from Duluth, Minnesota; Superior, Wisconsin; and Thunder Bay, Ontario. It came from fields in the northern prairies of the United States and from Canadian fields across the border. During the 1920s more than 185 million bushels of Canadian grain reached Buffalo.

Facing page, top
Neighbors help each other out in this typical shoveling-out scene after the "Great Blizzard of '77." Nine counties were designated as major disaster areas. Courtesy, Buffalo Courier Express/ Mickey Osterreicher.

Facing page, bottom left
A lone man plods through the snow during the disastrous storm which became known as the "Great Blizzard of '77." Courtesy, Buffalo Courier Express/ Ronald M. Moscati.

Facing page, bottom right
Four days after the 1977 storm, a typical city scene at the intersection of Bidwell and Elmwood reveals abandoned cars and children playing in a winter wonderland. Courtesy, Buffalo Evening News/Richard Roeller.

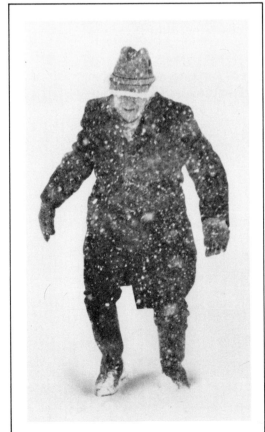

The decade of the 1920s broke all records, with 300 million bushels of grain arriving annually at the city's elevators and mills. The late 1940s saw even this figure exceeded because of World War II and the necessity of feeding western Europe in the immediate postwar years. Since that time, however, the decline in Buffalo's grain industries has been rapid and severe, and today the volume is barely 20 percent of what it once was. Elevators and mills have been abandoned or are operating at less than capacity, resulting in loss of jobs and of tax revenues for the city.

The reasons for these losses are complex, subtle, and largely beyond the control of any group or any institution in Buffalo. Two of the causes, however, are clearly related to waterways. In 1932 the Welland Ship Canal opened, permitting larger grain boats from northern Great Lakes ports to bypass Buffalo, carrying their cargo instead to Canadian or Northern New York cities for processing or transshipment. Hardly any Canadian grain has been transshipped from Buffalo since the opening of the Welland Ship Canal.

The opening of the St. Lawrence Seaway in June 1959 had an even more severe impact on Buffalo's grain trade as well as on other aspects of the city's economy. For decades Buffalonians were in the forefront of those opposing a project to enlarge the locks on the St. Lawrence River to accommodate larger oceangoing vessels. Every time the project was discussed in Albany or in Washington, Buffalo's leaders fought against it. When legislation authorizing construction of the St. Lawrence Seaway was finally passed in May 1954, these same leaders tried to make the best of the situation, predicting increased employment, new industries, and the benefits of world trade.

Unfortunately, these favorable predictions remained unfulfilled. For one reason, what local opponents of the seaway project had feared proved to be true—the loss of transshipment trade, particularly in grain. For another, it proved all too easy for ocean vessels, "salties" as they are called, to exit from the Welland Ship Canal at Port Colborne and turn west toward Cleveland, Toledo, Detroit, and Chicago, rather than east toward Buffalo, the only port at the eastern end of Lake Erie. Because of the Erie Canal, 19th-century Buffalo was on America's Main Street. In the 20th century, the Welland Ship Canal and the St. Lawrence Seaway have put Buffalo on a dead-end street.

The decline in the grain trade was accompanied by changes in Buffalo's heavy industry, including a number of plant closings with consequent loss of jobs and of tax revenue to the city. In 1958 the New York Car Wheel Company went bankrupt. The Buffalo metal-fabricating

Above
Abandoned grain elevators on the Buffalo River are seen in this 1979 view. The opening of the Welland Ship Canal in 1932 and the St. Lawrence Seaway in 1959 diminished the need for ships to pass through the Erie Canal. Courtesy, Buffalo Courier Express/Ric Delaney.

plant of ACF Industries, which at one time had employed 3,000 workers, closed in 1959. The next year the Buffalo plant of Allegheny Ludlum Steel Corporation closed. And in 1962 another 400 workers became unemployed as the Buffalo Steel Corporation shut down forever. During the 1970s, National Gypsum moved its corporate headquarters from Buffalo to Dallas, and Houdaille Industries left Buffalo for Florida. It was little consolation to Buffalonians that these developments were part of nationwide trends—the same kinds of things were happening to other cities in the arc of economic distress.

As Buffalo lost industrial plants and corporate headquarters, it also lost residents. In part, at least, this too was a reflection of broad national trends. The flight from city to suburbs following World War II was a nationwide phenomenon, and many former Buffalonians moved across city lines into adjacent communities. Declining birthrates in the 1960s and 1970s slowed population growth throughout the nation. Meanwhile, restrictions on immigration to the United States cut down on the number of newcomers who had added so dramatically to city populations in the late 19th and early 20th centuries. This combination of circumstances caused most cities in the arc of economic distress to lose population in the decades following the end of World War II.

But Buffalo's decline in population has been precipitous. Ranking 15th in population among American cities in 1950, by 1980 it had fallen out of the top 30. In the five years between 1970 and 1975, Buffalo lost 12 percent of its population, the highest percentage loss of any city in New York State. Among all the cities on the Great Lakes, only Cleveland's 15.8-percent decline surpassed that of Buffalo.

Thus at the time of the Great Blizzard, Buffalo suffered literally from the winter weather and figuratively from the winter of economic and population decline. Even in the dead of winter, however, there are occasional favorable signs that point to better days ahead. So it was with Buffalo by the late 1970s.

One of these favorable signs was the progress made in cleaning up Buffalo's waterways. Among these, the Buffalo River was the dirtiest and most polluted. Because of the industries and grain elevators crowded on both sides of its six-mile length, the river had long been a good friend of Buffalo's economy but an enemy of the public's health and welfare.

In the early years of the 20th century, raw sewage from Buffalo was dumped into the river, a practice in part responsible for the high typhoid rate prevailing from Buffalo north

Above
The Buffalo River, shown here in 1952, is lined with grain elevators, lake ships, and railroads. From the Fitzgerald Collection. (BECHS)

along the Niagara. On occasion storms and changes in water levels activated slugs of domestic sewage and industrial waste, causing them to move from the polluted river out to Buffalo harbor and into the Niagara. Down that river flowed the polluted material until it reached the open water of Lake Ontario, where it usually settled along the south shore. Public-health officials blamed these pollutants for outbreaks of waterborne diseases in towns downriver from Buffalo. Several times the New York Department of Conservation reported the sudden death of large numbers of fish at the eastern end of Lake Erie, in the Niagara River, and along the New York shore of Lake Ontario.

Fortunately, experts located the sources of pollution and aroused public opinion against the dangers to Buffalo's waterways. A new sewage-treatment plant took care of one source of pollution. Dredges deepened and widened the channel of the Buffalo River, increasing the water flow to prevent the buildup of pollutants in the formerly sluggish stream. State authorities began to regulate the dumping of toxic wastes. The federal Clean Waters Act of 1972 provided additional regulation. Treaties between the United States and Canada established procedures preventing either side from polluting international waterways to the harm of the other. Though still some distance from springtime freshness, Buffalo's waterways by 1981 were noticeably cleaner and safer than they had been a quarter-century before.

Nor was this the only favorable sign. As early as 1970, *House and Garden, Architectural Record,* and similar publications began drawing attention to plans for developing Buffalo's waterfront. When the Shoreline Apartments were built, a writer in *House and Garden* described them as a "New Way to Live: A Village in the Heart of the City." Buffalonians in the past have been less than enthusiastic about building apartment houses or about living in them. Nevertheless, plans for apartment houses along the waterfront and elsewhere in Buffalo may be a favorable sign that the city's residents are adapting to the necessities of 20th-century urban life.

Another necessary adjunct of city life is the department store. In 19th-century America, downtown department stores for the first time drew substantial numbers of women into an area previously given over largely to men going about their business. In the mid-20th century, however, development has tended to be in the opposite direction. Though women have remained downtown in business capacities of their own, the large retail establishments have been branching out into the suburbs.

Buffalo's University Plaza at Main and Kenmore was built in 1939 as a new concept in retailing. But it was the Thruway Plaza, opened in 1952 with 39 stores, that truly sparked the

Above
The Shoreline Apartments were constructed in 1971. Planned as "a village in the heart of the city," the complex has been part of the increased urban development witnessed by 20th-century Buffalo residents. Courtesy, Buffalo Evening News/Merrill Matthews.

Facing page, top left
After the Clean Waters Act of 1972, the regulation of wastes in Buffalo's water-ways was stepped up. This 1974 photograph shows research aids aboard the Great Lakes Lab ship pulling up plankton with a net used for gathering samples from Lake Erie. Courtesy, Buffalo Evening News. (BECHS)

Facing page, top right
By 1978 the Niagara River was deemed safe for fishing as evidenced by this tranquil scene near West Ferry. Courtesy, Buffalo Evening News/Stevie Benson.

Facing page, bottom
The Thruway Plaza opened in 1952, the year this photo was taken. With 39 stores and a large parking area, the Thruway Plaza set a precedent for the expansion of suburban shopping centers and malls. Courtesy, Buffalo Evening News/Schultz. (BECHS)

move to large suburban shopping centers. Over the past 20 years, six new or improved suburban shopping malls have ringed Buffalo, unintentionally acting as spikes driven into the coffin of the city's downtown shopping area. Eastern Hills Mall, the largest of the six, contains 90 national, regional, and specialty stores. Boulevard Mall, built in 1962, was metropolitan Buffalo's first covered suburban shopping mall. Later the Thruway Mall was enclosed. Southgate Plaza, Seneca Mall, and Summit Park Mall completed the ring, the last-named being 12 miles north of Sheridan Drive, in Niagara County.

Over the same 20 years, the only new shopper-oriented facilities in downtown Buffalo have been Main Place Mall and Courtyard Mall—attempts to duplicate the suburban plazas within the city. Older department stores such as Adam, Meldrum & Anderson, Hengerer's, and Sattler's have remained in downtown Buffalo, but each has also established branch stores in one or more of the suburban malls. Woolworth's, with its close connections to Buffalo, remains downtown, but national chains such as Sears, J.C. Penney, and K-Mart have either left Buffalo for the suburbs or never entered the city in the first place.

All this is not to say that building in downtown Buffalo has been completely ignored. Far from it. Lafayette Square underwent a facelift when the Tishman Building went up and Western Savings Bank began a new home across the street from it. To make room, the old Lafayette Theater was demolished. So was the old library building, to be replaced by the handsome new Buffalo and Erie County Public Library.

The Edward A. Rath building, named for Erie County's first elected county executive, was erected across from the old County Hall. To the east of the Rath Building, Erie Savings Bank built Main Place Mall, along with a 26-story tower to house the bank's offices and other facilities. Manufacturers and Traders Trust Company added its elegant M&T Plaza to Buffalo's downtown skyline, a combination bank and office building topped off by a popular restaurant, the Plaza Suite. Not to be outdone, Marine Midland Bank built a 40-story building that stands astride lower Main Street. In the 1980s, two more banks, Liberty and Buffalo Savings, have begun construction of new headquarters buildings in downtown Buffalo.

Meanwhile, the waterfront nearest to downtown has been undergoing extensive rejuvenation. Erie Basin Marina provides a modern and attractive launching and storage facility for Western New York boat owners. Near the marina, the Naval and Servicemen's Park features a World War II destroyer and cruiser as its principal attractions. A new Hilton Hotel and the beginning of new housing developments are further evidence that Buffalo's waterfront is replacing its dreary winter garb with a springtime appearance.

Above
Main Place Mall in 1970 was one of two shopping malls in downtown Buffalo patterned after the successful suburban plazas. Courtesy, Buffalo Evening News/Merrill Matthews.

Facing page, top
This view looking south on Main Street in 1950 shows the brilliantly lit Theater District. Attempts are now being made to revitalize this area. From the Fitzgerald Collection. (BECHS)

Facing page, bottom
Buffalo's dramatically changing skyline can be seen in this 1981 photograph showing the Hilton Hotel and the Erie Basin Marina on its waterfront. The basin serves as a storage port for Western New York boat owners. Courtesy, Buffalo Courier Express/Paul Pasquarello.

A third essential ingredient of a satisfying urban life is a lively metropolitan press. In 19th-century cities, newspapers helped provide a sense of community, filling the need for enlightenment and gossip previously exchanged face to face with friends and relatives in the smaller communities from which so many recent urban arrivals had come. In the 1920s residents of Buffalo could choose among six dailies—two morning papers and four evening—of which three had Sunday editions. By the time of the Great Blizzard a half-century later, these totals had shrunk to two dailies, the morning *Courier-Express* and the *Buffalo Evening News*. The *Courier-Express* also published a Sunday edition, from which it derived a major portion of its earnings.

Again this shrinkage of city newspapers followed a national trend, whose cause seems to have been mainly economic. In 1920 there were competing newspapers in more than 700 cities of the United States. By 1977 fewer than 50 cities had more than one newspaper, Buffalo being among this number. In fact, Buffalo shared another distinction: both its competing newspapers were owned and published by local families—the *Courier-Express* by the Conners family, and the *Buffalo Evening News* by the Butlers.

In 1977 this distinction disappeared when Warren E. Buffett, an Omaha, Nebraska, finan-

Above
This photograph of the main lobby at Shea's Buffalo Theatre shows the grand theater during the time before its very existence would be threatened. Now Shea's great theater has been saved. It remains an important landmark in the restoration of the Theater District. (BECHS)

cier, bought the *Buffalo Evening News*. Soon after, the *News* announced plans to publish a Sunday edition. Faced with this threat to his main source of revenue, and thus to the continued existence of his newspaper, William J. Conners III, publisher of the *Courier-Express*, began a series of legal actions against the rival paper, including an antitrust suit. Then came the startling news that Conners had sold the *Courier-Express* to outside interests—the Cowles group of publications—and Buffalo, too, dropped from the rapidly shrinking number of American cities with competing, locally owned newspapers. Although many thoughtful Buffalonians regretted those developments, in today's rapidly changing publishing world they probably ensured that Buffalo would at least continue to be a city with two competing newspapers.

Buffalo also remains a major printing center. The largest of several firms is Arcata Graphics, Buffalo Division, which prints *Reader's Digest*, the *National Enquirer*, and innumerable paperback books. Graphic Controls is a nationally known producer of business forms based in Buffalo. Greater Buffalo Press prints the Sunday comics and advertising inserts found in newspapers all over the country.

For most of the 20th century, of course, Buffalonians have gotten news, enlightenment,

Above
Edward A. Rath, pictured in 1961, was Erie County's first elected County Executive. The Edward A. Rath County Office Building is named in his honor. From the Rath Collection, Buffalo Evening News/Matthews. (BECHS)

and entertainment through radio and television, as well as through their newspapers. Buffalo's first radio station was WGR, still in existence, which began broadcasting in 1922 from the Federal Telephone building on Elmwood Avenue. The city's first television station, WBEN-TV, sent out its inaugural program on May 14, 1948. It was owned by the Butler interests, the call letters BEN standing for "Buffalo Evening News." The station has since been sold and changed its call letters to WIVB-TV (channel 4). Station WKBW, originally founded by the Churchill Tabernacle and subsequently sold, is now channel 7; WGR-TV is channel 2; WUTV (channel 29) is an independent commercial station; and Buffalo's own public television station, WNED, operates on channel 17.

Students of urban history have long recognized the role of spectator sports in providing city residents with a sense of community and identity. In the last quarter of the 19th century, organized professional baseball became the first urban spectator sport. Buffalo soon had its own professional team, playing in different leagues before settling down as one of the solid franchises in the old International League. The greatest days of Buffalo baseball were associated with Offermann Stadium before it was torn down in the early 1960s to make way for a junior high school. Within the intimate confines of that old ball park Buffalonians watched many a well-known ball player on his way up to, or on his way down from, the major leagues.

After Offermann Stadium was dismantled, the professional team played its games in War Memorial Stadium, a facility not well suited for baseball. After a few years there, the Buffalo team moved to Niagara Falls and finally went out of existence entirely—ushering in a long, cold winter for organized professional baseball in Western New York. But now there are definite signs of spring, with a minor-league professional team once more playing at War Memorial Stadium. Most baseball fans realize, however, that a new stadium better suited to baseball will be required to bring some future "Boys of Summer" to Buffalo in a league with a higher classification.

As the popularity of professional baseball declined in Buffalo, professional football came to town. Beginning in 1960, the new Buffalo Bills began to capture fan interest, increasing as the Bills won three divisional titles in the old American Football League. When the American and National football leagues merged, the Buffalo Bills became a member of the new league's American Football Conference. Buffalo made the playoffs for the conference championship in 1980—indicating that spring may be on its way here, too, after some long winters of football frustration.

Most recently the Buffalo Sabres hockey team has become the hottest sports attraction in the area. Once more the Knox family proved to be benefactors, for the Sabres came to Buffalo through the dogged persistence of two brothers, Seymour H. Knox III and Northrop R. Knox. These two and their associates worked long and hard to put Buffalo's first National Hockey League team on the ice, and they did not let up once this goal was achieved. Opening night for the Sabres in Memorial Auditorium was October 15, 1970, a game that began a decade of sellout hockey crowds throughout the regular season as well as on those occasions when the Buffalo team made the playoffs for the Stanley Cup. In fact, Memorial Auditorium literally had its roof raised to provide more seats for hockey fans coming from Western New York and from Canada to see the Sabres play.

Over the years Buffalo has earned a well-deserved reputation as a good sports town. Without a doubt the recent successes of the Bills and the Sabres, as well as the Buffalo

Stallions soccer team, have helped revitalize the spirit of the city and its surrounding communities. These professional teams have received national attention—international in the case of the Sabres—thereby helping to modify the negative image of Buffalo created by publicity given to the Great Blizzard of 1977.

Another necessity for the creation or rejuvenation of a city such as Buffalo is a good mass-transit system. City planners today regret past reliance on automobiles as a means of urban transportation, particularly in the inner city. The Niagara Frontier Transportation Authority now has major responsibility for transportation other than by private automobile or taxi in the Buffalo area. NFTA operates Buffalo International Airport, the metro bus system, and the intercity bus terminal in downtown Buffalo. Since the 1970s NFTA has had a major role in letting contracts and supervising construction for a 6.4-mile "Light Rail Rapid Transit Line" to run from Main and Bailey to the foot of Main Street downtown. Part of the line will run on the surface, and part underground.

Work on the "Rapid Transit" has already provided employment for hundreds of Buffalo construction workers. It is hoped that the opening of the system, now scheduled for 1984, will be a decisive step in the rejuvenation of downtown Buffalo. In later years the Niagara Frontier Transportation Authority may add other rail links to the line now being completed, providing metropolitan Buffalo with a modern, efficient rapid-transit system.

New construction is one indication that the springtime of Buffalo's renaissance has begun. In addition to the new banks, new office buildings, and the modern newspaper plant of the *Buffalo Evening News*, there is the new convention center, and plans for at least one more new hotel. The dazzling Rich Products headquarters building on Niagara Street, near West Ferry, shows that new construction is not confined to downtown Buffalo. Buffalonians should be proud to learn that the New York State Association of Architects named this as one of the state's 13 best recent works of architecture, praising the way the new building fits in with an adjoining, older Rich Products office.

This mixture of the new with the worthy old may be the most graceful feature of the Buffalo of the 1980s. Along with the effort that has produced new buildings downtown has come an equally desirable effort to save such landmark construction as Louis Sullivan's Prudential Building, David Burnham's Ellicott Square, the classic Old Post Office Building, and H.H. Richardson's twin-towered edifice that stands on the grounds of the State Psychiatric Center on Elmwood Avenue. Allentown, a community within a community, shows what can be done to revitalize an area by restoring fine old homes. Similarly, public-spirited corporate officials have preserved the exteriors of Delaware Avenue mansions while reworking the interiors as offices. In these ways the new Buffalo keeps continuity with its past.

"To Build a City: Buffalo, 1832-1957" was a poem written in honor of Buffalo's 125th birthday by Dr. Charles A. Brady. Its conclusion, celebrating the continuity of past, present, and future, is equally suitable for the city's sesquicentennial.

> Yes, we have builded a city
> And it is good.
> The task is not yet finished.
> We build it still.
> Buffalo is yesterday.
> It was tomorrow.
> Forever will it be today.

Facing page, left
This 1927 etching entitled Booth Alley No. 2 presents an unusual view of Buffalo's Old Post Office Building long before restoration became an issue. From the Schwanekamp Collection. (BECHS)

Facing page, top
This 1979 photograph shows a prime example of adaptive reuse. Buffalo's Old Post Office is to become the downtown site of the Erie Community College. Courtesy, Buffalo Evening News/ Robert L. Smith. (BECHS)

Facing page, bottom
Underground construction on Buffalo's rapid transit system is shown as of February 1981. It is expected that the transit line will contribute to the renewal of downtown Buffalo. Courtesy, Buffalo Courier Express/Mickey Osterreicher.

Above
The Art Theatre was located on Main Street before McDonald's replaced it, circa 1977. Photo by Charles Jamieson.

Facing page, top
Precinct Three on Main Street was once the old Bus Station. Photo by Diane Bush.

Facing page, bottom
Home of the new Tralfamadore jazz club on Main Street, 1981. Photo by Diane Bush.

Facing page
Named for Erie County's first elected county executive, the Edward A. Rath County Office Building was erected across from the old County Hall. Photo by Paul Pasquarello.

Top
The station of the Delaware, Lackawanna, and Western Railroad, opened in 1917, stands abandoned next to the Buffalo River in this 1979 photograph. Photo by Lawrence P. Gawoski.

Above
The New York Central constructed a huge terminal on Buffalo's east side in 1929, which was designed to service 200 passenger trains a day. The huge concourse and waiting room (pictured here) contain a statue of a buffalo. Photo by Lawrence P. Gawoski.

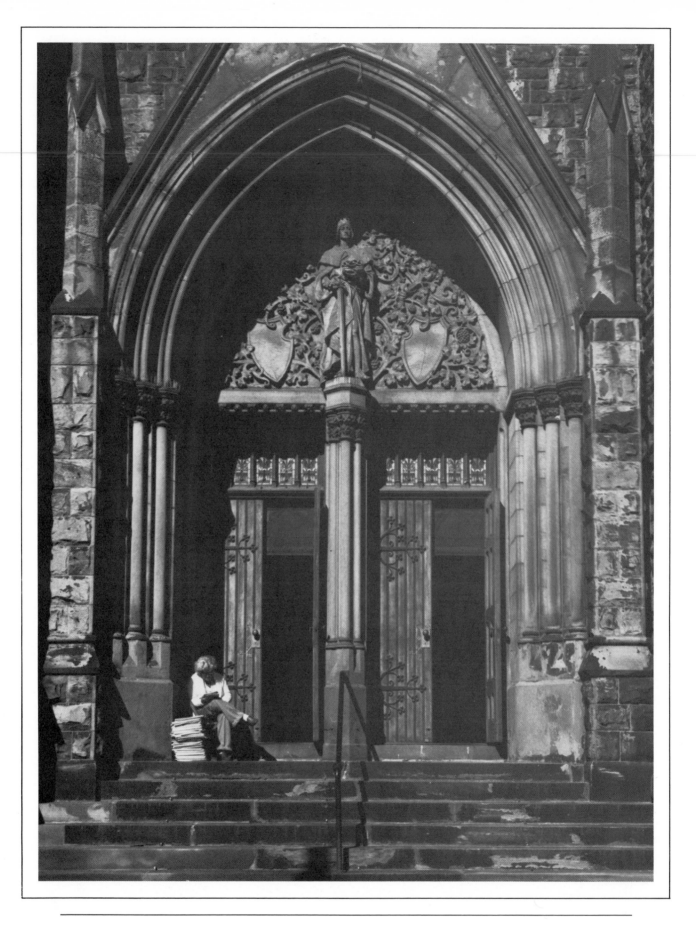

Above
St. Louis Church on a Sunday morning, spring of 1979. Photo by Charles Jamieson.

Facing page
Top
This angel monument, pictured from the front and back, may be found in Buffalo's Forest Lawn. Photos by Colleen Maroney Fahey.

Bottom left
Detail of the intricate carving that graces the Prudential (Guaranty) Building at Pearl and Church streets. Photo by Deborah Cassidy.

Bottom right
Examples of fine architectural detail may be found on numerous buildings throughout the city. Photo by Paul Pasquarello.

THE CHICKEN WING CITY

A distinctive feature of American culinary culture is the way in which certain cities have become associated with food items unique to their setting. This has been true since the days when Boston baked beans first emerged from the Puritans' version of the modern slow-cooker. Phoenix, Arizona, has recently become perhaps the only place where adventuresome diners can order "menudo," a soup made from the lining of a cow's stomach. Utica, New York, and nowhere else, features "white pizza," made without tomatoes. New Orleans has Creole specialties too numerous to list, but St. Louis, Missouri, has only one—toasted ravioli—while Lexington, Kentucky, is chiefly noted as the home of "burgoo," a kind of hunter's stew containing six different kinds of meat.

Buffalo is blessed with two of these city specialties. The older is the time-honored "beef on weck" served to several generations of Buffalonians who long ago learned to appreciate succulent beef served in a sliced roll with salt and caraway seeds on top. Beef on weck has been around so long that its origins are lost in the misty past, but most likely it was the creation of 19th-century German burghers transplanted from their native land to the City on the Lake.

The newer specialty is another kettle of fish—or, to be more precise, another bucket of wings. It is a matter of historical record that chicken wings—served as they are in Buffalo—originated in the Anchor Bar on Main Street. Though not everyone agrees, the majority has it that this delicacy was the serendipitous outcome of a mistake made by a bemused truck driver who, one day in 1964, delivered boxes of chicken wings to the Anchor Bar instead of the backs and necks ordered by manager Frank Bellissimo. Unwilling to use the wings in spaghetti sauce, Teresa Bellissimo, who did the cooking, cut them in two, deep-fried them, and served them with celery and blue-cheese dressing as hors d'oeuvres at the bar. They were an immediate hit. John Young, operator of a restaurant in the 1960s named Wings 'n' Things, credits himself with the added feature of serving chicken wings in a hot, spicy sauce known as "mambo."

Some years later an official proclamation of the city of Buffalo designated July 29, 1977, as Chicken Wing Day in honor of the "tasty experiment" at the Anchor Bar—an experiment that had grown to the point that "thousands of pounds of chicken wings are consumed by Buffalonians in restaurants and taverns throughout our city each week." In 1980 a seriocomic article entitled "An Attempt to Compile a Short History of the Buffalo Chicken Wing" appeared in the *New Yorker*—and Buffalo chicken wings had truly found their niche in the culinary annals of Americana.

Facing page, top
"John Young, the King of Wings." Courtesy, John Young.

Facing page, bottom
The Anchor Bar, "Home of Chicken Wings." Courtesy, Frank & Theresa's Anchor Bar, Inc. Photo by Patricia Brazill. (BECHS)

Top left
By the mid-19th century, the ethnic makeup of Buffalo had begun to change as German businessmen established themselves, and some, like Jacob Dold, rose to prominence. (BECHS)

Top right
Max Weisberg's Buffet & Rathskeller, advertised on this card, was located on West Chippewa Street between the years 1906 and 1911. (BECHS)

Above
Mildred C. Green's painting of the International Car Ferry at the foot of Porter Avenue depicts a time before the International Railroad Bridge was constructed. (BECHS)

Above
*This award-winning poster was created
for Buffalo's Centennial in 1932.*
(BECHS)

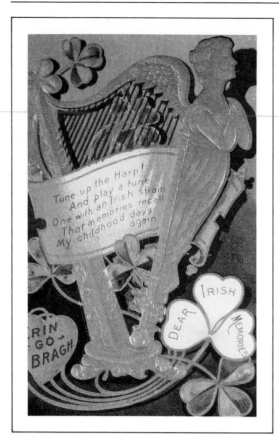

Top left

St. Patrick's Day is a day of much parading and celebrating by Buffalo's Irish population. (BECHS)

Top right

This certificate of confirmation was presented to Herman Milke in 1910 by the pastor of a German Evangelical Church in Buffalo. (BECHS)

Above

On the evening of November 30, 1843, the St. Andrews Society celebrated its fourth anniversary with a banquet at Buffalo's American Hotel. T.H. Cone caught the spirit of the evening, as his fellow Scotsmen celebrated on the anniversary of their patron saint. (BECHS)

Top
This Hindu wedding took place in 1974 at the International Institute of Buffalo. Courtesy, International Institute of Buffalo/Emil Mohorovicic.

Above left
This St. Stanislaus Church Corpus Christi Procession took place in 1980. Courtesy, Dr. Lydia Fish, Department of Anthropology, State University College at Buffalo.

Above right
Oleh Boreczak demonstrates traditional Ukrainian designs at an Easter Egg Fair at the International Institute of Buffalo in 1973. Courtesy, International Institute of Buffalo/Emil Mohorovicic.

Top
This view of Buffalo was taken from Fort Erie, Canada on February 15, 1981. Photo by Donna Jordan Dusel.

Above
Buffalo harbor scene. Photo by Dorothy L. Ralph.

Above
*This detail of City Court in downtown
Buffalo was shot in the summer of 1980.
Photo by Debra K. Hacken.*

Facing page, top left
Fish-eye view of downtown Buffalo.
Photo by Paul Pasquarello.

Facing page, top right
Downtown Cinema on Main Street in
Buffalo, 1980. Photo by Diane Bush.

Bottom
The old mill freighter at Buffalo. Photo
by Lucille Cranston.

Above
Sunset at the Buffalo docks in winter.
Photo by Paul Pasquarello.

Part III.
PARTNERS IN PROGRESS

by Ann Podd and Tim Murray

Buffalo was the land of opportunity in 1832. As the terminus of the Erie Canal, the new city linked the abundance of the country's West to the awaiting markets of the East. The hundreds of cargo-laden ships visiting the city were soon joined by dozens of railroads, making the city one of the greatest transshipment points in the world.

Young entrepreneurs poured into the booming city, a city formed when only 24 states constituted the United States. Those coming to the Niagara Frontier were bold in their willingness to try the untried. Buffalo was the first city in the country to light its streets with electricity and one of its stores became the first commercial establishment to use the new power. It was in Buffalo that the first commercial steel casting was successfully made, and where a young man was able to persuade railroader Cornelius Vanderbilt to allow him to try out Vanderbilt's

new railroad brake design.

New enterprises continued long after the Erie Canal lost its usefulness due to other modes of transportation. Here on the easternmost tip of Lake Erie, companies continue to prosper with new ideas. In the same city that spawned the invention of the grain elevator, a company was established that operates the world's largest fleet of self-unloading ships.

Buffalo, the city where an ice box manufacturer discovered a better way to store blood, is now headquarters for a company which innovated a way to freeze food without crystallization, allowing frozen food to be eaten without defrosting. The classic Pierce-Arrow automobile shares the same home, Buffalo, with the construction of the first aircraft to break the sound barrier.

The Niagara Frontier has long since moved westward and Buffalo has coped with its changing economy. A new wave of service-oriented and small high-technology companies was under way as the city entered its 150th year. Only 25 percent of the city's workers held factory jobs compared with more than 50 percent 30 years earlier.

Buffalo has grown from a frontier town to a mature city rich with history and culture. Many of the same business leaders who developed the city's industries also nurtured its culture: generously supporting Buffalo's museums, art galleries, zoo, public art, and magnificent architectural treasures. Read and enjoy the following stories of some of the selected businesses that played such a significant part in the rich heritage of the Queen City of the Lakes.

Facing page, top
Harnessing the mighty power of the Niagara Frontier allowed Buffalo to be the first city in the country to light its streets with electricity. Here, General Electric Company employees surround a model of the Electric Building. (BECHS)

Facing page, bottom
A leader in new ideas, Buffalo spawned the invention of the grain elevator and a company that runs the world's largest self-unloading ships. Here, scoopers inside a lake boat sweep grain into the path of an elevator marine leg. From the Agway Collection. (BECHS)

ADAM, MELDRUM & ANDERSON COMPANY

Robert B. Adam was just 10 years old when he began working in a hosiery and glove factory in Scotland. But even at that early age he had the desire to go to America and start his own business.

It wasn't until he was 24 that he was able to follow his dream to the United States. After working for 10 years in a wholesale company, one of Adam's employers agreed to loan him $5,000 to start a business. Adam could have gone anywhere, but he chose Buffalo because he believed the city would grow quickly. Together with partners Herbert A. Meldrum and Alexander Whiting, Adam opened a store at 396 Main Street on March 21, 1867. The total business that first day was $77, not very impressive even then. Whiting decided to withdraw from the partnership in 1872 and Adam, Meldrum & Whiting became Adam, Meldrum & Company. It wasn't until William Anderson became a partner four years later that the familiar name was formed—Adam, Meldrum & Anderson Company.

With business prospering, Adam encouraged his younger brother J.N. Adam to come over from Scotland. He did and, ironically, established a competing store directly across the street from AM&A. J.N. Adam also followed his brother's example of civic involvement and eventually served as mayor of Buffalo from 1906 to 1909.

Robert Adam was always ready to be part

Adam, Meldrum & Anderson Company's main store and headquarters is located across the street from the site of its first store.

The merchandise was displayed for all to see at AM&A's first store at 396 Main Street during the 1870s.

of Buffalo's pioneering days. This was evident in his success in making AM&A the first business in the city to use electric lights, on November 26, 1886.

By the turn of the century, Adam had bought out his two partners and Robert B. Adam II was learning the business. Adam II had been born in England in 1863 and was adopted and brought to the United States by his uncle Adam. When Adam died in 1904, the son took over as president and served as head of the company for 36 years. The third generation took over in 1940 when Robert B. Adam III succeeded his late father in the business at the age of 22.

AM&A had lost its top position among department stores in the city, but Adam III was willing to take chances that other merchants considered rash at the time. In 1947 he decided to open a branch store in the University Plaza on Main Street, the first suburban shopping center in the Buffalo area. Some stores waited too long to find out if the experiment would work and found themselves out of business. Other storey began rapid growth in the suburbs following young Adam's lead.

Then in a turnabout, when other stores were leaving downtown Buffalo, Adam decided to expand the downtown store's floor space by 35 percent and moved into the empty J.N. Adam building at 389 Main Street. These and other strategies worked. Since the 1960s, AM&A has been the leading regional department store chain. The family-controlled business, which had opened with 11 employees in 1867, had grown to more than 2,050 employees in nine Western New York stores as it entered the 1980s.

AMERICAN PRECISION INDUSTRIES INC.

There's an old saying, "A corporation is the extended shadow of one man's ideas." It was 1947 when Robert J. Fierle, a young graduate engineer from Northwestern University, just out of the U.S. Navy, drew together a few friends as investors and purchased a small, bankrupt job shop, Amherst Tool and Manufacturing Company, in Williamsville, New York. Fierle spent the next several years struggling to keep their investment afloat. But, because of his entrepreneurship, he was determined to build his own organization rather than work for larger, more structured organizations as he had upon graduation from college. The company survived through a combination of hard work, engineering skills, acquisitions, and the wise choice of talented people.

The company changed its name to Amherst Manufacturing as it acquired larger contracts, one of which was an order for 250,000 protective fuse dust caps for the navy. In keeping with the expansion into more exotic metals machining, the company's name was again changed to American Precision Industries Inc.

In 1953 API made its first major acquisition by purchasing a small coil company in Delevan, New York. This division soon became a leader in the electronics field as it

President Robert J. Fierle in 1962, when Amherst Manufacturing became American Precision Industries Inc. and a publically owned corporation.

produced high-quality coils and chokes for commercial and military markets. Delevan's products have been used in the Apollo spacecraft, the Viking unmanned space explorations, and in the Telestar program.

In the early 1960s, because of API's financial success, investment banking advisors recommended that American Precision Industries Inc. go public with a stock offering as sales edged past the $3-million mark. By reinvesting the proceeds of the stock sale, the company purchased Basco Inc. of North Tonawanda, New York, in 1961. This

move now diversified API into the manufacturing of heat exchangers. The Electro-Mechanical Clutch and Brake Company was added in 1964, and in 1967 Dustex, a producer of air pollution control products, was purchased.

Growing from a small 2-man shop to the present work force of nearly 800 with sales nearing $40 million, the API group of companies develop and manufacture high-quality products for industry and government. The Industrial Process segment of the business produces heat transfer products and mechanical and fabric filter collectors for air pollution control applications. The Electronics Components segment produces inductive coils and electromechanical clutches and brakes.

Bob Fierle had great hopes for his enterprise in 1947. His goal today is to build API into a $100-million corporation with worldwide involvements. The corporation looks forward to the 1980s as a decade of substantial growth that will return economic benefits to shareholders, offer opportunities for its employees, and guarantee long-term commitment to the Buffalo area.

Today, American Precision Industries Inc. headquarters and its Basco Division occupy this modern facility at 2777 Walden Avenue in Cheektowaga, New York.

AMERICAN STEAMSHIP COMPANY

In 1895 John J. Boland began a prominent career in Great Lakes commerce by organizing a vessel brokerage business in Buffalo. In 1902 he purchased his first vessel, the steamer *Yale*, and two years later formed a partnership with Adam E. Cornelius.

In 1907 the two Buffalo businessmen established their own steamship line, the American Steamship Company. By year's end, there was cheering in the offices of Boland and Cornelius. Their 400-foot steamer, the *Yale*, had survived a blinding snowstorm to make the last run of the navigation season into Buffalo Harbor. The *Yale*'s late-season voyage turned out to be the most profitable run on the Great Lakes that year.

The new firm launched a major building program and turned out six steamers over the next four years. The boom years continued, spurring additional building programs until the Depression of the 1930s threatened the existence of the line. But ASC averted disaster by taking the bold and risky step of converting three of its bulk freighters into self-unloading ships. These ships could unload faster than conventional vessels and eliminated the need for expensive shore equipment. While other lines floundered during the Depression, ASC expanded its list of customers with the capability of self-unloading vessels to serve small and remote ports.

The original partners, Boland and Cornelius, in their first office.

Today ASC operates the world's largest fleet of self-unloading ships, 20 in all, including the 635-foot M/V *Buffalo*, christened in 1979. And it has retained its innovative leadership on the Great Lakes by pioneering an intermodal transportation system to move western coal into the Northeast.

In 1967 the line was sold to the Oswego Shipping Company, and under the newly integrated management ASC expanded its fleet by buying three smaller Great Lakes lines, the Gartland, Redland, and Reiss steamship companies.

In the early 1970s, ASC undertook a major building program to assure its position as one of the major transport lines on the Great Lakes. In 1973 ASC was acquired by GATX, which immediately endorsed ASC's ambitious expansion program.

Under the current leadership of Thomas W. Burke and D. Ward Fuller, the now wholly owned subsidiary of GATX has added 10 vessels to its fleet at a cost of more than $250 million.

Headquartered in Buffalo, ASC coordinates its sprawling operations out of offices in Cleveland, Toledo, and Winnipeg, Canada. The expanded fleet now has an annual capacity of more than 30 million tons with service to ports throughout the Great Lakes.

The M/V Buffalo *with Buffalo's skyline in the background.*

ARCATA GRAPHICS, BUFFALO DIVISION

J.W. Clement Company, the predecessor company of Arcata, was founded here in Buffalo in 1876. Its printing shop was on the second floor of the smaller building in this picture of lower Main Street.

An unusual string of events led James Watson Clement to start a printing facility in Buffalo—a printing company that would eventually be one of the largest in the country.

Clement was operating a printing shop in Batavia in 1878 when he received a telegram informing him that his mother was seriously ill in Chicago. He rushed to her bedside and was relieved to find that her condition had improved considerably. He decided to stop in Buffalo on the trip home to talk business with printers he knew, including Christopher Abell and Daniel Penfield.

Impressed by the growing city, Clement began considering a move to Buffalo. Before the year was out, Penfield died and Clement joined Abell in buying the Penfield print shop at 201 Main Street. Two years later, when Abell withdrew from the partnership because of ill health, Clement was already building a reputation as a high-quality printer.

Clement died on February 20, 1907. His wife Sarah continued to operate the business until her death in October 1908. The J.W. Clement Company was then reorganized and incorporated.

During the next decade, the firm was Buffalo's leading producer of almanacs, catalogs, and folders. Customers included Singer Sewing Machine Company, Thomas Edison, Inc., Remington Arms Company, and Standard Oil Company. A 1914 fire at its 4-story Exchange Street building prompted the company's move into a modern printing plant at Seneca and Lord streets. That plant was expanded a number of times.

By the early 1960s, the J.W. Clement Company was one of the country's largest printers with plants in Buffalo, San Francisco, and Los Angeles. Its customers were, and remain, some of the largest publishers in the United States.

The facility has produced more than 10 million copies of the *Reader's Digest* each month since 1965. This production doubled at the end of 1981. In 1965 Arcata National Corporation of Menlo Park, California, acquired J.W. Clement. Renamed Arcata Graphics, Buffalo Division, the company is Arcata's oldest and second largest operating unit. The 800,000-square-foot facility is located on a 50-acre site in Depew. From 350 employees in 1928, the business grew to more than 1,800 employees in 1981.

In recent years the firm installed an advanced gravure facility to produce more than five million color copies of the *National Enquirer* newspaper. It also remains a leader in paperback book production, with a daily capacity of two million books. The all-time production record for the division is Dr. Spock's *Baby and Child Care*, printed for the Pocketbook division of Simon & Schuster more than 22 million times.

Many national publications are printed here in Arcata's Depew plant.

ARMSTRONG-ROTH-CADY CO., INC.

Frederick L.A. Cady purchased the oldest insurance agency in Buffalo in 1869, which later became Armstrong-Roth-Cady Company, Inc.

Charles B. Armstrong became the first president, in 1908, of the merging companies of Edward C. Roth & Company, Armstrong & Husted, and Cady & Perkins.

Armstrong-Roth-Cady Co., Inc., is Buffalo's oldest insurance agency, among the city's oldest continuous businesses, and—tracing its history to 1830—even older than the city itself.

Buffalo was a small frontier village, its population less than 9,000, when the Hartford Fire Insurance Company appointed George B. Webster its sole agent in the area.

Webster sold that agency, in 1849, to A.N.C. Smith in the first of a series of sales or mergers that would lead directly to the formation of the Armstrong-Roth-Cady Company in the next century.

George Stringer and Frederick L.A. Cady acquired the business in 1869, and operated as Stringer & Cady Insurance. By this time the agency represented 17 insurance companies. But in the fall of 1871, Mrs. O'Leary's cow knocked over the lantern, starting the Great Chicago Fire, which created millions of dollars in insurance claims. Only three insurance companies were able to pay the losses and survive.

Cady's stepbrother, Thomas Perkins, had joined the firm in 1881, and it became known as Cady & Perkins in 1894. Meanwhile, C.B. Armstrong and Edward Roth had formed agencies of their own. The three firms competed in the rapidly growing city. The small village Webster served 80 years before had grown to more than .25 million residents in the 1890s.

In 1908 the three firms—Edward C. Roth & Company, Armstrong & Husted, and Cady & Perkins—merged. Charles Armstrong became the first president. When the Marine Trust Building at the southeast corner of Main and Seneca streets was completed in 1912, the agency was one of the first tenants. After nearly 70 years of operation, the agency still has its headquarters on the ninth floor of the building, now called the Main-Seneca Building.

The firm was incorporated under its present name of Armstrong-Roth-Cady on June 2, 1921. Frank W. Fiske, Jr., who was a junior partner in the former Roth agency, was president from 1921 until 1950, when Charles M. Epes took over. C.M. Epes, Jr., has served as chairman of the board since 1972, when David H. Eslick became president. Both remain at the same positions at the present time.

In late 1980, the agency celebrated its 150th anniversary and had already begun investing in its future. A computer system was completed in 1979, making the firm one of the first fully automated insurance agencies in the Buffalo area.

ARVIN/CALSPAN ADVANCED TECHNOLOGY CENTER (ATC)

Calspan has grown from an aviation research and test facility funded by aircraft company donations to a multidisciplinary, high-technology division of Arvin Industries. Through the years it has preserved a tradition of independent research in the aerosciences, and has applied changing technology to the fields of electronics and avionics, information sciences, defense and space systems, transportation and vehicle research, and the environmental sciences.

The original Curtiss-Wright laboratory was built to house one of the nation's largest wind tunnels and the world's largest altitude chamber. On January 2, 1946, these facilities became the Cornell Aeronautical Laboratory of Cornell University (CAL), which continued its independent aeroscience research programs. Within months, CAL had five major contracts for the development of the Bumblebee-guided missile program. Growing government interest in this field led to additional support, and in 1948 CAL became a wholly owned subsidiary of Cornell University known as Cornell Aeronautical Laboratory, Inc., a nonprofit research organization.

During the 1950s and 1960s, CAL continued to expand its programs in systems research, operations analysis, studies of tactical air warfare and air defense, and new developments in terrain-following radar, automatic pattern recognition, crash injury investigation, defense penetration aids, target discrimination, inflight simulation, laser applications, and environmental studies.

In 1972 the company changed its name to Calspan Corporation, dropped its nonprofit status, and continued operation as a public company with Cornell University holding majority interest. In April 1978 Calspan was acquired by Arvin Industries. The former Calspan Corporation became the Arvin/Calspan Advanced Technology Center, a part of the Arvin Applied Technology Group.

Arvin/Calspan Advanced Technology Center is located near the Buffalo Airport.

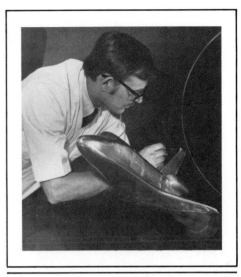

Models of the Space Shuttle have been tested in Calspan's facilities, which simulate the conditions of reentry into the earth's atmosphere from space.

Today, Arvin/Calspan continues its tradition of excellence, with a core of talented professionals and a wide variety of unique facilities such as hypersonic shock tubes and tunnels; a real-time, manned simulator for evaluating electronic warfare systems; a vehicle experimental test center; ordnance test ranges; a tire research facility; advanced optics and photogrammetry facilities; surface physics and surface chemistry laboratories; a laser laboratory; and a flight research center.

Calspan is well recognized for its support of such programs as the Space Shuttle, the Cruise Missile, the B-1 bomber and vertical take-off and landing aircraft; engineering support to the Air Force Aeronautical Systems Division in 14 major areas including structures, avionics, test support, logistics, and production analysis; and independent evaluation of automotive crashworthiness. Calspan engineers and scientists are also engaged in the design and implementation of advanced computer-based information systems in support of critical national intelligence and command and control projects.

Calspan also operates the Aerospace Flight Dynamics Testing Facilities at Arnold Engineering Development Center (AEDC), Arnold Air Force Station, Tennessee.

THE BANK OF NEW YORK WESTERN REGION

This 1941 photograph shows the Buffalo Industrial Bank's first drive-up banking facility at 694 Fillmore Avenue.

Two Buffalo Industrial Bank officers were visiting St. Louis, Missouri, back in the 1930s when they came across a new-fangled idea in banking. In fact, the St. Louis Bank was the first of its kind.

Later returning to the Queen City, the bankers decided to try out the innovation at the bank's Fillmore Avenue branch. The result—in 1939 the first drive-up banking facility opened east of the Mississippi.

Those two men probably had little idea how quickly drive-up banking would spread over the years as the bond between America and its automobiles grew. To the bankers, the drive-up facility just seemed the perfect way to highlight the fact that Buffalo Industrial Bank was the leader in financing automobiles. The bank still offers car loans today, but now as a part of The Bank of New York its range of services has broadened dramatically.

The bank grew from a modest start. On August 4, 1916, a group of prominent business executives, many connected with the Marine Trust Company of Buffalo, raised

$200,000 to start the Morris Plan Company of Buffalo. Like similar plans throughout the country, the Morris Plan focused on making personal loans. The only other services were savings certificates and Christmas Club savings accounts.

A 1933 brochure pointed out that one out of every 10 families in Buffalo used the Morris Plan. In the early '30s, a person could walk into the main office at Washington and Huron streets or the Broadway branch at 694 Fillmore Avenue and request a loan of up to $5,000. The interest rate for the 12-month loan was about 7 percent.

As the bank began doing more commercial business, it changed its name to the Buffalo Industrial Bank in 1936. By 1959 it was time to reflect another change. The institution moved from an industrial bank to a full-fledged state-chartered commercial bank. A sign bearing the new name "Bank of Buffalo" was hung at the Court Street main office in 1959. The bank had moved to its familiar 17 Court Street site 11 years earlier.

The last name change came in 1976. The Bank of New York, the first major chartered commercial bank in the state, with roots going back to 1784, had purchased the Bank of Buffalo from its shareholders. In December 1975 the Bank of Buffalo was merged with the Niagara Frontier Bank of New York, a member of Bank of New York Co., Inc., a holding company. Under a new state law effective January 1, 1976, commercial banks were allowed to branch statewide. Taking advantage of this law, the bank was merged into The Bank of New York and designated the Western Region.

In addition to bringing the first drive-up teller to Buffalo banking, The Bank of New York also claims to be the first to introduce the home improvement loan and student loan concepts to the area. More recently, in the 1960s, the bank introduced lines of credit attached to checking accounts and announced it would be the first in Buffalo to offer free checking accounts to persons over 60 years old. Today The Bank of New York offers a full range of commercial services and complete trust and investment service.

The Bank of New York's Western Region headquarters is located in this building at Court and Pearl streets.

BELL AEROSPACE TEXTRON

It was early morning on October 14, 1947, when Air Force Captain Charles E. Yeager climbed into the cockpit of an experimental aircraft called the X-1. He set off the craft's four rockets and the surge of the force threw him back in the seat. The speed of the plane increased until the X-1 and Yeager did what no one in the world had ever done before—flown faster than the speed of sound.

That supersonic aircraft was designed and manufactured in a Niagara Falls Boulevard plant of Bell Aircraft Corporation. Bell's X-1, now on display in the National Air and Space Museum of the Smithsonian Institution in Washington, D.C., is only one of a dozen history-making accomplishments of Bell.

Ironically, the company itself almost didn't make it off the ground. Lawrence Dale Bell, son of a hardware store proprietor, was a vice-president of Consolidated Aircraft in Buffalo. When the company decided to move its operations to San Diego in 1935, Bell convinced fellow Consolidated employees Ray P. Whitman, assistant general manager; Robert J. Woods, an aeronautical engineer; and his secretary, Irene Bernhardt, to stay in Buffalo and join him in forming a new company.

Bell Aircraft was incorporated on July 10, 1935, with Bell as president. But even as Woods was working on new plans in a tiny office, Bell was still pounding the pavement looking for investors willing to take a chance on the new enterprise. His persistence paid off and by September the company had the needed working capital.

The first contract came from the U.S. Army, which hired Bell to install engines in a Consolidated aircraft. Fifty men were put to work in an Elmwood Avenue plant. Five years later, Bell Aircraft broke ground on a $1.5-million plant at a Wheatfield site next to the Niagara Falls Municipal Airport. Production started in the new plant in May 1941, and within four months an $8.5-million addition was started. At the height of wartime production in 1942, nearly 30,000 men and women were working at Bell.

The company's growth didn't end with the war. Larry Bell's faith in a young

designer, Arthur Young, led to the postwar success of the helicopter for both military and commercial tasks. By 1951, a separate Helicopter Division—a spin-off from Bell Aircraft—was established in Fort Worth, Texas.

Bell Aircraft turned out more than 10,000 P-39 Aircobras in its Niagara Falls Boulevard plant during World War II.

A U.S. Army version of one of Bell's many high-speed amphibious air-cushion vehicles. This one can travel at speeds up to 62 miles per hour over water, land, snow, ice, marshes, and swamps. It will be in production at the Niagara Falls Boulevard plant through the mid-1980s.

Other Bell achievements include building the XP59A, the United States' first jet aircraft; developing the first jet-propelled vertical takeoff and landing aircraft; creating the first all-weather automatic aircraft landing system used on all U.S. Navy aircraft carriers; developing an air-cushion landing system and later, high-speed, amphibian air-cushion vehicles. Bell aircraft continued to break speed and altitude records.

Textron Inc., based in Providence, Rhode Island, purchased Bell's entire multimillion-dollar defense business in 1960. In 1976 the company officially became Bell Aerospace Textron, Division of Textron, Inc. The division headquarters remains on Niagara Falls Boulevard.

Bell continues to be an innovative company and one adaptive to new directions and goals. Its high-technology products include rocket engines, missile and spacecraft propulsions systems, rocket propellant tanks, inertial navigation instruments, high-energy laser systems, aircraft landing systems, air-cushion vehicles, and advanced machining of materials.

BUFFALO BRAKE BEAM COMPANY

Seth A. Crone, founder of the Buffalo Brake Beam Company.

At the turn of the century, Buffalo was a railroad center served by many different lines. The area was also a booming steel and iron center. So, to Seth A. Crone, Buffalo seemed the logical place to establish his new venture called Buffalo Brake Beam Company.

Before he decided to start his own business, Crone had worked for the railroad industry, rising through the ranks until he was assistant superintendent of rolling stock for the New York Central Railroad. He saw the need for quality brake beams—the part that transmits the braking force to the wheels of a railroad car. Crone was able to persuade Cornelius Vanderbilt, the railroad industrialist and financier, to allow his new company to manufacture Vanderbilt's design of railroad brake beams.

Buffalo Brake Beam Company was founded on August 15, 1902. The headquarters and sales office was located in New York City, then within walking distance of many railroad headquarters. The production facilities were located in a rented building on Chandler Street in Buffalo.

In 1907 Crone decided to build his own facility. He bought a site at what is now 400 Ingham Avenue in Lackawanna, still home in 1981 for Buffalo Brake Beam.

As in those early days of business, brake beams are the company's number one product, but the design has changed over the years. The railroads had been plagued by failure of the braking system parts. In 1940 Buffalo Brake Beam developed a unit brake beam as an integral part of the railroad car truck. This one-piece system eliminated the problem, and the design quickly became the industry standard.

Buffalo Brake Beam was also the first company to develop a 2-piece spring brake shoe key. This spring key holds the brake shoe tightly against the brake head, allowing for replacement of the brake shoe when it wears down.

These and other advances helped make the family-owned business one of the largest of its type. In addition to the Buffalo facility, the company has a plant in Hamilton, Ontario, and Buffalo Railroad Equipment Corp., a subsidiary in Charleston, South Carolina, makes other railroad equipment such as ladders and sill steps.

Buffalo Brake Beam moved its headquarters to Lackawanna in 1965. The company has continued to grow, with the number of units sold tripling during the 1970s. Seth's sons, Alfred and Lester, carried on the business for many years. The third generation of family leadership is assured by Walter Seth Crone, company president.

BUFFALO CHINA, INC.

From Bangor, Maine, to Honolulu, Hawaii, thousands of restaurant and hotel patrons are being served on Buffalo China each day. The china is easy to spot. The underside of every one of the millions of pieces made by the pottery since 1901 is marked with the firm's back stamp or the words "Buffalo Pottery."

The company was founded as Buffalo Pottery on October 23, 1901, as part of the great Larkin Company of Buffalo. The Larkin Company was a soap manufacturer which grew into one of the nation's largest mail-order businesses of its time. As part of its marketing strategy for its laundry soap, Larkin would give pottery to consumers as a premium. Larkin founder John D. Larkin decided that instead of buying the pottery, he would set up his own pottery facility in Buffalo.

Two years after he made that decision, the first piece of pottery was put into a kiln at the new complex at Hayes Place and Seneca Street. The eight original buildings formed the world's largest fireproof pottery in the world and the only one to operate entirely by electricity.

The 1915 Buffalo Pottery factory.

By 1915, the firm was focusing on a finer type of ware. It became one of only 12 potteries in the country to make the fine vitreous china. More than 100 potteries made semiporcelain, a coarser ware. The company was producing high-quality, artistic work such as Deldare Ware and Emerald Deldare. Today these products are sought by collectors and there is an active market for them.

The business was reorganized in 1940 and the name changed to Buffalo Pottery, Inc. Sixteen years later the name changed again, this time to Buffalo China, Inc., to reflect more accurately the type of product. Ownership moved from the Larkin family to a group of private investors on October 1, 1970.

Since then a number of multimillion-dollar expansions and modernizations enabled production to more than double during the 1970s. Employment grew from 300 to more than 450 in the United States. Buffalo China, with its headquarters at 658 Bailey Avenue, is one of the largest manufacturers of restaurant and institutional china in the country. In addition to John C. Heebner, president, the board of directors includes Harold M. Esty, grandson of John D. Larkin; Karl Hinke; Richard O. Hopkins; Samuel D. Magavern; and William D. Roesser.

The current home of Buffalo China, Inc.

BUFFALO COURIER-EXPRESS

The city of Buffalo was just two years old when its 10,000 residents were presented with their first daily newspaper. The *Western Star* arrived on the morning of July 21, 1834, and by the end of the month five other daily newspapers hit the street. Only the *Star* lasted more than a month.

From that surviving 4-page journal grew the *Buffalo Courier-Express*, the largest daily morning newspaper in upstate New York. With few exceptions, the *Buffalo Courier-Express* and its predecessors have been delivered to homes in Western New York every day for nearly 150 years.

The *Star* and its weekly predecessor, the *Black Rock Gazette* formed in 1824, were just two of the more than 100 newspapers published in the Buffalo area in the first half of the 19th century.

Another early daily, the *Express*, had begun publishing in 1846. In 1869 Samuel L. Clemens (Mark Twain) bought an interest in the *Express* and served as its editor for two years.

Until their merger in 1926, competition between the *Buffalo Courier* and the *Buffalo Express* was so fierce that, as one story put it, *Express* readers and *Courier* readers sat on opposite sides of the streetcars. And after the merger, a joke around town claimed newsstands folded the paper, *Courier* showing on half, *Express* on half, so readers could still buy their favorite.

William J. Conners is the man who brought the *Courier* and the *Express* together. He was born in Buffalo in 1857, quit school at age 13 to work on the docks, rose through the rough-and-tumble ranks, became affluent contracting out dock work, acquired various interests in Great Lakes shipping ventures, made a fortune and, in 1896, bought the *Enquirer*. A year later he bought the *Courier*. Both papers prospered into the 1920s, when radio news began to take its toll on circulation.

Conners approached the *Express*, which had fallen on hard times, with the idea of merger. The *Courier-Express* corporation was formed, and the first "C-E" hit the newsstands on June 14, 1926. Conners acquired all of its stock.

Plant and offices at Main and Goodell streets.

The paper did well and a building was planned at 787 Main Street, at the corner of Goodell. The building opened in December 1930 and, with renovations and additions over the years, still houses the newspaper more than 50 years later.

W.J. Conners died October 5, 1929, and his son, W.J. Conners, Jr., took over operation of the paper. A third generation, under William J. Conners III, continued publication from 1951 until 1979.

In 1974 a major overhaul was begun to convert the editorial and composing rooms from traditional printing methods to a computer system. By 1980 the new system was in place.

The paper remained in the Conners family until August 24, 1979, when it was sold to the Minneapolis Star and Tribune Company, Inc. Roger P. Parkinson, formerly a vice-president at the *Washington Post*, was named president and publisher. The editorial staff was expanded, and the paper's format modernized. In 1981 it became the first paper in the state to receive wire service reports over microwave equipment, and the paper once fought over on the old streetcars of Buffalo took the lead in newspaper technology and maintains its lead as the area's largest morning and Sunday newspaper.

a. *William J. Conners, publisher 1896-1926.*
b. *William J. Conners, Jr., publisher 1926-1951.*
c. *William J. Conners III, publisher 1951-1979.*
d. *Roger P. Parkinson, publisher 1980 to present.*

THE BUFFALO EVENING NEWS

For 76 years The News *was based in this building at 218 Main Street.*

Few dull moments have marked the 100-year-plus history of *The Buffalo News*. Its first edition never got to press because a printer dumped the handset type of Page One in an elevator just before the 2 p.m. deadline October 11, 1880.

A few days later, the founder, Edward H. Butler, collapsed in the street in "extreme pain" and was ordered out of action for two months by his physician. Then, the early newspaper chain, Scripps-McRae, opened the *Telegraph*, a rival evening paper, 19 days later.

Butler was back in his office in early December, and the *Telegraph* gave up the fight August 17, 1885. (In the next century, a successor chain, Scripps-Howard, would challenge *The News* with the afternoon *Buffalo Times*, which ended publication July 31, 1939.)

The rollicking early days were marked by coverage of drunken brawls at political rallies, a city editor who dashed out to cover stories, and a boisterous bunch of reporters who hoisted the British flag opposite a police headquarters filled with Irish-descended policemen.

Butler, a lusty man himself, presided happily over this activity until his death on March 9, 1914. His son, Edward H. Butler, brought a sound business sense to the proprietorship and on March 1, 1927, he named Alfred H. Kirchhofer managing editor. During the period before Butler's death in 1956 and Kirchhofer's retirement in 1966, they set the tone of today's *News*—credible reporting, spiced with meaningful feature stories.

The original home of the daily *News* at 214 Main was expanded quickly to 218 Main. By the mid-20th century, it was cramped and antiquated. The widow of the younger Butler, Kate, moved into his office and in 1971 presided over planning for the present modern structure that Edward Durell Stone designed at Washington and Scott streets. It became the home of *The News* in 1973.

Paul E. Neville took over the editorial helm in 1966, but his career ended with his untimely death in 1969. The news department now is run by Murray B. Light, vice-president and editor, who came to *The News* in 1949 as a reporter; and Foster L. Spencer, managing editor, who joined the copy desk in 1966. Henry Z. Urban succeeded Kate Butler as president and publisher, and his care for detail has earned him the title of a "reader's publisher." Stanford Lipsey is vice-chairman.

On April 15, 1977, *The News* was purchased by Blue Chip Stamps, Inc., whose principal stockholder, Warren E. Buffett of Omaha, Nebraska, became chairman of the board of *The News*. Buffett pledged to maintain *The News* tradition of solid, fundamental journalism, and brought the paper into a new era by reinstituting a Sunday edition in 1977. *The News* now publishes in the afternoons Monday through Friday and in the mornings on Saturdays, Sundays, and holidays. Now publishing every day of the year, *The News* looks forward to the 21st century.

The Buffalo Evening News *moved into its new headquarters in 1973.*

BUFFALO FORGE COMPANY

William F. Wendt was still a teenager in 1878 when he strode up five flights of stairs at 78 Washington Street and worked out a deal to become part owner in the new and somewhat shakey Buffalo Forge Company. The name described exactly the type of enterprise young Wendt was getting involved with—Buffalo Forge made forges.

The firm's name hasn't changed over the past century. And indeed, it still produces a small number of efficient blacksmith forges. But Buffalo Forge has grown to be a leading producer of air-handling equipment, pumps, and machine tools. Its equipment heats and cools major buildings throughout the world, including Houston's Astrodome, New York City's massive World Trade Center, and Buffalo's Kleinhan's Music Hall.

After buying out his former partner Charles Hammelmann in 1883, William Wendt brought his brother Henry W. Wendt into the prospering business.

Although the corner blacksmith was slowly disappearing, the brothers were ready to take advantage of America's industrial expansion. Buffalo Forge's forges were efficient because they had gear-driven blowers instead of the traditional blacksmith bellows. Using that forge fan as a start, Buffalo Forge moved into air movement on a larger scale.

As early as 1884, Buffalo Forge discovered a way to warm air by circulating it through pipe coils which were heated by exhaust steam. By moving air over ice, the company created a primitive type of air conditioning. Another Buffalo Forge product relieved industry of poor air in plants by introducing ventilation. As Buffalo Forge improved its wide range of air-moving products, the Wendts found they needed specialized

---

This artist's sketch shows a small blacksmith shop using Buffalo Forge's portable forge.

machine tools such as punches, shears, and bar cutters. Reasoning that other forge companies must also be in need of such tools, the Wendts began marketing the new line successfully.

This pioneer in the development of moving large masses of air purchased a pump company in 1904. In this North Tonawanda facility Buffalo Forge produced centrifugal pumps capable of moving large quantities of liquids and semiliquids.

With its three basic products—pumps, machine tools, and air-handling equipment—Buffalo Forge grew to become a $125-million business. In addition to being one of the largest employers in the city of Buffalo, Buffalo Forge has several other plants in the United States, Canada, and Mexico. The Wendt family retained company ownership until 1941, when the ownership was broadened by a public stock offering.

BUFFALO GENERAL HOSPITAL

On July 15, 1858, the first patient was admitted to the Buffalo General Hospital on High Street. According to hospital records, John Russell, a tailor, was suffering from a disease loosely translated as "arm bone trouble." The records of his stay were fairly thorough, ranging from statements revealing that he paid $2.50 a week for his bed to a note that said his habits were "bad."

The admittance of the first patient to Buffalo General came nearly 12 years after a group of Buffalo doctors first tried to establish a public hospital. For years, money was short and enthusiasm low. But persistence paid off and on the cold, windy night of November 21, 1855, six civic leaders and 11 doctors accomplished what others had failed to do. The Buffalo General Hospital was formed.

Within several years of its opening, Buffalo General Hospital was named a United States Army General Hospital, eventually treating more than 869 sick and wounded Civil War soldiers. The 1870s saw the establishment of a training school for nurses—the first in the state outside of New York City. The continued operation of the school makes it the second oldest school of nursing in the country.

The following decade was a time of expansion. A new main building, children's ward, maternity building, and an isolation extension were built.

Buffalo General proudly received its first ambulance on April 1, 1883. The hospital used this horse and carriage for many years.

By its 50th anniversary, Buffalo General Hospital had become a major medical center with a wide range of facilities. During the next 50 years, the hospital continued to grow and contribute to medical science. Buffalo General sponsored an army hospital in World War I and again in World War II, when more than 50 doctors and 40 nurses cared for nearly 554,000 patients in northern Africa and Europe. The hospital pioneered the use of a new blood dialyzer in 1954 as well as a new technique for heart examination. Its first open-heart surgery was undertaken in 1960. Within 20 years, open-heart surgery had become the most common elective surgery performed at the Buffalo General.

In 1974 Buffalo General incorporated a 60-bed community mental health center into its system. Five years later, it merged with Deaconess Hospital on the city's east side to form a 1,070-bed health care facility. With the new partnership, Buffalo General provided nearly 25 percent of all adult medical-surgical services in Erie County.

The beginning of the 1980s brought the realization of a $166.4-million construction, consolidation, and renovation program to the hospital's High Street site. The program includes a 16-story medical tower at High and Ellicott streets, allowing the Buffalo General Hospital to continue as one of the largest and most modern hospital systems in the country.

Nurses and doctors pose for an 1897 picture in the men's ward of the Buffalo General Hospital.

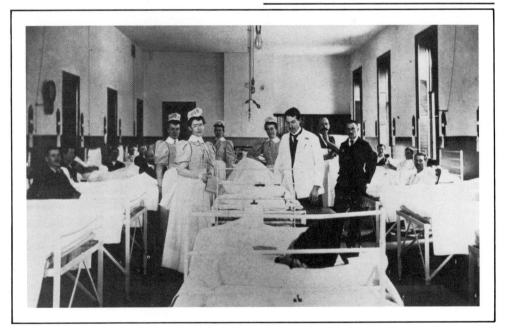

BUFFALO HILTON

The Buffalo Hilton Hotel officially opened—in grand style—November 7, 1980. The pageantry included an 8-course, black-tie dinner, as part of the weekend-long celebration at the new waterfront hotel.

Ground had been broken in August 1978, but the story began years before.

In the late 1950s, Buffalo, like other major urban areas, was hit with urban renewal fever. Old buildings were torn down in the idea that modern structures would go up in their place. The idea didn't always work. And a plot of land at Lower Terrace and Church stood vacant for years.

Then, in 1972, a California developer came to Buffalo, interested in building a hotel in the city. Negotiations started, but then died.

A fountain greets guests at the Buffalo Hilton Hotel, built on Buffalo's waterfront.

Guests and visitors dine in the hotel's airy atrium.

Nearly five years later, at the urging of community leaders and bankers, the developer, Clement Chen, Jr., returned to try again. Working closely with the city to arrange federally backed, low-cost loans, Chen began negotiations, which this time proved fruitful. A legion of lawyers worked long hours to get the project moving. Finally agreements were reached, papers signed, and Buffalo was set to become home to a $17-million hotel complex of 500 rooms and an adjoining indoor athletic club.

The entire complex was designed by Chen. He came to the United States from China in 1949 and designed and built hotels on the West Coast. What brought him to Buffalo, he later explained, were the opportunities he saw in the city which other developers failed to perceive. The city's waterfront and downtown areas were entering a revival, and Chen decided to play a leading part.

Tons of Italian marble were imported. Miles of carpets were laid. Chen's design included an 80-foot-wide waterfall in the hotel's atrium and an outdoor fountain. And, as part of his plan to be a major contributor in Buffalo's downtown revival, the new Hilton Hotel includes two restaurants, a dazzling nightclub, six meeting rooms, and a formal ballroom. The adjoining athletic club, available without charge to all guests, includes six tennis courts, an indoor pool, one-sixth-mile jogging track, two official squash and handball courts, four racketball courts, steam rooms, masseurs, and saunas.

What had been vacant land for more than 25 years is now a jewel on Buffalo's waterfront.

THE BUFFALO SABRES HOCKEY CLUB

The world's fastest team sport—ice hockey—came to Buffalo in major league dress at the beginning of the 1970s, thanks to the persistence and community pride of the Knox brothers.

Seymour and Norty Knox had wanted to bring the brilliance of the National Hockey League to their hometown for years, and had persisted against adversity in their efforts to obtain a big league franchise for Buffalo. They wouldn't take "no" for an answer, and when the "yes" finally came, the Knoxes quickly set up what has become one of professional sports' most successful and dynamic franchises.

Through the '70s the Sabres excelled on the ice and fans on the Niagara Frontier turned out to fill every seat for every game, making Buffalo a benchmark for other young and growing sports franchises.

Artistically the Sabres have been one of the best teams in the NHL in their first 11 seasons, compiling a win-loss record at the top echelon of the league. And those wins were translated from some of the most spectacular plays and players in the NHL. The incomparable Gil Perreault still thrills crowds with his grace and skill as he did since being the Sabres' first amateur player picked in their first draft. Goalie Roger Crozier, the first player selected to the Sabres Hall of Fame, was a bulwark in those early years, an incomparable stylist in sports' most demanding position.

The Sabres later put Perreault with wingers Richard Martin and Rene Robert to form the French Connection, the most explosive and famous offensive unit of the '70s. The new Sabres entering the '80s are under Scott Bowman, hockey's most successful active coach, who was hired by the Knox brothers at the end of the decade. And Bowman has fast assembled a young and talented squad with depth that promises even more success on the ice in the decade ahead.

Off the ice the Sabres have been close to the heart of the community since their first days. Under the leadership of the club's first coach and general manager, Punch Impach, the Sabres began programs which brought the club, the players, and the sport close to young and old alike.

Gil Perreault of the Buffalo Sabres swings into action to gain control of the puck. Perreault has been with the club since it was organized in 1970.

The Sabres were the first team in sports to annually produce their own half-hour highlights film; the club runs an annual open practice for thousands of youngsters and their parents and has successfully operated hockey clinics for young players and a number of other programs showing involvement and commitment to the community. And recently the Knoxes even bought a twin hockey rink to help support area amateur hockey, and named it Sabreland.

The Knoxes brought the NHL to Buffalo because they believed in the community, and the community has shown it believes in the Sabres.

The club was first located in a suite of temporary offices on Niagara Street, with a small staff which used to occasionally pass the time by playing floor hockey at lunchtime. Today the Sabres operate out of a modern set of offices tucked into Buffalo's Memorial Auditorium, where they play all of their home games, but the atmosphere has never changed, though floor hockey has disappeared. The people of the Sabres remain concerned with providing the best version of the world's fastest and most exciting team sport.

BUFFALO SAVINGS BANK

Buffalo Savings Bank's first day of business on July 6, 1846, gave little indication of events to come. The only accounts were opened by Robert Pomeroy, his wife Elizabeth, their four children, and a housemaid. Pomeroy had one of the best reasons for wanting the new bank to succeed—he was its only employee.

By January 1, 1847, the small office on the corner of Main and Erie streets held the grand sum of $18,585.57 for 149 depositors. One-third of that amount was already lent back out to the community for home mortgages. Now, more than 135 years later, Buffalo's first and largest savings bank holds more than $2.8 billion in assets and ranks as the country's seventh largest savings bank. Over the years it has established itself as the greatest single mortgage lender and the primary consumer banking institution in Western New York.

The institution's philosophy was spelled out in one of its early bankbooks. Buffalo Savings Bank wanted to "encourage the industrious and prudent, and to induce those who have not hitherto been such, to lessen their unnecessary expenses, and to save and lay by something for a period of life when they will be less able to earn a support." In other words, the residents of the young city were urged to save now for the uncertain future.

The future was uncertain for banks, as well, but Buffalo Savings was destined to survive—and to grow. Since 1816 when the first bank opened in Buffalo, savings institutions generally had a short lifespan. But a group of prominent citizens were determined that Buffalo Savings Bank would survive. Among them was Millard Fillmore, a founder and trustee of Buffalo Savings, later to become President of the United States.

Early records show that Buffalo Savings Bank "promptly met all the demands on its deposits even in the panic seasons of 1857, 1873, and 1893 and on the occasions when heavy drafts were made upon it by reason of false rumors regarding its solvency." In 1907, the bank avoided another run when it

piled money in the windows for all to see.

Jitters naturally reappeared during the Depression. But Buffalo Savings tellers were told to ask those withdrawing money, "Do you want gold, bills, or a check?" And, as one banker recalled, a common reply was, "Can I get it that easily? Then put it back in my account." By 1933 Buffalonians trusted the bank enough to deposit more than $8 million in nearly 100,000 accounts.

As Buffalo Savings Bank grew, it moved to larger quarters. After six years at a rented office at Main and Erie streets, the bank moved into a 4-story brick building on Main Street, just north of Court. On January 25, 1865, during a violent storm, the building was destroyed by a fire that had started in a nearby restaurant. The vault and its con-

Buffalo Savings Bank's gold-domed headquarters, constructed in 1901.

tents were saved, but the bank had to find a new home. On May 1, 1867, Buffalo Savings Bank moved into a new 2-story brownstone on the northeast corner of Washington Street and Batavia (now known as Broadway).

By the end of the century, the trustees decided to build again on "a greater scale and in a nobler style." The decision was made as Buffalo prepared for the grand Pan-American Exhibition; it resulted in one of the city's most famous landmarks. The grandeur of the Beaux-Arts building at Main and Genesee streets reflects the importance of

Customers on the main banking floor, circa 1920.

Buffalo at the dawn of the century, and the strength and stability of the bank itself.

Like the great Pan-American Exhibition, the bank headquarters opened in 1901. At first, its great dome was covered by green tile. But for reasons of maintenance and beauty, it was covered in pure gold leaf first in 1954, and again in 1979. Beneath the gold dome is a magnificent marble banking floor, hand-painted murals, and the signs of the zodiac.

Over the past 50 years the bank's headquarters have been expanded as needed. In 1980 the board of trustees decided to consolidate primary banking operations into a new 12-story facility adjacent to the gold-domed building. The structure will not only serve as the new headquarters for Buffalo's largest savings bank, but will be a cornerstone in the city's massive redevelopment of upper Main Street.

When Robert Pomeroy opened the bank for business on that lonely first day in 1846, Buffalo Savings Bank very simply took in savings deposits and lent them back to the community. Since then the financial services offered have expanded into areas that Pomeroy could have never imagined. Buffalo Savings Bank now has dozens of different savings and investment instruments and can make a wide variety of consumer, commercial, and mortgage loans.

Many of the financial world's most important services were actually pioneered by Buffalo Savings Bank. Automatic payroll savings deposits—now offered throughout the nation—were first developed by the bank in 1928. School savings plans were initiated jointly with two other local banks in 1947. In recent years, Buffalo Savings Bank has established the region's largest in-store banking system under a single bank name; and has introduced the rest of the nation to depositor discount plans, guaranteed investments with changing daily rates, and the nation's first complete telephone banking service.

Buffalo Savings Bank, which continues to grow, has merged with a number of smaller savings and loans and acquired a statewide real estate network and mortgage company within and beyond New York State. Long-range plans call for more growth and diversity, and more service innovations.

The new corporate headquarters is a symbol of the bank's promising future; but, one that remains linked to a symbol of the past. The great gold dome represents strength and achievement—a tradition that will not be forgotten in the years to come.

F.N. BURT CO., INC.

F.N. Burt Company's products enter millions of homes each year, yet F.N. Burt is not a household name. The explanation is simple—F.N. Burt makes set-up boxes and folding cartons for a wide range of products. For years, the job of F.N. Burt has been to promote customers' names, not its own. Company packaging skills and the technological advances it pioneered have made F.N. Burt the leader in custom packaging.

For years, F.N. Burt was the leading manufacturer of boxes for cigarettes. The firm now prints a variety of packaging, from attractive jewelry boxes for Avon Products to elegant holiday gift packages for Seagram's liquors. Most of its products are stamped with a bit of Buffalo—a standing bison is the firm's trademark.

Company founder Frederick N. Burt was a member of one of Buffalo's pioneer families. After high school, Burt learned the printing trade by traveling around the country. By August 1886 he returned to Buffalo to set up a small printing shop at 440 Main Street to print legal forms and labels for boxes.

Frederick N. Burt, founder of F.N. Burt Company, Inc.

Frederick Burt first entered the paper box business by purchasing small drug boxes and attaching his own labels. But when business began growing, Burt decided it would be more profitable to make his own boxes. He developed a machine for this purpose around 1901.

In 1909, when Frederick Burt was 46 years old, he sold his growing business to Moore Corporation Limited of Canada, which provided capital to build more machines. Cigarette boxes for brands including Helmar and Pall Mall were produced. At one point, 200 million boxes were made each year, about 98 percent of all such boxes. Also in 1909, Burt retired and Mary R. Cass became general manager, one of the area's first female executives.

In 1917 F.N. Burt produced an order for the California Perfume Company, and in 1939 that company became Avon Products. F.N. Burt has become a major supplier of packaging to Avon.

The firm was the world's largest producer of small paper boxes. Over the next few decades F.N. Burt manufactured products such as cone-shaped paper cups, paper decorations, puzzles, and fancy cosmetics boxes.

In early 1936 F.N. Burt was the first company to manufacture lithographic printed cartons. Beginning in the 1970s, the firm became recognized as the developer of a unique ink-drying process for carton printing, ultraviolet curing. The company has also applied the process to printed surface coatings. F.N. Burt is now the leading supplier of high-quality folding cartons.

Although the company has a plant and several sales offices outside the Buffalo region, its headquarters has remained in the area. Since 1959 F.N. Burt has been based in a modern plant and office complex on 25 acres in Cheektowaga. Nationally known local customers include Zippo Manufacturing and Westwood Pharmaceuticals.

By the 1930s, F.N. Burt Company had five printing and warehouse facilities. The building at Seneca and Hamburg streets was its main headquarters and factory for many years.

CANISIUS COLLEGE

In 1870 a group of Jesuits left Europe in response to Bishop John Timon's call for a Catholic institution of higher learning to serve European immigrants settling in western New York. The Jesuits founded Buffalo's first Catholic college and named it after St. Peter Canisius, a distinguished Jesuit theologian, scholar, and educator of the 16th century.

For the more than 110 years since that founding, Canisius College has been an integral part of the educational, cultural, religious, and social service mosaic of the Niagara Frontier.

According to the original charter issued by the Regents of the State of New York, the college was to be "an institution of learning in the City of Buffalo ... for the instruction of youth in the learned languages and in the liberal and useful arts and sciences." The charter, received in 1883, made it possible for Canisius to confer its first bachelor of arts degree on six graduates.

In its earliest days, the main courses of study were classical languages, literature, and philosophy. Premed, prelaw, and predental courses were added in 1914 and the first bachelor of science degrees were conferred that year. The college's current Continuing Studies Division began as the Normal School of the Diocese of Buffalo in 1919 with inauguration of summer school for teachers, many of them nuns. Classes were extended into the evening that September and have continued since.

The first bachelor of business administration degree was conferred in 1935. A masters of education program was started in 1939, followed by a nursing program in 1940, and a masters of business administration program in 1968.

Over the years, Canisius College's mission has broadened to include high quality coeducational programs in the arts, sciences, education, and business administration, on both the undergraduate and graduate levels. Major programs are now offered in 36 areas including psychology, computer-science, criminal justice, gerontology, medical technology, pre-engineering, and pre-environmental science and forestry.

The campus has also changed dramatically from the 2-story building at 434 Ellicott Street in 1870. The building was large enough for classes of 25 young men. By 1872 the college moved to more spacious quarters at Washington and Tupper streets. They shared that location with Canisius High School for 40 years.

Development of the present campus began in 1911 with the start of construction

Churchill Academic Tower, now a Main Street landmark, punctuates the modern Canisius College campus. The college's Old Main building is in the background.

of the golden-domed Old Main, still the center of campus activity. More than 4,200 students study on the 18-acre campus at 2001 Main Street. Included among its 14 buildings are Bosch and Frisch residence halls, a 200,000-volume library, science and health buildings, student center, neo-Gothic Christ the King chapel, Koessler Athletic Center, and Churchill Academic Tower.

Canisius College first held classes in this building on Ellicott Street.

CANNON DESIGN INC.

A few eyebrows might have raised when a young architect named Will Alban Cannon was chosen to design the new Niagara Falls City Hall built in 1922. Cannon had graduated from the University of Pennsylvania only six years before, but he met the challenge with his design of a stylized classic building. From that one-man office grew one of the nation's leading architectural and engineering firms, now known as Cannon Design Inc.

For about 25 years after Cannon first hung his shingle outside a small Niagara Falls office in 1916, Cannon's work centered nearly exclusively in the Niagara Falls area. He designed a number of residences in Niagara County as well as residence halls at Niagara University.

After World War II, several events occurred which changed the nature of the firm. Will Alban Cannon, Jr., received a degree in architecture from the University of Michigan and joined his father and two other architects to form Cannon, Thiele, Betz & Cannon in 1945. John Donald Cannon, with an engineering degree from the University of Michigan, joined the firm in 1950.

At about the same time, the federal government started a program to help small communities develop local hospitals. The Cannon firm was the first in the state to

Young Will Alban Cannon designed Niagara Falls City Hall in the classic style of the day. This photograph was taken about 1925.

receive a contract for a hospital under the program. It soon was the architect for dozens of health care facilities and is now listed as one of the country's top 10 design firms for hospitals.

By the mid-1960s the company was ready to take another giant step. It merged with

another Niagara Falls firm to become Cannon, Thiele, Betz, Cannon, Shackleton & FitzGerald in 1965. The additional personnel gave the organization the strength to move from a regional firm to an interstate business. The expansion plan worked. From 40 employees in 1964, the company grew to 80 employees in 1968 when it changed its name to the simpler, The Cannon Partnership. By 1972 employment had jumped to 120. It was time to consolidate its offices in Niagara Falls, Buffalo, and Niagara Falls, Ontario, Canada. The firm built a corporate headquarters at 2170 Whitehaven Road on Grand Island, a site about halfway between its Niagara Falls birthplace and Buffalo.

The company decided to incorporate in 1974 and the name was changed once again. As it entered the 1980s, Cannon Design Inc. was a multidisciplinary professional organization with four divisions and two subsidiaries and 250 employees.

In addition to Will Jr., chairman, and John D., president, other board directors are Robert R. FitzGerald, James H. Finley, Jr., Mogens M. Hertz, Franz S. Veit, Mark R. Mendell, and Robert L. Bailey.

Cannon Design Inc. is one of the foremost architects of health care facilities. This is its rendering of the planned addition to Buffalo General Hospital, scheduled for completion in 1984.

COLUMBUS McKINNON CORPORATION

The late 1870s was a time of the horse and buggy. Outside the small hardware shop in St. Catharines, Ontario, Lachlan Ebenezer McKinnon was proudly hanging the new sign that read "McKinnon & Mitchell, Manufacturers and Importers of Carriage Makers Supplies." In the rear of the store, four employees were busily setting up the production equipment for manufacturing saddlery hardware, wagon gear, and horse harnesses. It was a momentous opening day for a business that would soon flourish and expand across international boundaries.

Within a decade, the young company had established a Buffalo subsidiary, The McKinnon Dash Company, and by 1907, it had become the largest single employer of skilled labor on the Niagara Frontier.

Shortly after the turn of the century,

Employees of the Columbus Chain Company in Ohio make a chain using the fire-welded method. Photograph circa 1910.

McKinnon Dash was using an innovative technique, electric welding, in the assembly of some of its products. Through experimentation, it was discovered that when electric welding was applied to the chain-making process, the chain became stronger. There was already a need for more rugged chain in industry and the new product proved incredibly successful. In 1909, The McKinnon Chain Company Ltd. was launched to meet the flood of orders and plants were set up in Tonawanda, New York, and St. Catharines, Ontario.

The year 1917 was a landmark one. Through merger with the Columbus Chain Company of Columbus, Ohio, the Columbus McKinnon Chain Company was born. As the world was thrown into World War I, Columbus McKinnon supplied the U.S. Army with both traditional cavalry equipment and with the armaments for a new artillery style of warfare that would soon make fighting on horseback obsolete. After the war, Columbus McKinnon made an easy

Workmen use a Cyclone to install an airplane motor in 1926.

transition to manufacturing parts for the budding automotive industry. Radiators, windshields, and transmission gears were all made at the Buffalo plant.

Columbus McKinnon Chain was sold to Columbus, Ohio, interests in 1922 and three years later resold to board member Julius Stone. Stone promptly started reshaping the corporation. Corporate offices were moved to Tonawanda in 1927, and by 1931 the Columbus operation was closed completely. The 1928 acquisition of Chisholm Moore Company, a leading hoist manufacturer, enabled Columbus McKinnon to diversify its line and to supply industry with two closely aligned products—chain and hoist.

Columbus McKinnon next entered a period of expansion and product development that, despite sagging sales, was to pull it through the Depression. The post-World War II years brought increased exporting activities and solid international growth. Today Columbus McKinnon hoists, chains, and farm hardware are sold in more than 70 countries through a network of more than 3,000 domestic and foreign distributors. Subsidiaries and affiliates are located throughout the free world.

Now into its second century of operation, Columbus McKinnon has recently moved its corporate headquarters to Amherst, New York, less than 30 miles from the site of L.E. McKinnon's first hardware store, where it all began.

COMPUTER TASK GROUP, INC.

In 1966 two IBM Corporation employees decided to team up on an idea. They noticed that many small companies had computers but limited staff; their idea was to start a business to provide computer programming services to these companies.

Well, it turned out that the results weren't exactly what founders Randolph A. Marks and G. David Baer had in mind. They were even better. Instead of just small firms looking for computer services, the large Fortune 500 companies came knocking on the new venture's door. Their typical customers became Fisher-Price Toys, Marine Midland Bank, Xerox, and Westinghouse Electric Company.

Even with the business of large corporations, it took Computer Task Group five years to attain one million dollars in sales and then another five years to reach $5 million, in 1976. But it took only four more years for that $5 million to increase fivefold to $25 million. Computer Task Group's astonishing growth has ranked it consistently among the top 100 fastest growing small companies in the country, according to national business publications.

As Computer Task Group's sales grew, so did the number and size of its offices. From

This second renovated mansion at 844 Delaware Avenue contains a modern data processing training facility.

This renovated Buffalo mansion at 800 Delaware Avenue became Computer Task Group Inc.'s national corporate headquarters.

its first 500-square-foot rented office at 5585 Main Street in Williamsville, the company expanded to 18 branch offices by its 15th year in business.

In 1979 the firm became one of the first Buffalo corporations to move into a renovated Delaware Avenue mansion. Computer Task Group bought the former Knox residence at 800 Delaware Avenue for its national corporate headquarters, and by the end of the year announced plans to acquire a nearby mansion at 844 Delaware Avenue for a modern data processing training facility. The CTG Institute for Technical and Management Training teaches men and women to design, implement, and manage software systems for computers. The company believes this special training for professional growth is one reason why its personnel turnover rate is only one-half the national average in the competitive computer industry.

Computer Task Group acquired Neoterics Inc. of Cleveland, Ohio, in October 1980. The merger of the company that provided computer services in seven cities coupled with Computer Task Group's internal growth elevated Computer Task Group into one of the largest firms in the United States whose primary business is commercial programming services.

In addition to its professional software services, Computer Task Group's Application Products Division sells and programs minicomputer systems for small and medium-size businesses. Its Service Bureau Division offers direct mail services and batch processing of accounting applications.

Since June 1979, Marks has been chairman and chief executive officer. David N. Campbell, who joined Computer Task Group in 1968 as manager of market development, was named president and chief operating officer. Cofounder G. David Baer was named executive vice-president in charge of human resources and education, and John P. Courtney, former vice-president of marketing who joined the company in 1968, was named executive vice-president for the computer and professional services divisions.

DELAWARE NORTH COMPANIES, INC.

Delaware North sells snack foods to big league sports fans and serves gourmet fare to the Queen of England at Ascot Racecourse. It operates parking lots, dining rooms, flight kitchens, and gift shops at airports. The company owns racecourses filled with fast-paced horses and greyhounds and operates a shipping company transporting North-Pacific seafoods from the Aleutians to Seattle. It is engaged in publishing sports program magazines; oilfield safety services; typography; operation of bowling and recreation centers; and steel, aluminum, and zinc processing. In all the firm has more than two dozen separate operations, annual revenues of $500 million, and a seasonal work force of 30,000 internationally.

And it all grew from peanuts.

The story begins around 1915. Things were difficult for Marvin, Charles, and Louis Jacobs, sons of an immigrant tailor from Po-land. "If I wanted to eat and go to school," Marvin once recalled, "I had to work." So, the Jacobs brothers sold peanuts at theaters and ballparks, and quickly took their concessions wherever large numbers of people gathered.

Much of the company's explosive growth came after brother Louis took full ownership and control in the early 1950s. Louis invested in nonfood-related businesses such as racecourses and the Joseph Strauss appliance distributorship in Buffalo. By the mid-1960s annual revenues had reached $100 million.

In 1968 Louis died, passing the presidency to his youngest son, Jeremy M. Jacobs. Under Jeremy's tutelage, the corporation

Employees pose for a picture during a company picnic in Emery Park in June 1929.

was guided to new levels of growth and diversification. Delaware North ventured into metals processing, publishing, ocean shipping, wilderness feeding, and typography, and recruited a professional management team to handle its growing interests. In just 12 years, the firm's annual revenues increased fivefold.

Locally, Delaware North provides food services at Buffalo International Airport, Memorial Auditorium, Erie County Fair, and Buffalo Raceway, which it also owns and manages. The corporation continues to operate the Joseph Strauss Company on Union Road.

Jeremy Jacobs is chairman and chief executive officer of Delaware North. Donald S. Carmichael is president. Jeremy's brothers, Max W., an author and philanthropist, and Lawrence D., a neurologist, are shareholders.

THE JOHN W. COWPER COMPANY, INC.

Since 1915 The John W. Cowper Company, Inc., has been making a visible impact upon the growth of the Niagara Frontier. Quick proof can be gained by a walk around downtown Buffalo.

The company was formed on March 31, 1915, in Buffalo by John W. Cowper. The founder was born in 1871 into a prosperous family in Suffolk, Virginia, but at age 17, he decided to go off on his own in search of an independent career. His first job was as a rodman in the city engineer's office in Chattanooga, Tennessee. Within six months he moved to a railroad company, rising quickly to assistant engineer, a job he learned by studying on his own. Finally in 1901, at age 30, he received the chance to prove his skills. James Stewart and Company hired him and sent him to England as a superintendent and later as manager of the company's contracts. Almost immediately Cowper was put in charge of the construction of an $8-million facility for Westinghouse Electric Company in Manchester. From there, he compiled an impressive track record by supervising the electric-power conversion of the Mersey Railroad, directing the building of the Midland Hotel in Manchester, and supervising construction of an addition to London's Savoy Hotel. Cowper's ability to finish the construction speedily was considered so unusual that the *New York Herald* wrote a news article about him.

In 1907 Cowper returned to the United States and became manager of Stewart's Pittsburgh division. Two years later he moved on to become vice-president of the Milwaukee construction firm of Warden-Allen, Inc. Shortly thereafter Cowper moved again—this time to the area he adopted as his home. Cowper arrived in Buffalo to become vice-president of the Lackawanna Bridge Corporation.

Cowper recognized the opportunities in the bustling Great Lakes city. Buffalo was a center of the rail, steel, and grain mill industries. The successful manager decided to turn entrepreneur. With $500,000 capital he formed The John W. Cowper Company, Inc.

Cowper's reputation brought him his first contracts. One of the early projects was an addition to the General Railway Signal Company facilities in Rochester. Cowper is said to have made the record book by completing the one-and-one-half story concrete and steel building in 43 days.

An early ambitious project was the construction of new $7-million manufacturing facilities for commercial dye and chemicals at the Buffalo plant of the National Aniline and Chemical Works.

Those early years linked Cowper with some of the Buffalo area's diverse and best-known buildings. Cowper was chosen to build the 28-story office and bank building for the Marine Trust Company in 1928. The structure, on Lafayette Square, now known as the Rand Building, was the city's tallest skyscraper at the time. Another early building was Foster Hall. Built in 1921, it was the first structure on the University of Buffalo campus. The following year Cowper built the Buffalo Athletic Club on Niagara Square.

When the Depression hit in the 1930s, construction in the area came to a virtual standstill. John Cowper was faced with the possibility of ending the corporation. Instead, he personally carried the organization through the slow times and maintained the nucleus of persons who helped him build his company.

When war broke out in Europe in 1939, it became obvious that this country had to be prepared. In September 1940 the U.S. government announced plans for the expansion and redevelopment of Pine Camp near Watertown, New York, to provide a suitable training area for one of the newly formed U.S. Armored Divisions. Cowper was chosen to do the bulk of the construction work. Almost immediately, hundreds of railroad cars began to funnel into the area. Farmers were retrained as construction workers, and housing was put up for the laborers.

As winter moved in with its high winds, sub-zero temperatures, and heavy snow, the work continued on schedule. The project was substantially under way when the government announced in February 1941 that its initial plans were inadequate. About 75,000 more acres were purchased for the camp. By March more than 6,000 were employed at the Pine Camp site. Four months later the camp was officially turned over to the government.

The coming of World War II spurred millions of dollars worth of new construction on the Niagara Frontier. One of the projects was a $7.5-million airplane factory in Cheektowaga for the Curtiss-Wright Corporation. Ground was broken for the 30-acre plant on November 19, 1940. The job was completed within the 230-day deadline. That plant now houses the Westinghouse Electric Company motor operations.

Wartime construction totaled more than 25 jobs for the government and specific agencies in defense production, earning the Cowper firm a congressional citation. The construction contracts awarded during the 1940s also ensured the company of its title as the largest construction contractor in upstate New York.

John Cowper had remained active in his firm until his death in 1944. Daniel B. Niederlander, a Buffalo native who joined the Cowper company in 1919 as a job superintendent, became president until March 1963 when he moved up into the position of chairman of the board.

D.B. Niederlander was succeeded as president by David Donald. Donald, a native of Scotland, who moved to Buffalo when he was 16. After graduation from business school, he joined The John W. Cowper Company as an assistant bookkeeper and clerk in 1921. And in the tradition of the best Horatio Alger stories, the son of poor parents worked his way up to the presidency of the large construction company.

I.C. Francis became the Cowper company's fourth president in 1970. His father, Fred O. Francis, had been an officer in the organization for many years and brought his son up in the industry. I. Francis, a native of Buffalo, first joined the company in 1941 in its timekeeping department. After gaining experience in field engineering, supervision, estimating, and purchasing, he was appointed general superintendent in 1957. He was named a director in 1963 and five years later was selected as executive vice president.

The Marine Midland Tower in Buffalo, the tallest building in upstate New York, was constructed by The John W. Cowper Company, Inc.

Warren R. Strong was named president of The John W. Cowper Company, Inc., in 1981.

Irving C. Francis progressed through several positions with The John W. Cowper Company, Inc., assuming the chairmanship in 1981.

Under I.C. Francis, the company continued to build some of the most ambitious construction projects in the area, including major portions of the $650-million State University of New York at Buffalo's Amherst campus, Buffalo City Court, Bethlehem Steel Corporation's Lackawanna offices, Rich Stadium in Orchard Park, the Niagara Falls Convention Center, Marine Midland Tower, and presently under construction, main headquarters buildings for Buffalo Savings Bank and Liberty National Bank, together with major portions of the Light-Rail Rapid Transit System. The Marine building became the tallest building in upstate New York.

Since the 1960s, I.C. Francis has encouraged the idea of Construction Management, where a team works with the building owners, architects, and construction crews to keep the project running smoothly and on budget. Cowper became the first construction company in upstate New York with a specialized construction management department.

As the firm entered the 1980s, I.C. Francis was elected chairman and Warren B. Strong became the company's fifth president in its 65-year history. When he joined Cowper, W.B. Strong had more than 25 years' experience in the construction industry, including a top management position with Gilbane Construction Company and presidency of Zapata Construction.

Cowper has always done out-of-town work, such as the Francis Marion Hotel in Charleston, South Carolina; additions to the famed Greenbrier Hotel in White Sulphur Springs, West Virginia; U.S. Army camps in Fort Benning, Georgia, and Fort Knox; and Calvery Street Bridge in Washington, D.C. But the company is expanding its geographic horizons. Although Buffalo remains its headquarters, Cowper's reputation is growing nationwide. Some of its projects in other parts of the country include three University of Wyoming campus buildings, a nursing home in Michigan, a U.S. Army Corps of Engineers project in Fort Carson, Colorado, and five major environmental works in Virginia.

D'YOUVILLE COLLEGE

D'Youville College, founded in 1908 by the Grey Nuns, has a heritage rich in academic excellence and community service. The college, named for Marguerite D'Youville, foundress of the Grey Nuns, has carried on her spirit as a pioneer in health care and social welfare.

D'Youville was the first college for women in Western New York, and the second Catholic college for women in New York State. Beginning as a general liberal arts school, it has grown into a coeducational institution offering a wide range of studies. Commitment to the future has led the college to introduce new courses and programs to meet the needs of a changing society. Programs in management, criminal justice, computer science, bilingual education, and gerontology are some of D'Youville's responses to the signs of the times.

With a lecture series in 1913, D'Youville began a tradition of leadership and cooperation in her community in the areas of culture and service. The recently renovated theater of the college continues this cultural thrust. D'Youville works closely with her west side neighbors for local developments and building projects, and has acted as a catalyst for area growth.

The college's four academic divisions—humanities; nursing; mathematics and natural sciences; and social, behavioral and professional sciences—continue to offer programs to prepare today's youth and adults to undertake leadership roles as productive, integrated, and interdependent members of their society.

As D'Youville adjusts to the challenges of contemporary society it remains firmly rooted in its Judeo-Christian heritage and commitment to the growth and well-being of those within its sphere of influence by remaining the small, personal, but dynamic community institution it has become.

Pauline Garnett, Mary Brennan, and Elizabeth Gosselin received the first undergraduate degrees conferred by D'Youville College, in 1912.

After 63 years as a women's college, D'Youville admitted its first male students in 1971.

Theater productions complement the academic programs offered by D'Youville.

ERIE SAVINGS BANK

At 9 a.m. on September 1, 1854, Erie County Savings Bank first opened the doors of its small rented office at Main and North Division streets. Even the safe was rented. The minimum deposit was officially one dollar. But the bank, unwilling to turn away any new deposit, offered what it called the "10-cent system." A record card was maintained for all deposits of less than one dollar. When that sum was attained, a regular passbook savings account was opened.

The bank prospered immediately. It withstood a civil war and two world wars, several financial panics and depressions, relocations, and banking law changes to grow into one of the largest savings banks in the country. When Erie Savings reached its 125th anniversary in 1979, its assets exceeded $2 billion.

Bank growth necessitated relocation to larger quarters. After three years in its first small home, Erie Savings moved to Main

Inventor Thomas A. Edison was the consulting engineer for the electrical installation when Erie Savings Bank's first home was constructed at Main and Niagara streets.

and Erie streets, remaining there for 10 years. It was there during the Civil War years that the bank's deposits first reached one million dollars. By 1867 deposits were more than $2.5 million and the bank constructed its own building. After 26 years at Main and Court streets, Erie Savings announced it would build again—this time on a grander scale.

New York architect George B. Post won a competition to design the new structure at Main and Niagara streets. Inventor Thomas A. Edison was chosen as the consulting engineer for the electrical installation.

Decades passed before the bank moved again. This time it was to a $26-million banking and retail complex completed in March 1969. Main Place, the name chosen from more than 500 suggestions, was a highlight of the city's redevelopment efforts.

The bank's investments in downtown Buffalo and its mortgages throughout the area have had a significant impact upon the community. Erie Savings' innovations, which have always left their mark, began in

the early 1900s when the bank placed its first order for an adding machine—a newfangled device that was only grudgingly accepted by dubious accounting personnel. One of Erie Savings' most noteworthy achievements in recent years was its advocacy of electronic banking facilities. Its network of 125 banking facilities in supermarkets and retail stores had become widespread by 1980, but only four years earlier Erie had been the first savings institution in the state to obtain approval for such a facility. Its early confidence in the program helped turn its subsidiary, Metroteller Systems Inc., into the largest sharing point-of-sale network in the United States.

In 1977 the bank changed its name from Erie County Savings Bank to Erie Savings Bank to reflect its expanded service area. Four years later its name was amended slightly when the bank changed from a state to a federal charter. On July 1, 1981, the bank's official name became Erie Savings Bank, FSB (Federal Savings Bank).

Main Place, a $26-million banking and retail complex completed in March 1969, is a highlight of Buffalo's redevelopment program.

FERGUSON ELECTRIC CONSTRUCTION CO., INC.

Whitworth Ferguson, Jr., president (left) and Whitworth Ferguson, Sr., chairman.

In 1956 the state of New York was ready to begin one of the most massive undertakings ever in the history of electricity. Millions of dollars would be spent building the Niagara Power Project to generate hydroelectricity. When it came time for the first large electrical construction contract to be awarded, it was Ferguson Electric Construction Company, Inc., which received the million-dollar order. The Buffalo firm eventually did $12 million of work on the project.

Although the job of helping to harness the power of Niagara Falls was one of the more spectacular electrical construction jobs done by Ferguson Electric, its other work is just as well known on the Niagara Frontier. The company has installed the electrical wiring in such industrial complexes as the Ford Motor Company's Stamping Plant, General Motors' two Harrison Radiator plants, and four Chevrolet plants. Bell Aerospace has been a longtime customer, as have Hooker, Union Carbide, Arcata Graphics, Anaconda, Niagara Machine & Tool, and many other corporations located in Western New York.

On the commercial side, Ferguson Electric was the electrical contractor for the 40-story Marine Midland Center, 27-story Main Place Tower and Plaza, and the Western Savings Bank Tower, all on Main Street in downtown Buffalo. The Amherst Campus of the State University of New York, Millard Fillmore Hospital, Veteran's Hospital, and the Niagara Falls Convention Center are among other projects. Ferguson lays claim to the title of the largest electrical construction company in Western New York.

The firm has been successful since it first opened for business on August 1, 1935, in a small office at 204 Oak Street. Whitworth Ferguson, Sr., who had been a vice-president and chief engineer for a large electrical contracting company, decided to start his own business. The native of Victor, Iowa, who came to Buffalo after graduating from Iowa State University and doing graduate work while teaching at MIT, believed this city could support another electric contracting company specializing in engineering.

The decision to form the new electrical company had come at a fortuitous time. The advent of World War II in the 1940s created one of the largest construction booms in the history of Western New York. The small Oak Street office soon became cramped and the firm moved to 333 Ellicott Street, which in the late 1800s had been a livery stable. Its headquarters has remained there for nearly 40 years, adding adjoining property for offices, warehousing, and parking. Ferguson's Niagara Falls office, the dominant electrical force in Niagara County, has been in operation since 1956, when it was set up to handle the Power Project work.

After more than 45 years since the company's founding, Whitworth Ferguson, Sr., remains involved in the business as chairman, turning over operations to his son, Whitworth Ferguson, Jr., as president, and a fine team of engineers and project managers headed by vice-presidents W. Richard Duffy, Robert A. Fredricks, and Donald A. Reiter.

FISHER-PRICE TOYS
A DIVISION OF THE QUAKER OATS COMPANY

In a modern laboratory in the East Aurora countryside, there are no scientists in white smocks working with test tubes. Instead, the focus is on a nursery school filled with young children playing with a large variety of toys. Fisher-Price's research is learning what makes a child smile.

Fisher-Price is the world's largest maker of infant and preschool toys. An estimated 97 percent of the toy-buying public has purchased at least one Fisher-Price toy, and other marketing studies have shown that an average American family with preschool children owns more than 14 Fisher-Price products.

And what makes those figures all the more remarkable is that Fisher-Price has never "swamped the market" with its products to make fast sales. It spends roughly twice the time of other major toy makers in research and testing before its products leave a Fisher-Price plant.

Quality, with emphasis on durability and safety, was the original goal of Herman G. Fisher, Irving L. Price, and Helen M. Schelle, who formed the company in a small East Aurora shop in 1930.

The trio knew the odds were against success. The toy business was fiercely competi-

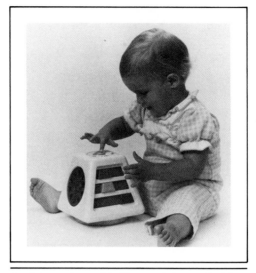

An infant plays with Turn and Learn Activity Center.

tive, and the Depression had already set in. They announced, as part of their new firm's philosophy and their proposed formula for success, that each product would have "intrinsic play value, ingenuity, strong construction, good value for the money, and action." Sixteen toys—all made of wood— were designed and sold that first year, and all the rest that have followed reflect that understanding of practicality and value.

The firm struggled during the Depression, losing two-thirds of its capital in its first four years. But it stayed afloat and engendered confidence in the quality of its products.

Early in the 1950s Fisher-Price recognized the expanding role of plastics in toy making and purchased the plastics firm of Trimold Inc. in the Buffalo suburb of Kenmore. Fisher-Price continued its plastics operation there until 1962, when it opened another plant in Holland, New York.

In 1966 Herman Fisher resigned as president, and Henry H. Coords, formerly of Western Electric, became the firm's second president. In 1969 Fisher-Price was acquired by The Quaker Oats Company, and the company began rapid expansion through the 1970s.

This growth included the purchase of a plant in Medina, New York, formerly owned by the H.J. Heinz Co., which provides fabrication, molding, and assembly capabilities.

In 1972 the firm broke ground on a manufacturing facility in Murray, Kentucky, where the hard goods of the Crib & Playpen line are produced. That same year marked the opening of twin manufacturing facilities on the Texas-Mexico border, which produce the soft goods line. In 1976 Fisher-Price acquired majority ownership of the Plastimarx Company of Mexico City to expand its sales throughout Mexico and Latin America. In 1977 the company acquired Montron Corporation, now a Fisher-Price facility in San Diego, California. This plant and its sister facility in Tijuana, Mexico, provide resources for an expanded audio-visual line.

The firm has since added manufacturing centers in Kaulille, Belgium, and Peterlee, England. Its products are sold in nearly 100 countries.

Also in the 1970s, Fisher-Price expanded its product line to offer toys for children beyond the preschool age, including Crib & Playpen products for infants, an assortment of playsets for school-age children, a special line of "Muppet" toys, dolls, trucks, and most recently, Arts & Crafts.

In 1981 Franklyn S. Barry, Jr., became the third president in the history of Fisher-Price, replacing Coords who retired after 14 years as president.

Fisher-Price Toys headquarters, East Aurora, New York, with "Reflective Child" sculpture in the foreground.

S. M. FLICKINGER CO., INC.

From a turn-of-the century grocery store, S.M. Flickinger Co., Inc., has grown into Western New York's first billion-dollar company.

But the Flickinger company is also responsible for another achievement that has had national implications. Its founder, Smith M. Flickinger, is known as the father of the voluntary chain concept in supermarket retailing.

The idea evolved over a number of years. Flickinger had started a wholesale food and grocery operation in May 1900 in conjunction with his own grocery store. A 1908 invoice still displayed on the company's walls gives this typical list of products sold: corn flakes, bird seed, sugar by the barrel, corn meal, oats, and cream of tartar.

Flickinger's business grew and he opened more grocery stores. At the same time he came to know many of the independent store owners from the wholesaling operation. He recognized the advantages of owners running their own stores, but he also saw the positive side of buying in bulk, which owners of individual stores couldn't afford to do.

Flickinger came up with the voluntary chain concept to utilize the best of both

A current Super Duper supermarket serviced by S.M. Flickinger Co., Inc.

A typical early grocery store serviced by S.M. Flickinger Co., Inc.

systems. In 1934 he began selling the stores his company owned to the store managers. The Flickinger company then focused on buying the needed products in bulk to sell to the independent stores and organizing the independents together for such considerations as advertising.

Fifty years after Flickinger thought of this revolutionary idea, an estimated half of the nation's supermarkets use the voluntary chain concept. In Western New York, one of the supermarket chains working under

the independent ownership concept is Super Duper Markets. The Flickinger company has been supplying and sponsoring Super Duper since the 1950s, when modern supermarkets were developed.

The 1960s were years of rapid growth for the company. During that decade sales grew from $67 million to $283 million. These years also saw the firm change from a privately held enterprise to a public corporation when it issued stock to the public on December 19, 1968.

By 1975 sales had passed the $500-million mark, and within five years the company reached one billion dollars. The following year the Flickinger Company announced it would build a new corporate headquarters on Transit Road in West Seneca.

S.M. Flickinger remained chairman until his death in 1939. His son, Burt P. Flickinger, assumed that position upon his father's death; he was succeeded by his brother, Glenn W. Flickinger, in 1965. Other chairmen were Hildreth C. Olney, Clarence R. Baker, and Robert F. Norris. In February 1981 Jerry D. Metcalf became the firm's seventh chairman. At that time, four members of the Flickinger family remained active in the business. They were Burt P. Flickinger, Jr., Peter Flickinger, Thomas Flickinger, and William Flickinger, all grandsons of the founder.

FOREST LAWN CEMETERY

The Grand Archway at Forest Lawn's Main Street entrance was erected in time for the 1901 Pan American Exposition.

Forest Lawn is located on land acquired from the Seneca Nation circa 1797 by William Johnston, a retired British Army captain who had married a Seneca woman and wielded a considerable influence among her people. In 1806 title passed to Erastus Granger, agent to the Six Indian Nations, and it was on this land that Granger met with the Great Council of Nations and persuaded the Council to refuse an alliance with the British in the War of 1812. Some 30 years later, when the young city of Buffalo was rising into prominence, a need was felt increasingly by her populace for a large, parklike burial ground. Accordingly, in 1849 the public-spirited entrepreneur Charles E. Clarke purchased approximately 80 acres of the Granger estate at $150 per acre and began the following spring to grade and survey the land as a park/cemetery.

The first burial was made in the afternoon of July 12, 1850, for John Lay, Jr., who had been an old and greatly esteemed member of the community. The purchase of lots by other early Buffalonians followed in rapid order. In 1855 Clarke conveyed the unsold cemetery grounds to a group of lot owners known as the Forest Lawn Cemetery Association, which acquired more land from the surrounding farms and incorporated in 1864 under the name of the Buffalo City Cemetery, known commonly as Forest Lawn. Since then the cemetery has been guided by a board of trustees under 11 presidents and four chairmen.

The first offices of the Buffalo City Cemetery were at No. 4 West Swan Street. In 1866 the offices were moved to Main and Court streets and the grounds, by then greatly improved and enlarged to 203 acres, were dedicated on September 28. Improvement followed improvement: a chapel built with stone from the cemetery's own quarry, 1882; a bridge across Scajaquada Creek, 1888; the present iron fence begun, 1892; a second bridge, 1895; the Main Street and Delaware Avenue arches, 1900 and 1901; the present office building, 1908; the superintendent's house, 1926; a crematory and columbarium added to the chapel, 1932; the quarry filled and landscaped, 1939; a modern service building, 1949; Oakwood Community Mausoleum, 1973; Birchwood Mausoleum, 1976; and Rosewood Mausoleum, 1980.

Today Forest Lawn has grown to 267 acres which have become the final resting place for thousands of the men and women whose deeds have inspired this book: the farmers, teachers, industrialists, and statesmen who raised Buffalo up from a wilderness. Of particular interest are the many superb examples of Victorian memorial sculpture, especially the memorials of General Albert J. Meyer, founder of the U.S. Weather Bureau and the Army Signal Corps; William G. Fargo, cofounder of the Wells Fargo Bank and the American Express Company; America Pinckney Peter Williams, great-granddaughter of Martha Washington; Red Jacket, the Seneca orator; and J.J. Albright, donor of the magnificent Albright Art Gallery.

A complete list of memorials would fill about 300 pages of this size, for as of this writing some 128,000 people from every sector of the Buffalo population have been buried or entombed at Forest Lawn. Despite this already large number it is projected that at the current rate of burial Forest Lawn will not be filled for another 200 years. In fact, there are extensive areas within the cemetery that have never been surveyed. Here is where deer used to wander a century ago, gone now only because the surrounding land has become citified. The cemetery, by contrast, is more heavily wooded today than it was at the time of the Pan American Exposition, which explains why Forest Lawn is a haven for over 200 species of song and game birds from the chickadee to the great blue heron.

Visitors should bring a camera and binoculars, since many of the thousands of birds and small animals here are quite tame and vastly amusing. Every visit to Forest Lawn should include stops at the Millard Fillmore Shrine, the Blocher Memorial, and Mirror Lake, which can be found on maps available at the cemetery office. The Blocher Memorial is world famous for its life-size figures carved from Italian marble. Mirror Lake is the year-round home for a flock of mallard ducks, and it is the focal point of the Forest Lawn Arboretum, a living source of beauty and refreshment in the heart of the city.

GENERAL MILLS, INC.

The history and growth of General Mills' Buffalo operations are closely aligned with the city's development into the world's largest flour milling center and with the growth of General Mills itself.

The story began in 1887 when 17-year-old Frank F. Henry came to Buffalo to work for a shipping company. Five years later, executives of the Washburn Crosby Company of Minneapolis, Minnesota, asked him to operate a waterfront office for the milling company. For 10 years, the Washburn Crosby operations were primarily warehousing. But Henry finally convinced the firm that it was not economical to ship flour to Buffalo in bags and repack it there into paper sacks. Instead, he suggested, why not bring the grain directly to Buffalo for milling and packaging?

The opening of the mill at Michigan and Ganson streets on January 28, 1904, added to the growing excitement on Buffalo's waterfront. As the new employees came to work that winter, they had to be wary of the runaway dog teams of the ice fishermen that dotted the lakefront. During the warmer months, they watched as new construction rose along the lake and saw the steady stream of lake ships enter the Port of Buffalo.

By 1928 Buffalo had grown into a major milling center. That year General Mills, Inc., was organized, with Washburn Crosby as a nucleus. Henry, who had been director and officer of the Washburn Crosby Company, was elected director. He later became chairman of General Mills' operating board.

Meanwhile, the operation he had suggested continued to thrive, eventually producing one-fifth of all of General Mills' flour. The Buffalo operation continues to make the famous Gold Medal brand flour, the same flour it packed into 5-gallon cans for Admiral Richard E. Byrd's historic South Pole expedition.

The packaged foods plant, opened October 6, 1941, still on South Michigan Street, was one of the first GM facilities to make the famous Cheerios cereal (originally called Cheerioats). The Buffalo operations also produce thousands of cases of Wheaties, Bisquick, and Betty Crocker mixes every day.

Although that first flour mill was torn down in 1969, its chimney still stands, a monument to initiative seen daily by the nearly 900 employees who work in the packaged foods and flour mill plants.

Employees of the flour mill pose for a group photograph taken sometime during the 1920s. The plant hired its first women in 1910.

GIOIA MACARONI COMPANY, INC.

Antonio Gioia, founder of Gioia Macaroni Company, Inc.

Anthony H. Gioia, trustee, Buffalo Savings Bank.

You wouldn't think you'd have to look outside Italy to find the world's finest pasta, but in Rome they do just that. The Gioia Macaroni Company of Buffalo has been winning awards for years at the acclaimed Italy Food Fair.

The family-owned company began in 1910 in Fredonia, a small town west of Buffalo, when brothers Antonio and Alphonse Gioia began making pasta in their home. Their first tentative steps toward selling the homemade pasta met with enormous success. The Gioias' spaghetti was the best in town. Business was so successful that the fledgling firm outgrew the small community and moved, in 1919, to Rochester. Steady growth continued, and the Gioia family began to expand its market throughout the Northeast.

Following World War II, Gioia Macaroni moved to Buffalo, opening its current office and production facilities at 1700 Elmwood Avenue. The original plant was 75,000 square feet. While the Gioia address has re-mained the same, the size of the plant has nearly doubled to 130,000 square feet.

As the firm grew, varieties of pasta were added to the line so that the company now markets 75 types of macaroni. Gioia also sells three types of spaghetti sauce and a pizza sauce. By the 1970s the firm had become one of the 10 largest pasta producers in the United States, selling more than 45 million pounds of pasta each year.

Gioia's major marketing area is within a 500-mile radius of Buffalo, but its sales have been increased through acquisitions of several other firms. In 1960 Piscitello Macaroni Company of Rochester was bought by Gioia. In 1976 a majority interest in Gioia itself was sold to the British-based transnational food company of Ranks Hovis McDougall (RHM). Total acquisition of Gioia by RHM was completed in 1978.

Throughout the corporate changes the Gioia family has continued to oversee the firm's operation. Antonio's son, Horace, was president from 1958 to 1972 and was in turn followed by his son, Anthony, who served as president from 1972 to 1981, when he became president of an RHM holding company for macaroni operations. Anthony Gioia's brother, Richard, became president of Gioia in 1981.

Under the merger with RHM, the Gioia family's know-how in the macaroni business became supported by the assets of an international company. One of the first benefits of the merger came the following year, in 1977, when RHM acquired Rochester-based Bravo Macaroni. Its production facilities were added to those of Gioia, and the expansion allowed Gioia to meet its rapidly growing consumer demands, a demand which doubled during the 1970s.

While word of mouth was enough to spread news of Antonio Gioia's recipe in 1910, the competition and expanding markets of the modern Gioia company require major advertising. And Richard Gioia, in addition to operating the company, retained his role as its chief advertising spokesman. Thus the Gioia tradition, which began generations ago in Italy and was transported to the United States at the turn of the century, continues today.

GREATER BUFFALO PRESS, INC.

Walter Koessler was a 25-year-old reporter in 1926 when he decided to quit working for newspapers and set out on his own to start printing them. He managed to put together $3,000 and buy a small printing operation located in the basement of a Niagara Street home. He called it Greater Buffalo Press.

Young Koessler had never been trained as a pressman. Along with his father and brother, he learned his new trade by doing. The work in those beginning years was all done on a flatbed press. Printing small community newspapers was the mainstay of the fledgling business. Among them was the *Cold Spring Advertiser* (circulation 7,000) and the even smaller *International Gazette* (circulation 1,300).

It was the tiny *Gazette*, a publisher of legal notices, that gave Koessler's firm its only steady stream of business during the Depression. While other companies failed in the worsening economy, Greater Buffalo Press kept afloat by publishing the increasing number of foreclosure notices. By 1932 the operation outgrew the Hertel Avenue shop it had moved into and Koessler made another move into larger quarters at 1245 Niagara Street on Buffalo's west side.

In the same year, Greater Buffalo Press began color reproduction work and won contracts to print the comic sections of the *Syracuse Herald* and the *Buffalo Courier-Express*. In 1935 it began printing the comic section of the *Chicago Times*.

In 1936 Koessler made another move into a larger facility at 302 Grote Street, which still serves as the firm's corporate headquarters.

About this time, Walter's father, John, and his younger brother, Kenneth, bought out the two partners who had contributed the start-up capital, and the entire operation came into family hands. More Sunday comics were added to the accounts, including the *San Antonio Express*, which was the firm's first major southern customer.

Business grew during World War II despite a newsprint shortage, and in 1947 a subsidiary plant was opened, Great Lakes Color of Dunkirk, some 45 miles south of Buffalo. When comic books gained in popularity, Greater Buffalo Press supplied

The heart of a printing plant is its press. There are 27 at Greater Buffalo—18 letterpresses and nine offset presses.

them. It printed the first issues of *Superman* and *Batman* comic books and *Mad Magazine*.

In 1956 another subsidiary was established in Lufkin, Texas, about 100 miles from Houston. Dixie Color Printing was es-

tablished at Sylacauga, Alabama, in 1963 to serve the increasing number of southern accounts.

In the mid-1960s the company turned from printing comics exclusively and began printing 4-color advertising circulars for national companies such as Sears, Montgomery Ward, Woolworth, and JC Penney.

Greater Buffalo has become one of the top two producers of color comics in the U.S. and employs 1,300 people, with 600 of them in the Buffalo area.

In 1972, under the leadership of Kenneth L. Koessler, the firm branched into the Canadian printing market by opening Greater Canada Colour Corporation in Stevenville, Ontario, a few miles from Niagara Falls. In 1981 two new printing plants, one in York, Pennsylvania, and one in Marengo, Iowa, were opened.

Long established as a leader in letterpress work, GBP has expanded into high-volume commercial heat-set offset work.

The company has remained privately held, with more than a half-dozen members of the Koessler family holding key positions. John W. Koessler, Jr., is president.

Walter Koessler began Greater Buffalo Press in 1926.

Today J.W. Koessler, Jr., is the firm's president and chief executive officer.

GRAPHIC CONTROLS CORPORATION

As Graphic Controls Corporation enters its silver anniversary year in 1982, it holds two national reputations. One is as a major manufacturer of recording charts, instrument marking systems, disposable medical products, and coated imaging papers. The other is as a recognized leader in improving the quality of modern working conditions. The common element in both is innovation.

Although April 1957 was the incorporation date of the present-day firm, its roots go back to the early 1900s. A small Canadian company, Staebler & Baker Ltd., made recording instruments and found that it needed to produce its own charts for the instruments. It began chart production in a tent on an island in the St. Lawrence River.

As technology increased during the 20th century, so did the need for charts to use with the newly invented instrumentation. Chart-making companies began to open in various parts of the northeastern United States and Canada.

About 50 years after Staebler & Baker started, three entrepreneurs, George Elliott Clarkson and two of his sons, consolidated six chart and printing enterprises, including Staebler & Baker, into Graphic Controls Corporation.

The headquarters of the new corporation was at 189 Van Rensselaer Street, the same location where, 17 years earlier, George Clarkson had moved his small chart business from Halesite, Long Island. At that time the operation was so small that everything was able to be loaded onto one large truck for the move to Buffalo.

Graphic Controls Corporation continues to maintain its headquarters at 189 Van Rensselaer. The company now owns the building and occupies most of the 600,000 square feet of work space. Its operations have grown to include plants in various parts of the United States and in 10 other countries.

Graphic Controls still makes charts similar to those printed on the island in the St. Lawrence River. However, it now produces over 90,000 different kinds of strip, circular, and folded charts used wherever production processes are monitored, seismic tests are taken, satellite performance is traced, oceanographic and meteorological ac-

Graphic Controls Corporation, a subsidiary of the Times Mirror Company, has its world headquarters in Buffalo.

Graphic Controls' charts and marking systems are used worldwide in industry, business, research, and medicine.

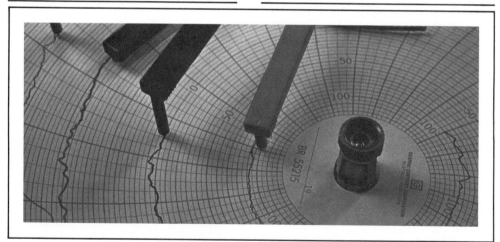

tivities are evaluated, and pollution is measured. A natural area for product expansion was into marking systems used with the thousands of charts produced. Graphic Controls recently introduced disposable marking pens, which eliminate the often

messy and inconvenient job of refilling ink in recording instruments. In addition to recording charts and marking systems, the company manufactures and markets a complete line of disposable medical products for cardiographic, encephalographic, and

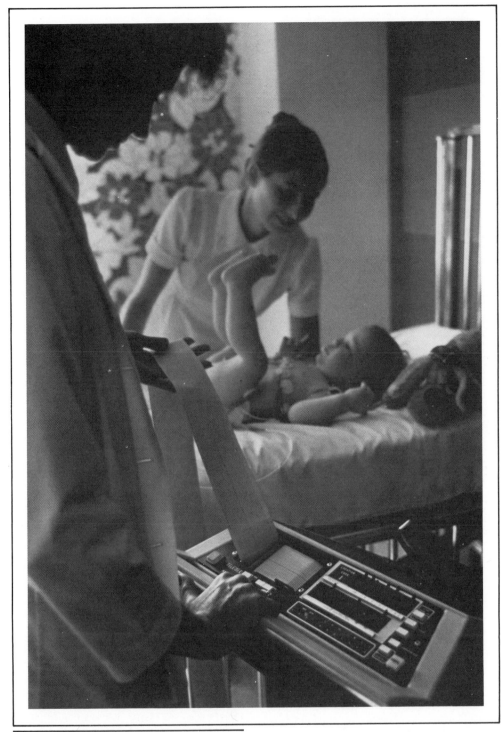

Graphic Controls' health monitoring and recording systems provide the documentation needed for efficient diagnosis and treatment.

medical laboratory applications; pH and Ion selective electrodes used in laboratories and industrial process control measurement; and specially coated papers used for high-speed communications, including the facsimile transmission of photographs

around the world and for monitoring the Space Shuttle launchings at Cape Kennedy.

In its 25th year, Graphic Controls is the world's leading manufacturer of recording charts. Employment has also grown steadily, increasing from 90 in 1950 to over 1,800 today. More than 25 percent of Graphic's people are located at the Buffalo headquarters. It is there that the company for-

mulated its distinctive management style. The management policies have attracted such national recognition as the 1978 Phillips Award for Management-Employee Relations. The award was established to foster a greater awareness of social and ethical values in business.

The firm began veering from traditional management-employee relations soon after its establishment. Chairman George Elliott Clarkson and his sons, Max B.E. Clarkson, then president, and William M.E. Clarkson, then executive vice-president, believed that if employees are satisfied with their work, the company will also benefit. As Will Clarkson wrote, "A full-time person spends over 2,000 hours a year at his or her work place. It is important that people feel that their varied needs have an opportunity of being satisfied, concurrent with meeting the organization's objectives."

An early Graphic Controls innovation was the elimination of the time clock for production workers. Plant employees were put on a weekly salary just as the managers and office staff. This was soon followed by making benefits for production and clerical people the same as benefits for management and sales.

Graphic Controls made a significant contribution to management theory by its evolving use of consensus management. The formal name is Decentralized Participative Management by Objectives. The basic value-system concepts are the authority of knowledge, the sharing of decision-making authority, the need for individual and group responsibility, informed choice, and the commitment that results from effective participation.

The health of a corporation is determined, not only by its financial results, but also by its relationship with its people. In 1975, 1977, 1979, and 1981, Graphic Controls has gathered and audited information on how people feel about their jobs, their coworkers and supervisors, their pay and working conditions, and their community activities. These quality of work life surveys are a measurement of the human side of the corporation. Better data enables better management of human resources to occur.

Graphic Controls was a privately held company until 1966, when it became publicly listed. In 1978 the firm was acquired by the Times Mirror Company of Los Angeles. Two years later, Will Clarkson, who had been president since 1970, became chairman and Walter H. Greenholt became the third president in the corporation's history.

THE JEWETT REFRIGERATOR COMPANY, INC.

This photograph, taken around 1930, shows the plant of Jewett Refrigerator Company, Inc., one of the city's oldest firms.

The Jewett Refrigerator Company, Inc., a pioneer in the development of home refrigerators, has become a leader in refrigerators and equipment for health care.

How the company changed its focus from home to health care is an interesting and important part of its history. As the story goes, a pathologist was in a bar one night in 1941 when he noticed Jewett's Bevador. The round metal refrigerator showcased bottles of wine and soda on its revolving shelves.

The pathologist's idea, which he took to Jewett, was to make a similar revolving refrigerator for blood storage. Up until then, blood had been stored in conventional refrigerators. But hospitals found they had to throw away much of the blood after bottles were pushed back into corners and not chosen for use until after the blood had spoiled. The revolving shelves ensured that no blood was forgotten.

Jewett started making the new blood-bank storage units just as World War II broke out. The federal government chose the Jewett product as its standard for blood storage and sent the refrigerator to battlefields all over the world. The exposure later led to requests from private hospitals and laboratories for the Jewett refrigerators. By the early 1960s, Jewett decided to concentrate on appliances designed for medical use.

The company's focus has changed greatly since its founding as the John C. Jewett Manufacturing Company, Inc., in 1849 in Buffalo. John Cotton Jewett had grown up on the family farm in Moravia, New York, and conducted a mercantile business in Michigan before coming to Buffalo at the age of 29. The new enterprise made a wide range of household items, from iceboxes and bathtubs to bird cages and spittoons.

John Jewett was later joined in the business by his eldest son, Edgar Boardman Jewett. After successively becoming a brig-adier general in the U.S. Army and president and general manager of the family business, Edgar Jewett was elected mayor of Buffalo in 1894.

When iceboxes were developed into refrigerators, Jewett took a leading role and innovated new circulating systems. Its top-of-the-line, solid porcelain refrigerators were sold to the country's luxury hotels and to such persons as Cornelius Vanderbilt and John D. Rockefeller, Jr., in New York City; George Eastman in Rochester; Marshall Field III in Long Island; H.S. Firestone in Akron, Ohio; Henry Ford in Detroit; Joseph Pulitzer in St. Louis, Missouri; and actor Harold Lloyd in Beverly Hills, California.

One hundred years after its founding, Jewett was bought by Ruslander and Sons, Inc., another of Buffalo's oldest companies. Ruslander, a maker of food service equipment, was founded in 1870 by Abraham S. Ruslander. Harold S. Ruslander, grandson of the founder, is chairman. Marshall L. Glickman has been president of the Jewett company since 1973.

KITTINGER COMPANY

When the nation's top officers needed a table for their high-level Cabinet meetings, when President Nixon wanted a suitable gift to present to visiting foreign dignitaries, and when the White House staff decided to give a departing gift to Rosalynn Carter, wife of the President, they all turned to Buffalo's Kittinger Company.

The name "Kittinger" has become a legend in the furniture industry for its reproductions of English and American antiques. Although Kittinger is perhaps best known as the only authorized manufacturer of the American-style furniture of Colonial Williamsburg, the contract to reproduce the traditional furniture wasn't signed until 1937—after the company had been in business for 71 years.

The history of one of Buffalo's oldest companies is literally a rags-to-riches story. The Kittinger Company's roots go back to 1866 to a paper and rag warehouse on East Seneca Street. The firm, Thompson, Colie & Company, was run by partners Levi O. Thompson and Oliver S. Colie and his son George W.

By 1870 the company had changed its name to Colie & Son and listed its business as upholsterers. The small enterprise moved to various locations around the city until finally settling into its first real factory in 1885. In the 4-story building on Front Avenue (now Busti Avenue), George Colie, now president, expanded from single wooden frames for upholstery into other wood furniture such as tables.

Business was cyclical and although the last years of the 19th century were booming years for the firm, the beginning of the 20th century was not very good. On top of this Colie was ill. These circumstances led to Irvine J. Kittinger joining the company in 1904. Born October 25, 1874, on Buffalo's west side, Kittinger was married to Colie's niece, Gertrude.

After a few years with the firm, Kittinger was joined by his brother, Ralph G. Kittinger. The business was acquired from the Colie family, and the name changed to the Kittinger Company in 1913. Irvine was president and general manager and his brother was vice-president and factory manager. Enjoying a business upswing, the brothers

Irvine J. Kittinger, Sr.

Ralph G. Kittinger.

moved to larger quarters at 1893 Elmwood Avenue, where the company still maintains its headquarters. By 1929 Kittinger attained one million dollars in sales, and had completed several expansion projects on Elmwood Avenue. On this backdrop of rapid expansion, Irvine Kittinger reaffirmed the company's commitment to quality: "While our plans for the future are ambitious, we will never grow so large that highest quality shall give way to quantity production."

During the growing years in the 1920s, the Kittinger Company entered the office furniture field. It was during these years that Spencer C. Kittinger began to work for the family business. He became president when his father died in 1941. Frederick J. Batson, Sr., also joined Kittinger in the Roaring '20s. For many years he was executive vice-presi-

dent until succeeding Spencer C. Kittinger as president in 1968.

The business was sold to General Interiors Corporation in 1966. During its ownership Raymond W. Killian became president. After General Mills, Inc., of Minneapolis acquired Kittinger in 1975, Frederick J. Batson, Jr., son of the former executive, was named president.

Kittinger's main plant remains on Elmwood Avenue. In addition the company now has plants in Castile, New York, and Richmond, Virginia, producing its famous replicas, reproductions, and adaptations of 18th- and 19th-century English and American antiques.

By the 1930s, Kittinger Company's plant on Elmwood Avenue had been expanded several times.

LIBERTY NATIONAL BANK AND TRUST COMPANY

Robert J. Donough and Mayor James D. Griffin at the Erie Basin Marina.

When the new German American Bank opened its doors in 1882, it met with immediate success. Within a year, the bank found it had to move from its basement office at the southwest corner of Main and Court streets to larger quarters on the west side of Main Street, a half-block north of Court.

In 1890 the bank had expanded to the point that it was able to purchase the entire building housing its original small basement office. The bank's growth continued into the early 1900s, when the United States entered World War I. With public sentiment running high against the German Army, the bank changed its name to the Liberty Bank of Buffalo on April 15, 1918. A little more than a year later, Liberty acquired its first branch office through merger with the Union Stockyards Bank. The new office was on the corner of Broadway and Fillmore.

The most visible sign of Liberty's successes came on June 2, 1924, when construction began on a 22-story headquarters and office building at the southwestern corner of Main and Court. Just 15 months later, on October 13, 1925, the new building was opened to the public. Unforeseen amid the celebrating was the coming of the Great Depression.

The 1929 stock market crash did not reflect immediately on the bankers' statements. Many economists and bankers still believed better days were "just around the corner"—Liberty's deposits continued to grow and by the end of 1930 the bank had deposits of more than $95 million. It was the 60th largest commercial bank in the United States.

But by 1932, as the bank was entering its second half-century' of operation, the realization of what was happening in the country set in. Nationwide, bank deposits plummeted and loan charge-offs skyrocketed. The economy was in a state of chaos when the Federal Reserve Bank declared the Bank Holiday and ordered banks closed on March 6, 1933.

A special session of Congress created emergency banking legislation. One of the actions was the creation of the Federal Deposit Insurance Corporation, which still protects deposits today. Congress also created the Reconstruction Finance Corporation, which granted loans to banks and other businesses.

The bank's net worth had dropped from $17 million in 1930 to just under $5 million in 1940. The number of banking offices fell from 22 to 18. But, unlike many other banks in the country, Liberty continued to serve its market during the Depression years.

The country slowly began to recover by the beginning of the 1940s. The years during World War II saw the bank's deposits

Looking over historical Liberty documents and photographs are (left to right) Joseph T. Trapp, executive vice-president; Robert J. Donough, president; Robert B. Shanahan, executive vice-president; and Robert B. Mayer, executive vice-president.

nearly triple. By the end of the decade, Liberty was ready to expand. In 1949 Liberty opened a branch office in the village of Williamsville, its first office outside the city.

The bank sold its Main and Court headquarters building in 1957 and used the new funds to meet the increased demand for loans. Liberty's net worth increased by 50 percent and its loan portfolio grew by more than 200 percent.

During the 1960s, Liberty began acquiring additional offices through mergers. In March 1961, as it acquired the National Bank of Fredonia, Liberty Bank of Buffalo changed its name to Liberty Bank and Trust Company. The new name showed the bank's commitment to expand its service area outside Buffalo. By 1965, Liberty had completed eight mergers, which added 10 branches and more than $85 million in deposits. During this period it also received a national charter.

Liberty and the State Bank of Albany announced their intentions to form the United Bank Corporation of New York in July 1971. The holding company, with head-

The 10-story, 195,000-square-foot Liberty Bank headquarters is located at Main and West Huron streets in downtown Buffalo.

Main Street looking north from Court Street around 1882. The German American Bank (Liberty's original name) is on the left foreground.

quarters in Albany, officially started operation on January 2, 1972.

Early in 1973, E. Perry Spink, president and chief executive officer of the bank for 16 years, retired. Spink was an up-in-the-ranks career employee of Liberty who had started with the bank in 1924. During his years as chief executive officer, the bank's total resources increased from $156 million to $544 million.

Spink was succeeded by Avery H. Fonda. Upon Fonda's retirement in 1976, Robert J. Donough was elected president and chief executive officer.

As Liberty readies for its 100th anniversary on May 10, 1982, its assets are more than $700 million. The bank also took the dramatic move to build a new downtown Buffalo corporate headquarters as a cornerstone to Buffalo's redevelopment. The 10-story shining structure stands just a few blocks from the corner where Liberty had opened its basement office a century earlier.

M&T BANK

Buffalo in 1856 was a booming frontier city of 75,000, bursting with a youthful vitality and an urge to grow. The city was a center of lake commerce, spurred on by the construction of the Erie Canal. Enthusiasm for the railroads ran high in those days. Terminal tracks and switches of rail lines sprawled in every direction throughout the city; through-train service to major eastern cities was established. Buffalo was well-known as a milling center and a great grain market in 1856—the aggregate of grain received annually in Buffalo exceeded that of any other port in the world.

One winter day early in that year, two returning Buffalo businessmen boarded a New York Central train in New York City. Both Pascal P. Pratt and Bronson C. Rumsey were still in their thirties, but were already recognized as leaders in Buffalo's civic and business communities.

During the long trip back, the two inevitably talked business. Eventually, their discussion turned to the lack of adequate banking facilities in Buffalo to accommodate the needs of the city's growing business and manufacturing community. By the time the train had reached its destination, the two had decided to spearhead an effort among the business community to establish a new bank—the Manufacturers and Traders Bank, known today to Western New Yorkers as M&T Bank.

Pratt and Rumsey took their idea to other leading businessmen, who viewed it favorably. When the board of directors for the new bank was assembled, it included such prominent Buffalonians as Stephen Van Rensselaer Watson, railroad investor, elevator manufacturer, and real estate developer; manufacturer Sherman S. Jewett; and merchant William H. Glenny.

On March 24, 1856, the new bank was incorporated by the state, with a paid-in capital of $200,000, and five months later, on August 29, Manufacturers and Traders Bank officially opened its doors for business in a rented storefront at 2 East Swan Street.

The progress of the bank was rapid, paralleling that of the city. Before it was a year old, it had increased its capital by 250 percent, and outgrowing its Swan Street quarters, moved to a larger facility at 275

Pascal P. Pratt, cofounder of M&T Bank, foresaw the banking needs of the growing Buffalo area.

Bronson C. Rumsey met with Pratt in 1856. This meeting led to the establishment of M&T Bank.

Main Street to keep pace with the expanding volume of business. In fact, between the time M&T Bank opened and the start of the Pan American Exposition in 1901, it relocated a total of four times, in each instance to meet the increasing financial needs of the community.

During those initial 50 years of its existence, M&T Bank took an active role in providing the capital essential to encourage the growth of area businesses. The bank played a vital part in bringing various short railroad lines together, forming the basic companies from which major railroad systems developed. Leather goods manufacturers of Buffalo during those years became the predominant source nationally as a result of the financial assistance of M&T Bank. The institution contributed substantially to the further development and expansion of the Port of Buffalo as a world grain and milling center.

In the first half century, M&T passed through various periods which affected the area economy—wars, depressions, recoveries. It also passed through a period of transformation. Industrial activity was taking on a new, comprehensive form. As busi-

nesses expanded, they became more complex; companies grew and extended their operations throughout large territories. Industrial corporations began placing plants in the area. Such activities required financing of a higher order. M&T supplied it. And today, many of those same industries conceived during that time continue to prosper with M&T as their bank.

As the bank grew during the last decades of the 19th century, it began once again to feel the need for the additional space required to expediently transact business. To obtain this space, the bank purchased two parcels of land on the southwest corner of Main and Swan streets in March of 1899. On this site an imposing 3-story, gray-granite building was erected, into which the bank moved in May 1900; and there, with the subsequent addition of the Prosser Building, it remained headquartered until 1928.

The 20th century started off well for the bank as it began to expand through mergers. In 1902, M&T merged with the 23-year-old Merchants Bank of Buffalo. The Third National Bank was absorbed in December 1916.

However, those two mergers were small compared to what was to come in the 1920s. M&T had grown rapidly during the first 20 years of the new century, benefiting from the prosperity of the entire city. The funds supplied by the bank during this period were essential in helping many local industries and manufacturers move from peace to war and back again without serious financial harm. By 1925 its resources approached $65 million.

In that same year, the Fidelity Trust Company, head of the syndicate then underwriting the financing of the Peace Bridge, joined with the Manufacturers and Traders Bank to form the familiar Manufacturers and Traders Trust Company (M&T Bank). Eighteen months later, in May 1927, M&T merged with another larger commercial bank, Peoples Bank of Buffalo. In January 1928, following this merger, a new home for M&T Bank on the northwest corner of Main and Swan streets was completed.

The existence of branch bank offices in upstate New York was extremely rare at the turn of the century, until the opening of a branch office by Fidelity Trust in 1901 on the grounds of the Pan-American Exposition. This marked the actual beginnings of M&T bank's present extensive branch network in Buffalo and throughout the six

M&T, at the corner of Main and Swan streets, opened on May 14, 1900, and served the expanding needs of Buffalo businesses for nearly the next three decades.

counties of Western New York. Thereafter, branching became part of an ordered pattern of growth. The mergers of Fidelity Trust and Peoples Bank brought a total of 11 branch offices into the M&T system and to the doors of businesses, industries, and homes of the communities in which they were located, marking the beginning of its retail banking operations.

The frenzied pace of mergers and acquisitions came to a sharp halt in 1929. Like all other financial institutions, M&T felt the grim realities of the stock market crash and subsequent Great Depression of the 1930s. But, as in previous periods of financial depression, M&T Bank was able to bring stability to existing conditions. Through the support it gave to businesses and individuals, the most disastrous effects of the Depression were avoided, allowing M&T Bank customers to remain in a position to take advantage of general economic conditions as they improved.

World War II was a period of great activity and pronounced growth. Hundreds of millions of defense dollars flowed into the Niagara Frontier. Businesses expanded overnight. Heavy demands were made on all the banks in the area to finance the production of war goods from our plants and factories. All banks—large and small alike—met those demands.

M&T's rapid growth, both during and immediately following the war years (deposits had nearly doubled between 1942 and 1946), was also highlighted by more mergers and expanded branching.

Since 1960 M&T has continued to build on its century-old foundations. Branching continued into the Buffalo suburbs and into adjacent Western New York counties. Deposits grew and by 1981—the year of its 125th anniversary—M&T was a $1.7-billion bank with more than 50 banking offices and nearly 2,000 employees, serving 450 corporations and 410,000 households.

In 1969 M&T Bank became the major subsidiary of First Empire State Corporation, a bank holding company which later acquired the $116-million First National Bank of Highland in downstate New York and a real estate lending subsidiary. *continued*

One M&T Plaza headquarters was designed by Minoru Yamasaki, an American architect. This 21-story marble building opened in 1967, and is part of the continuing rebuilding in downtown Buffalo.

Summer entertainment at One M&T Plaza head-quarters on Main Street, where since 1969 the daily noontime Plaza Event Series has attracted large enthusiastic audiences.

In an effort to offer the best banking services available, M&T Bank began an office redesign program in 1979. The bank's Elmwood Plaza office, opened in December 1979, meets the needs of the community both today and for the future.

In M&T Bank's 125th year, the institution remains committed to the goals that have guided it since its inception—sound banking principles and a high ideal of service to the community. Many of the small businesses it helped years ago have grown into some of the area's most successful companies. Many of the businesses which are being established today are the result of the financing it provides. Its 21-story One M&T Plaza headquarters on Main Street, built in 1967, was a primary factor in the initial stages of Buffalo's continuing downtown revitalization. Its civic and community activities have been wide-ranging, from corporate and employee financial and volunteer support of community groups and cultural organizations to sponsorship of its popular summer entertainment series on its plaza.

Since 1856 M&T Bank has been proud of its contribution in providing the enterprise and business wisdom to help agencies, associations, and, most importantly, people shape Western New York, not only conceptually but financially as well. It looks forward to an even greater future, assured that it will, in years to come, continue to be an important factor in the area's progress.

MARINE MIDLAND BANK N.A.- WESTERN REGION

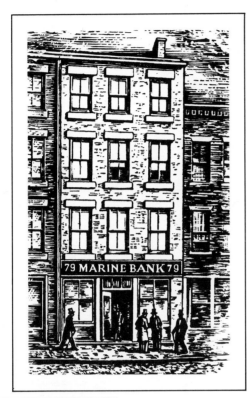

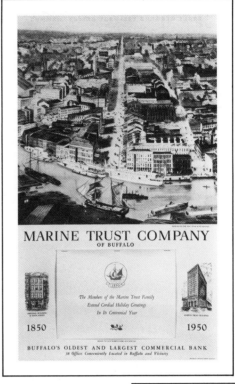

The first Marine Bank opened in this office at 79 Main Street.

To commemorate its 100th anniversary, Marine Midland sent out this Christmas calendar. By 1950 Marine had become the city's oldest and largest commercial bank.

In the summer of 1850, eight men gathered in Buffalo to form a new commercial bank. They had come from throughout the state—General James S. Wadsworth of Geneseo, J.P. Beekman of Kinderhook, John Arnot of Elmira, John Magee and Constant Cook of Bath, William R. Gwinn of Medina, and George Palmer and James M. Ganson of Buffalo. The geographic diversity of the men indicated that the plan was to extend eventually the bank's services across the state.

Marine Midland Bank N.A. accomplished that goal and has gone even further. It is the nation's 13th largest commercial bank with about 300 banking offices in more than 200 New York communities and about 25 offices in foreign countries.

Marine Bank was founded as a state-chartered bank on July 10, 1850, with a capital of $170,000. Palmer was elected president and Ganson was named cashier. The new institution was called Marine Bank

because much of its early business depended on the economic vitality of the city's lakefronts and riverfronts. From the first day it opened its doors on August 27 at 79 Main Street, Marine was the prominent bank for the thriving grain and milling industry on the waterfront.

By the turn of the century, Marine Bank of Buffalo began to expand through merger. In 1897 it absorbed the American Exchange Bank and in 1902 it acquired the Buffalo Commercial Bank. That same year it became a national bank and changed its name to Marine National Bank of Buffalo.

The next acquisition came in 1913 when Marine absorbed Columbia National Bank. Six years later Bankers Trust was acquired. Marine chose to become a state bank again, this time under the name Marine Trust Company of Buffalo. By the mid-1930s, Marine had acquired eight other banks.

Marine had also taken the lead in the formation of Marine Midland Corporation, a holding company for affiliating 17 banks throughout New York. That first multibank

holding company in the state was formed October 4, 1929.

As a result of 11 mergers throughout Western New York, Marine Trust Company became Marine Midland Trust Company of Western New York in the 1950s. The name was changed again in the 1960s to Marine Midland Trust Company of Western New York and again in 1970 to Marine Midland Bank—Western.

On January 1, 1976, all previously independent Marine Banks were merged into a single Marine Midland Bank with headquarters in Buffalo. The new bank was divided into regions, with Marine Midland Bank—Western Region based in Buffalo.

Marine Midland Bank became a national-chartered bank in early 1980. As it entered the 1980s, assets were close to $20 billion.

MATTHEWS, BARTLETT AND DEDECKER, INC.

Matthews, Bartlett and Dedecker was formed with a toss of a coin. But the story actually started about 30 years before.

Evans Ellicott Bartlett was fresh out of Yale University in the 1920s when he joined the small real estate firm of Harvey Harrison. The company was located in Buffalo, the city laid out by Bartlett's ancestor, Joseph Ellicott.

In that small office, young Bartlett handled the insurance transactions that often were a part of the real estate business. He enjoyed this side of the business and decided to pursue it full time.

In 1929 Bartlett founded the Rich, Bartlett and Comack Agency. The timing, however, was inauspicious in view of the Great Depression. It was mutually decided to dissolve the firm.

Bartlett then founded the Bartlett Agency in 1946, locating at 298 Main Street. Simultaneously, Adrian F. Dedecker, Jr., of

Gerald C. Saxe, co-owner of Matthews, Bartlett and Dedecker, Inc., serves as secretary-treasurer (left). Adrian F. Dedecker, Jr., president of Matthews, Bartlett and Dedecker, Inc. (right).

Millburn, New Jersey, a graduate of Rutgers University, was involved in the insurance business as a representative of the Firemen's Insurance Company. Dedecker was transferred to Buffalo in 1950 as liaison with his company's agents. There he met Bartlett and both decided to form Bartlett and Dedecker Insurance in 1953. After two years, realtor George E. Matthews joined the pair.

The time then came to create a name for the new alliance. That is where the coin toss comes in. The trio decided to flip a coin and the one who won would be listed first. Matthews, who was vice-president, won. Treasurer Bartlett came second; and the president, Dedecker, won the honors of rounding out the title.

In 1953, as Firemen's Insurance agents, the company occupied a 2-desk cubicle and employed a part-time secretary. The firm now represents numerous insurance companies and has a staff of 17. In addition to the general lines of insurance, MBD is the longtime administrator of certain professional group coverages for members of the Bar Association of Erie County.

MBD moved in 1968 from the White Building at 298 Main Street, to the Niagara Frontier Building on the corner of Main and Swan. Growing pains struck again and in 1978 the firm moved to larger quarters in the Rand Building on Lafayette Square.

As the company continued to grow, one of the persons hired on July 11, 1959, was Gerald C. Saxe. By mid-60s, Dedecker had acquired the shares of Matthews and Bartlett. As Gerald Saxe became more involved with the company's success and management, he became co-owner and serves as secretary-treasurer.

THE MENTHOLATUM
COMPANY, INC.

This 1937 poster promotes the use of Mentholatum for tired, aching feet.

It was 1912 and for most American companies the thought of doing business in a strange land called Japan wasn't very inviting. But The Mentholatum Company of Buffalo was already there, selling its famous Mentholatum ointment. Today the company sells its products in over 120 countries and Japan remains one of its largest markets.

In addition to being one of the city's major exporters, Mentholatum has the distinction of being one of the largest family-owned businesses in Buffalo. It was founded in 1889 by Albert Alexander Hyde. He had traveled from Massachusetts to Kansas to help start a bank. When a depression caused the bank to fail, he turned to a new venture called the Yucca Soap Company. Hyde made and sold a variety of products. When he came across the formula for the Mentholatum ointment, other products became much less important.

Family members say there's no formal record of how A.A. Hyde found the formula for the ointment made of camphor, menthol, and petrolatum. The most accepted story is that A.A. received the ointment from a Kansas doctor to soothe all kinds of discomforts.

In any case, A.A. found mass production of the formula profitable. Before long he decided to expand his operations in the East. Buffalo was chosen for the new plant, and eventually for the company's headquarters, primarily because of its advantageous location and efficient transportation system.

After spending a short time on Seneca Street, The Mentholatum Company moved to its present site at 1360 Niagara Street in 1919. Many years later, the ointment was joined by several other product lines.

A.A. was a deeply religious man. While it was customary to tithe 10 percent of one's earnings to Christian charities, A.A. chose to give away 90 percent of his income. But he did leave equal shares of The Mentholatum Company to each of his six sons and three daughters. A.A.'s grandsons now run the family business. George H. Hyde is president, Theodore A. Hyde is executive vice-president, and Arthur H. Hyde is secretary.

Although this picture of The Mentholatum Company headquarters was taken decades ago, the building at 1360 Niagara Street still looks much the same today.

MERCY HOSPITAL

Mercy Hospital opened the doors of its first facility on September 24, 1904, in this house on Tifft Street.

The Abbott Road facility has undergone numerous additions and renovations over the years.

As the tight-knit and community-minded neighborhoods of South Buffalo have grown over the years and spilled into suburbs, Mercy Hospital has kept pace. As much as the hospital is a landmark and old friend to Buffalo's south-side neighborhoods, the people still marvel at the number of times Mercy has expanded and added services to meet their needs. As the 1980s begin, the hospital is implementing plans to improve its emergency and outpatient services and has opened a satellite ambulatory care center to serve communities in the south towns area.

Mercy Hospital first opened its doors in the autumn of 1904 at another South Buffalo location. The Sisters of Mercy, mindful of the need for a hospital in Buffalo's then-burgeoning south side, purchased a private home on Tifft Street and opened a 30-bed hospital. Within a few months, arrangements were made to begin a horse-drawn ambulance, technicians installed the hospital's first X-ray machine, and a School of Nursing was founded.

Early hospital records show that the illnesses most commonly treated during that first decade included typhoid fever, malaria, rickets, galloping consumption, and St. Vitus's dance.

As early as 1913, the Sisters of Mercy saw the need for a much larger facility and began, with the aid of area business executives, to raise money to build a 165-bed hospital closer to the center of South Buffalo. The hospital's present site at 565 Abbott Road was purchased. Finally, in 1923, the citywide fund drive raised $120,000, and ground was broken the following year.

The first patients were admitted in 1928 and in its first decade on Abbott Road, Mercy Hospital treated more than 100,000 patients. That is 10 times the number of patients helped during the 24 years on Tifft Street.

During World War II, Mercy Hospital trained nurses to serve in combat areas. A newspaper account, datelined "Somewhere in the Pacific," reported: "Many Buffalo Angels in white who entered the Army are caring for wounded men evacuated to rear area hospitals from blood-drenched Iwo

Jima and Okinawa."

In 1949 three new wings increased the hospital to 360 beds. In the 1950s the hospital received private funds to modernize its front entrance and expand the medical library. Ground was broken in 1967 for the $11-million, 4-floor McAuley Building—named for Catherine McAuley, foundress of the Sisters of Mercy. By 1979 the fifth through eighth floors of the McAuley Building were completed. Plans now call for renovation of the third and fourth floors of the adjacent Main Building.

Mercy Hospital's new Emergency Ambulatory Care Center in Orchard Park represents one more extension of Mercy's promise to its growing and changing community.

"Each year we treat patients by the thousands, yet we remain dedicated to treating each as an individual," explained Sister Sheila Marie Walsh, hospital administrator. "In the tradition begun in the homelike atmosphere of the Tifft Street hospital, we strive to maintain an atmosphere of warmth and individual care for individual needs."

MOLLENBERG-BETZ MACHINE COMPANY

Buffalo's Mollenberg-Betz Machine Company has been providing essential equipment for the best-known names in the food industry for decades. It is the Mollenberg-Betz equipment that freezes nearly every food item consumers buy for their home freezers. And if the Buffalo equipment didn't freeze the food initially, there's a good chance it played a large part in keeping the food cold in warehouses, supermarkets, and hotels.

Like many of Buffalo's oldest companies, Mollenberg-Betz didn't start out in the business where it eventually made its mark. As its name implies, Mollenberg-Betz initially was a machine shop.

It was formed in 1910 by Henry J. Mollenberg, a former superintendent for a manufacturer of refrigeration equipment and electric elevators, and by Jacob Betz, who worked for an ice machine company. Because the pair thought the ice machine business was too troublesome, they decided to set up a machine shop at Washington and Perry streets. But before a few months had gone by, a dairy owner in Lockport asked them to install a refrigerating machine.

After some deliberation, they agreed to take the job. Before long, business in both the refrigeration and machine shops flourished. The refrigeration shop expanded into new areas such as meat industry equipment, while the machine shop kept busy by doing much of the work for the lake steam freighters.

In 1912 Mollenberg-Betz entered still another field. The firm began building artificial ice rinks. The first was for ice shows in the old Teck Cafe on Buffalo's Main Street. Over the next 50 years, the firm installed more than 80 rinks throughout the United States. From 1912 to 1968, Mollenberg-Betz moved twice to larger quarters to take care of the expanding business. The refrigeration division branched into a mechanical contractor and included air conditioning, heating, and process piping, as well as refrigeration. At the same time, the machine shop division designed and constructed special machinery, rebuilding all types of industrial machinery and performing general machining.

By 1968 sales had reached the millions of dollars and the company consolidated its operations at 300 Scott Street, where it remains today. Ironically, it was in this building that Henry J. Mollenberg learned his trade while with another firm. The second- and third-generation descendants of the founders continue to run the closely held company.

After more than 70 years of operation, Mollenberg-Betz still does business with the survivors of its first 25 customers.

Mollenberg-Betz Machine Company, located at 300 Scott Street. The Niagara section of the New York State Thruway and the downtown Buffalo skyline are in the background.

MOOG INC.

While working as an engineer at the former Cornell Aeronautical Laboratories in the late 1940s, a young man named William C. Moog was asked to create a device for the automatic steering of missiles and aircraft. Bill Moog went to work and created the first models of a new electrohydraulic valve. His prototype was a breakaway design which greatly advanced servotechnology and is today an indispensable component in the aerospace industry.

His employers were impressed and offered licensing rights to manufacturers, but when there were no takers for the newfangled device, Moog took a leave of absence from CAL and set up shop in the basement of his home. It was a shoestring operation, without capital, without a market, and in a facility better suited to hanging laundry than to developing guided

The main complex of Moog Inc. in Elma, New York, as it appears today. The original airport hangar, which is the building on the far right, now houses the corporate offices.

William C. Moog, Jr., president of Moog Inc.

missile parts. But the early tests were successful, and Moog sold his first four valves to Bendix Aviation.

In 1951 Moog rented a corner of an unused airplane hangar just outside East Aurora, about 20 miles south of Buffalo, and opened business as the Moog Valve Company. Part of the firm's headquarters facilities still occupy the same site. Bill Moog was joined by his brother, Arthur, and a fellow engineer from CAL, Lewis Geyer.

Then, in 1952, just as a few orders began coming in, fire struck, wiping out all of the young firm's testing equipment. Employees worked around the clock making repairs to get the project back on schedule. Sales and profits grew steadily. In 1959, the company changed its name to Moog Servocontrols, Inc., and sold common stock to the public.

The firm's growth has been meteoric. In 1952 Moog employed 11 people. By 1981 employment approached 3,000 and Moog had manufacturing operations in the United

States, West Germany, France, Japan, Ireland, and England; sales and service offices in Italy, Sweden, Canada, Brazil, and Australia; and a research center in Monterey Park, California. Net sales reached $160 million for fiscal year 1982 and the company gained status as one of the 1,000 largest U.S. industrial corporations.

These facts and numbers tell only a small part of the Moog operation. The greater part of the story lies in the corporation's unique and admirable relationships with its employees. When Bill Moog designed his electrohydraulic valve, he envisioned not only a business empire, but an employee's empire as well.

From the start Bill Moog considered people as important as profits. He dreaded the thought of a clock-punching assembly line of automatons. Instead, he has sought successfully to encourage creativity and pride in every Moog employee and to create an atmosphere of mutual trust and confidence.

There are no time clocks at Moog; employees complete their own time cards. Informational meetings are held frequently to apprise employees of developments in all aspects of their work fields so that they will understand the how and why of the jobs they perform.

Moog's business has remained primarily the design, manufacture, and marketing of electrohydraulic components and systems, but the firm has expanded the industrial applications of its products. It has designed flight-control systems for fighter planes, including the F-15, and was the sole developer of control parts of Trident submarine-launched missiles.

The Space Shuttle's dramatic flight, in the spring of 1981, was guided by Moog-designed servoactuators which position the shuttle's main engines, rocket boosters, and aerodynamic control surfaces.

Moog has been selected by Boeing to furnish a control system for a new transport plane which is expected to dominate the skies well into the 1990s.

The company has branched into N/C and CNC machine tools, controls for plastics machines, NDL digital radio controls, and systems for coil-winding machines, sheet steel, and rolling mills.

Robotics is one of Moog's fastest growing markets. Robots today are used primarily where repetitive functions are required and in hazardous environments. For example, Moog controls are used on auto assembly line work for spot and arc welding. In mining operations, Moog-designed radio con-

The pitch and roll control assembly of Moog's F-15 flight control package. The F-15 is one of the largest programs in Moog's Aerospace Division.

trol systems allow operators to remain in safe areas while difficult work is performed.

With a creative spark and his entrepreneurial savvy, Bill Moog transformed a "basement outfit" into a multinational corporation employing nearly 3,000 people.

Through the years of rapid growth, Bill Moog's original valve design has seen many changes and applications. But his vision of a company where engineers and other employees can work in a creative and encouraging atmosphere has remained constant.

A servoactuator electronic console used by Moog to test servoactuators on all three stages of the Trident Missile Program.

NATIONAL FUEL GAS COMPANY

Although for centuries man has been intrigued with "burning springs," it wasn't until the 19th century that natural gas was tapped and used as a source of heat and light. And it was in Western New York that much of the pioneering developments in the natural gas field occurred. National Fuel Gas Company is the modern outgrowth of innumerable small local gas works that passed in and out of service in the early years of discovery of the potential of natural gas.

The first documented commercial use of natural gas in the United States came in

1821 in the village of Fredonia. A local gunsmith drilled a 27-foot hole, laid a pipe, and brought light into one home. Four years later natural gas was used for street lighting in Fredonia. Throughout the region, towns and crossroad communities developed independent gas systems to supply local homes. A gas well or two and a couple of miles of pipe were all that was needed. The Fredonia system was one of nearly 170 small systems in Western New York and Pennsylvania that were eventually consolidated into the National Fuel Gas Company.

The New York-Pennsylvania area, known as the "Cradle of Natural Gas," has a history of "firsts" in the natural gas industry. One of the most significant developments took place in 1886. United Natural Gas Company, later part of the National Fuel system, constructed an 87-mile wrought iron gas transmission line from gas-producing fields in McKean County, Pennsylvania, to Buffalo. It was the world's longest natural gas pipeline and considered one of the great construction feats of the time.

Crews laying 20-inch steel pipe to carry more gas from producing areas in Pennsylvania to Buffalo.

Another National Fuel predecessor, the Iroquois Gas Corporation, proved for the first time in 1916 that a significant quantity of natural gas could be stored in gas-tight depleted gas fields. Zoar Field, located 40 miles south of Buffalo, became the country's first underground natural gas storage reservoir.

Less than 70 years later, National Fuel has the capacity to store over 100 billion cubic feet of natural gas for its 667,000 customers in 472 communities in Western New York, northwest Pennsylvania, and a small area in eastern Ohio.

Although the natural gas systems had been consolidating for many years, the largest combination in the area came in 1902. Eight of the largest companies became owned in part or completely by the newly formed National Fuel Gas Company. The eight held by the public stock company were Buffalo Natural Gas Company, Commercial Natural Gas Company, Oil City Fuel Supply Company, Pennsylvania Gas Company, Pennsylvania Oil Company, Provincial Gas Company, Salamanca Gas Company, and United Natural Gas Company.

In July 1974 National Fuel restructured its subsidiary firms into a single distribution corporation called National Fuel Gas Distribution Company. National Fuel Distribution has divisional headquarters in Buffalo and Erie, Pennsylvania. It is responsible for delivering natural gas to its customers. Another subsidiary, the National Fuel Gas Supply Corporation, obtains and stores natural gas for later distribution to customers. Penn-York Energy Corporation supplies gas storage to nonaffiliated utilities.

National Fuel Gas Company had revenues of more than $725 million as it neared its 80th anniversary.

Because natural gas was not always readily available, manufactured gas, produced from coal, was the only alternative. The country's first gas-manufacturing facilities were built in Buffalo in 1848. This is the Buffalo Servicenter as it looked shortly after completion. Some of the buildings still stand today, particularly the fortress design facing West Genesee Street.

NIAGARA FRONTIER SERVICES

The story of Niagara Frontier Services, Inc., began in 1952 with two men, Thomas A. Buscaglia and Armand J. Castellani. They had first met years earlier when Buscaglia, then a food salesman, came to call at Castellani's family-owned grocery store in Niagara Falls.

Their formal partnership began with the formation of the T.A. Buscaglia Equipment Company, which sold and serviced food store equipment. The pair expanded into the food store construction business and later they entered into food warehousing.

Because the partners needed a corporation to be the parent company of the operations, Niagara Frontier Services, Inc., was formed in December 1960. Corporate headquarters was established at 60 Dingens Street. Buscaglia was named chairman and Castellani became president.

Under the N.F.S. parentage, Norm and Ed Dusel, Ted and Lou Shelley, Al and Len DiMino, Irv and Joe Cooper, and Al Cowan joined with Buscaglia and Castellani in forming a regional food chain combining company-owned and franchised stores. The

larger units were called Tops Friendly Markets and the smaller superettes were called B-Kwik food stores.

Within five years, there were over 19 Tops and seven B-Kwik stores in operation, making it the leading food chain on the Niagara Frontier. Total sales of the corporate and

Pictured here is one of the company's more than 60 Tops Friendly Markets.

franchise stores amounted to more than $71.6 million when Castellani became chief executive officer upon the death of Buscaglia.

The corporate growth continued. Niagara Frontier Services of the 1980s operates and franchises more than 63 Tops, 15 B-Kwik, and 46 Wilson Farms convenience stores. It is also the parent company of G&G Sales and Services of Western New York, a nonfood supplier to the food retailing industry; J.G. Pieri Company, specializing in institutional foods; Ferrante's Restaurant; as well as the equipment company now called T.A. Buscaglia Company, Inc. Total combined sales near $800 million.

From its modest start, Niagara Frontier Services has grown to be one of the top 10 employers on the Niagara Frontier, with more than 6,000 employees.

But the company's story doesn't stop with its business side. Following the example of its founders, Niagara Frontier Services is active in the community. Its civic involvement ranges from sponsoring little league teams and supporting the arts, schools, and hospitals, to recognizing police officers for community service and sponsoring an annual Food & Nutrition Expo.

Along with Thomas A. Buscaglia, Armand J. Castellani founded Niagara Frontier Services, Inc., in 1952. He now serves as chairman of the board and chief executive officer.

Savino P. Nanula is the president and chief operating officer of the company.

NIAGARA MOHAWK POWER CORPORATION

A turn-of-the-century photograph of Niagara Falls Power Company employees, a forebear of Niagara Mohawk Power Corporation.

Niagara Mohawk's huge Huntley station on the Niagara River was under construction when this picture was taken in 1916.

The debate was worldwide in the late 19th century. How can the great discovery of electricity be transmitted over long distances?

An early pioneer in transmitting electricity was Jacob Schoellkopf, a successful Buffalo leather tanner and flour miller who formed the Niagara Falls Hydraulic Power and Manufacturing Company in 1878. The firm successfully used a direct current to power industry and the town of Niagara Falls. But the electricity couldn't be carried for much more than a mile.

Another company, Brush Electric Light Company, established a power station with one of the world's first alternating current generators on Buffalo's Wilkeson Street. On November 26, 1886, the generator was used to light up the Adam, Meldrum & Anderson store. It was the first commercial installation of an alternating current electrical system in the United States.

But what everyone really wanted to know was if it were possible for the power generated by Niagara Falls to flow into Buffalo, more than 25 miles away?

Two more small Niagara Frontier firms, the Niagara Falls Power Company and the Cataract Construction Company, joined up to find the answer. Edward Dean Adams, president of Cataract, and Dr. Coleman Sellers, a distinguished American engineer, believed that the only way to transmit power was to use transformers in Niagara Falls to raise the voltage of electricity for transmission and then use transformers on the receiving end in Buffalo to reduce the voltage for commercial use.

Construction started in 1893, and three years later Adams and a small group of others who realized the significance of what was to happen, gathered in downtown Buffalo. At the first stroke of midnight on November 11, 1896, Mayor Edgar Jewett threw a switch and the street lamps glowed. "The power is here," Jewett said, not only to the residents of Buffalo but to the world.

The companies that led the way to this event and to the eventual widespread use of electricity throughout the world were forebears of the Niagara Mohawk Power Corporation. During the first half of the 20th century many of the local electric companies merged. On December 13, 1949, three of the largest in upstate New York—the Buffalo Niagara Electric Corporation, the Central New York Power Corporation, and the New York Power and Light Corporation—merged. Central New York Power, the surviving company, then joined with the Niagara Falls Power Company. The result was the formation of the Niagara Mohawk Power Corporation on January 5, 1950. The new venture had 216,330 customers. More than 30 years later, that number has grown to 1.36 million across the state.

Niagara Mohawk has its corporate headquarters in Syracuse, but its regional headquarters in Buffalo is a local landmark. The Electric Building at 535 Washington Street at the corner of Genesee and Huron was built in 1912 for the Buffalo General Electric Company, another predecessor of Niagara Mohawk. The striking building, even more dramatic during the holiday season with its colorful lights on display, was patterned after the Electric Tower built for Buffalo's Pan-American Exposition in 1901.

As it entered the 1980s Niagara Mohawk served 220,000 customers in the Buffalo area, more than it served systemwide when it was founded 30 years earlier. It is one of the nation's largest investor-owned utilities. And although electricity is now generated from oil, coal, and nuclear power, a large portion of Niagara Mohawk's electricity is still generated by low-cost hydro power.

O-CEL-O- DIVISION OF GENERAL MILLS, INC.

Each week, General Mills' O-Cel-O Division in the Town of Tonawanda produces millions of sponges for use throughout the world. Not only has the company been an innovator in the sponge business, but it is considered a leader in worldwide sponge sales.

O-Cel-O was started in the 1940s. Three young men, who were working at a chemical company in Buffalo which was manufacturing sponges but not strongly pursuing the consumer market, decided to quit their jobs to start the new venture. These men were Jack Bitzer, Gerald Murray, and Chester Hardt (two chemical engineers and a chemist). They saw the opportunities in the sponge market. Natural sponges, commonly used for so many years, were getting harder to obtain because of sponge blights and supply cutoffs caused by World War II. By February 1947 the plant was ready to begin production. The business was a success after that first year. In 1952 O-Cel-O caught the eye of General Mills, Inc. The corporation bought O-Cel-O and turned the company into the leading seller of sponges in supermarkets and discount stores throughout the United States. The division is also the number one manufac-

Millions of sponges are produced in the O-Cel-O plant each year.

O-Cel-O employees work on the production line during the 1950s.

turer of sponges for mops. The plant at 305 Sawyer Avenue has been expanded a number of times to accommodate the firm's steady growth. Between 1975 and 1980 personnel has nearly doubled.

The name O-Cel-O is derived from the chemical components of the sponge: Oxygen—CELlulose—Oxygen. O-Cel-O sponges are manufactured by soaking cellulose from wood or cotton in a caustic solution, which is reacted with other chemicals to produce viscose. Viscose is then mixed with salt crystals, vegetable fibers for strength, and colored. When the salt crystals are dissolved out of the cellulose, they leave the holes, which make the sponge porous and absorbent.

PHILLIPS, LYTLE, HITCHCOCK, BLAINE & HUBER

Phillips, Lytle, Hitchcock, Blaine & Huber is Buffalo's largest and among the nation's oldest, most successful, and most prestigious law firms. Founded as a one-man office by Orsamus H. Marshall in 1834, its 83 lawyers now occupy offices on three floors in the towering Marine Midland Center and a suite of offices in Jamestown, and have a national practice.

The firm's history spans the sweeping changes that have taken place in the prac-

This is a portion of an undated newspaper article about a predecessor of Phillips, Lytle, Hitchcock, Blaine & Huber.

tice of law over the past 150 years. One of the key figures in this history was Grover Cleveland, a partner during the late 1870s and early 1880s, who became Mayor of Buffalo in 1881, Governor of New York State in 1883, and President of the United States in 1884 and again in 1892.

Another firm partner, Wilson S. Bissell, served as Cleveland's Postmaster General.

This photograph of the Weed Block was taken while President Cleveland was a partner in the firm. It occupied the second-floor offices and President Cleveland had his living quarters on the third floor.

Bissell continued with the firm after his Washington years, and in 1897 a young lawyer named Walter P. Cooke became a partner. Following Bissell's death, Cooke invited Supreme Court Justice Daniel J. Kenefick to become a partner with Cooke and James McCormick Mitchell, under the firm name of Kenefick, Cooke & Mitchell, later to become Kenefick, Cooke, Mitchell, Bass & Letchworth.

The Kenefick, Cooke years established the foundation for the firm's present practice. During these years, Buffalo became a major financial and industrial center and the home of Marine Midland Banks, Inc., New York's first statewide bank holding company. These years also saw the enactment of new and complex laws and regulations affecting business and labor and imposing income and other taxes. These developments in turn created the need for specialized legal services, in response to which the firm increased the numbers of its lawyers and their skills in new areas of the law which were important to clients. The firm's policy of responsiveness continues today, as evidenced by its expertise in the modern fields of environmental and energy law.

The firm's development during the Kenefick, Cooke years was to serve its clients well during the two world wars, the Great Depression, and the turbulent second half of the 20th century.

In the early 1960s, following the death of the last of Kenefick, Cooke, Mitchell, Bass and Letchworth, the firm adopted its present name.

The activities of the firm are not restricted solely to the practice of law. The firm lawyers traditionally engage in public and community service, including service in the Erie County, New York State, and American Bar Associations.

In continuous operation since Orsamus H. Marshall opened his office in 1834, Phillips, Lytle, has had a long history of professional excellence, of adaptability to the changing needs of its clients, and of civic service.

Orsamus H. Marshall, who founded the firm in 1834.

A copy of the firm's letterhead at the time Grover Cleveland was a partner.

PRATT & LETCHWORTH DIVISION OF DAYTON MALLEABLE INC.

In early 1848, two brothers, Samuel F. Pratt and Pascal P. Pratt, were operating Pratt & Company, an importer and dealer of hardware and metals. Business was booming as the migration west created a huge demand for such items as saddlery and coach hardware.

It was a logical step for the Pratts to make the items themselves instead of transporting them from New York City. They invited William Pryor Letchworth of New York, known for his knowledge of iron work and saddlery hardware, to join them in a partnership.

That was the start of Pratt & Letchworth Company, Inc. During its more than 130 years of operation, Pratt & Letchworth has manufactured a wide range of items, from kites to heavy railroad castings. Products changed as times changed.

By the early 1850s the partners saw that the use of iron and steel was expanding, and

This turn-of-the-century soup kitchen in the Pratt & Letchworth plant is said to have been the first in the nation.

opened one of the country's first foundries at 189 Tonawanda Street. The company is still located on that 23-acre parcel of land.

By the 1870s, Pratt & Letchworth had begun another period of change and expansion. In 1861 the firm produced steel castings on a commercial base, believed to be the first in the country. Some of these first castings were used in the construction of the first steam locomotive built in Buffalo.

The company grew into a major producer of steel castings for the railroad market all over the world. Today, more than 140 years after its founding, the firm's main product is draft sills, used as part of the coupling mechanism for railroad cars. More than 400 people are employed at the busy Tonawan-

da Street complex.

William Letchworth retired from the business in 1873 and devoted himself to philanthropical affairs. He assembled land in a picturesque spot on the Genesee River and deeded the site to the state. The land is now known as Letchworth State Park.

Samuel Pratt died in 1873. Pascal Pratt retained his interest until 1896, when the old partnership expired and a corporation was formed. Dayton Malleable, Inc., a large Ohio-based metal-producing conglomerate, acquired Pratt & Letchworth in 1924.

In addition to its production accomplishments, Pratt & Letchworth was an innovator in Buffalo labor relations at the turn of the century. The company claims to be the first institution of its kind to set up a soup kitchen for its employees. The firm also established recreation facilities, including billiard tables, a piano, and a reading room, for its management personnel.

RICH PRODUCTS CORPORATION

This Niagara Street house was the original corporate headquarters of Rich Products. It had been the home of John and Carolyn Butterfield Wells and, it is believed, where Wells and William G. Fargo met to form the famous Wells-Fargo freight lines.

Rich Products Corporation, known nationwide as an innovator in the frozen food industry, entered the frozen food business through a series of chance happenings.

Robert E. Rich was a young entrepreneur who had an idea of making a whipping cream from soy bean oil. A Buffalo research team came up with the formula and soon Rich was on his way to New York City to present his new product to a local distributor.

Anxious for everything to turn out well, Rich had put too much dry ice in the packing case containing the new liquid. "When I got ready to put my demonstration on the next morning I found I had a frozen product on my hands instead of a liquid." Rich recalled. "I had no other choice but to try to whip the product by hand after quickly thawing it. Well, it whipped to perfection and three months later, we were in the frozen food business and our marketplace became unlimited almost overnight."

People throughout the country began buying the frozen bakery specialties which used Rich's whipped topping as the prime ingredient. After years of development, the firm innovated with another new product in

1963. Coffee Rich, a non-dairy creamer, was developed in Rich's Buffalo headquarters as a low-cost replacement for the cow's product. And because it had an indefinite frozen shelf life, it was considered an outstanding new product in the rapidly expanding frozen food industry.

Being an innovator isn't always easy. Rich Products has had to go to court 40 times to fight dairy interests that have attempted to restrict or severely limit the company's marketing of non-dairy products. Rich was successful in all cases.

The firm's latest development is its revolutionary Freeze Flo process, unveiled in 1980. This natural process allows food to freeze without solidifying. No thawing is needed before use.

From its Buffalo headquarters at 1150 Niagara Street, Rich Products runs three non-dairy, one dessert specialties, seven frozen dough, and five seafood-processing operations in the United States and Canada.

The 4-person company founded in 1945 has grown into one of the nation's largest privately owned frozen food packers. Its frozen dough products comprise the na-

Rich Products' new headquarters on Niagara Street in 1981 is a visible sign of the company's commitment to Buffalo.

Robert E. Rich, Jr., and Robert E. Rich head the family-owned business.

tion's largest line of that food item. By the early 1980s, Rich Products Corporation's sales exceeded $350 million.

The company expressed its commitment to its hometown by building a new headquarters facility in the city in 1980. Seven years earlier, Rich Products had purchased the rights to name Erie County's new Orchard Park stadium, calling it Rich Stadium.

SEN-WEL INDUSTRIES, INC.

The residents of South Buffalo knew George V. Hayhurst's small garage as a good place to get bicycles fixed. Now, nearly 40 years later, Hayhurst's customers are among the largest companies and institutions in the state. From the garage at Seneca and Bailey Avenue called the Seneca Welding Company, the business has grown into Sen-Wel Industries, Inc., one of the largest metal fabricators in upstate New York. The projects the company handles are often 10 times the size of that 400-square-foot Seneca garage.

When Hayhurst started the company on September 23, 1944, he had just $750 in war bonds, an innate skill of welding, and a notion that he'd rather have his own business than work for another. By taking welding jobs as they came along, Hayhurst slowly built up his reputation and the business. By 1957 he found he had to build a 5,000-square-foot plant at 35 Dole Street to house the influx of business and the 15 employees. In 1964 another 4,000 square feet were added. And by the end of another year the

This small garage housed the beginnings of what would grow into a multimillion-dollar business.

company had moved to its present location at 11 Hubbard Avenue, the former plant of Lackawanna Steel Construction Corporation.

During those years of rapid growth, the company changed its name to Sen-Wel Industries, Inc., to reflect its diversification. Among other services, the firm fabricates and erects structural steel for buildings, constructs tanks, and, of course, does welding. Some of its projects include work on Buffalo Light Rail Rapid Transit System, the Erie Community College City Campus (formerly the Main Post Office building), the State University of New York at Buffalo's Amherst campus, the Churchill Academic Tower at Canisius College, and the addition to Children's Hospital.

Sen-Wel's facility includes 100,000 square feet of shop space and 200,000 square feet of storage area. Its corporate offices are located at 1395 Clinton Street. Employment at both locations averages about 250 persons. Hayhurst likes to point out that without many of his longtime employees, the company may have never grown as it has. "I have only two hands and one head; we succeeded because of good people," he said.

In 1944 George V. Hayhurst founded Seneca Welding Company, precursor to today's Sen-Wel Industries, Inc.

SERVOTRONICS, INC.

The products of Servotronics, Inc., and its subsidiaries are found in such diverse locations as the control systems of the country's most sophisticated missiles/aircraft and on many kitchen tables. The company's Advanced Technology Group designs, develops, and manufactures servo control components and other products in the forefront of the technological "state of the art." The firm's wholly owned subsidiaries, located in Arcade and Franklinville, New York, and Titusville, Pennsylvania, design and manufacture precision dies, metal stampings, a variety of exclusive and standard cutlery, hunting and pocket knives, and special-purpose knives of various types. These subsidiaries also supply the federal government with machetes, Air Force survival knives, and related items.

In 1959 Nicholas D. Trbovich, Sr., at the age of 24, founded Servotronics, Inc. Prior to that time, Trbovich held various engineering and supervisory positions in Western New York, was manager of a servo products division at an electronics firm in Oklahoma, and was an independent engineering consultant. He has been awarded over 30 United States and foreign patents in the fields of electromagnetic technology, fluid power, and consumer products. He holds both an MBA and a doctoral degree from the University of Rochester and has completed all the course requirements for a second earned doctorate. In addition, D'Youville College awarded him an honorary doctor of science degree in 1972. A former director of the Buffalo Chamber of Commerce, he has received numerous civic and other awards, including being selected in 1967 as one of the "Five Outstanding Young Men in New York State."

The company was founded because Trbovich was convinced that there was a better way to design and manufacture electromagnetic actuators that were being used in control systems for automatic pilots, aircraft, missiles, auxiliary power units, and jet engines. With a well-prepared economic presentation which also included new product designs, he proceeded to sell his ideas to four private investors. Two of them remain as major shareholders in the company today—C. Arnold Kalman, senior vice-president of Booz, Allen & Hamilton,

and William M. Weaver, Jr., partner of Alex Brown and Company. Trbovich and the four investors committed $80,000 to the firm with the understanding that their total commitment might be required to go as high as $300,000. It never was required. Thus, Servotronics, Inc., was organized and incorporated on August 20, 1959.

Trbovich, the chairman and president of the new enterprise, studied other areas before deciding to build in Buffalo. He leased a 5,000-square-foot newly constructed building for the firm's initial operations. By the end of the first year, the employees included two engineers, a model maker, a draftsman, a secretary, and Trbovich. Among the early employees who are still active in the firm (in addition to Trbovich) are William H. Meyer, senior vice-president, and Frederick Schabert, model shop director.

The company was organized to manufacture various types of control devices. The first and principal products developed were electromagnetic devices and proportional

The founder, chairman, and president of Servotronics, Inc., is Dr. Nicholas D. Trbovich, Sr.

An environmentally controlled area for precision assembly and final test of servo control components.

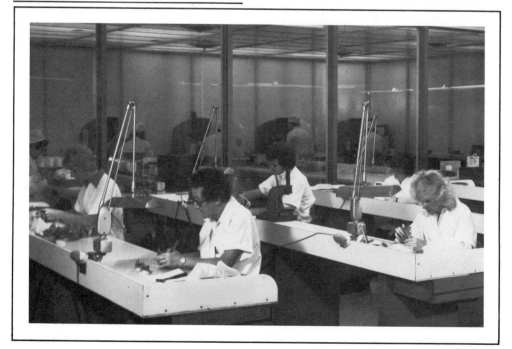

solenoids. These types of products, in some form, are used in all electrically actuated servo systems and have a wide range of control applications.

As a result of adopting a philosophy of new product development, Servotronics experienced significant growth and soon outgrew its original plant. Additional space was leased at the former Wildroot Company plant and other locations.

Servotronics also designed, developed, and produced metallic seals for use in various missile and jet engine programs, nuclear applications, and earth-circling satellites; electrical connectors for use in tactical missiles and rocket engines; and numerous special purpose servo control components.

Servotronics grew and made its presence felt in the country's defense and space efforts. By 1962 it had a number of patents pending and maintained a research and development program which manufactured new products, including an electromechanical actuator with the capability to operate continuously at 1200°F in a nuclear radiation environment. Servotronics

Servotronics, Inc., corporate headquarters is at 3901 Union Road, Buffalo, New York 14225.

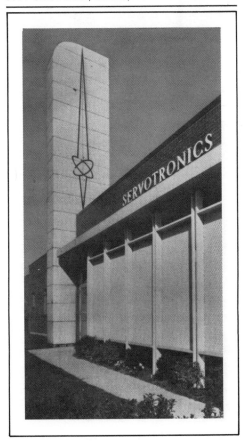

received the highest award granted by *Material in Design Engineering* (a technical trade journal) in recognition of this achievement.

In 1963 the company filed a registration statement with the Securities Exchange Commission, offered its shares for sale, and became a public corporation.

In August 1965 Servotronics moved to its present location and consolidated its operations. Completely equipped to serve the aerospace industry, its laboratories and "White Room" represented the state of the art in assembly and test facility technology. Staffed with experienced personnel dedicated to the maintenance of high quality and continuing product development, the new plant significantly increased Servotronics' ability to serve the developing demand for its new products.

Despite its continuing success, Servotronics decided that its future should not be entirely dependent on government business. In 1967 a total of 98 percent of Servotronics' sales were to the government, as compared to less than 50 percent today. That was the year Servotronics made its first acquisition. The company purchased the 79-year-old Ontario Knife Company in Franklinville, New York. Ontario Knife produces fine cutlery, special-purpose knives, and the "Old Hickory" brand of carbon steel cutlery.

In 1969 it was announced that Servotronics had acquired all of the outstanding shares of Queen Cutlery of Titusville, Pennsylvania. Founded in 1922, that firm specializes in the manufacture of high-quality stainless steel pocket and hunting knives for both the retail and exclusive "collector" markets.

Servotronics' growth of the '60s continued into the '70s as the company began its second decade. During the mid-1970s Servotronics renewed its concentration in the direction of developing its advanced

technology and cutlery product areas and diminished similar activities (to the point of exclusion) in other acquired product areas.

Production quantities of proprietary and patented components were and are being supplied for such significant missile and aircraft programs as the Standard Missile 1, Standard Missile 2, Standard ARM, F-14, F-15, F-16, F-18, DC-10, Boeing 727, 757, 767, and numerous private aircraft.

Sales and earnings are continuing strong into the 1980s—the firm's third decade. New programs and applications are emphasized, as evidenced by the company's commitment to significant prototype and design activity. Examples of new developments are a vacuum control valve for precisely controlling the removal of foreign material from the human eye, an electromagnetic actuator that is used in an automatic blood analyzer, a pneumatic servo valve for a "Gatling Gun" drive, and a servo device for a torpedo control system.

The firm's product quality is evidenced by the receipt of General Dynamics Corporation's Superior Supplier Award for seven consecutive years. During the past year, over 5,000 electromagnetic actuators for the Standard Missile program were delivered with zero rejects.

Naturally, being in a technical field, Servotronics prides itself on the high level of technical competence of the people employed in the Buffalo area. The company encourages its employees to continue their education by providing tuition refunds and sponsoring in-plant college courses.

During the past 22 years, Servotronics has demonstrated a resilience and adaptability to successfully meet all challenges and to continue to grow in a receptive and progressive community.

The company's shares are listed on the American Stock Exchange.

Advanced Technology products.

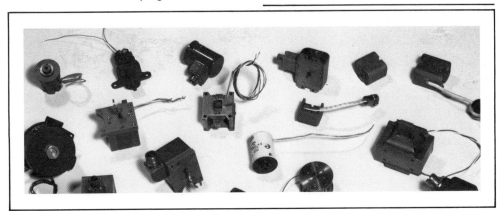

STRITT & PRIEBE, INC.

Co-founder John W. Priebe.

Stritt & Priebe warehouse and offices in the oldest church building in Buffalo at 44 Breckenridge Street.

Since 1922 Stritt & Priebe, Inc., has been supplying pipes, valves, and fittings in the Buffalo area from its 2-story brick building on the city's west side. The building, constructed in 1827, is older than the city itself. It served as a Black Rock union meeting hall during the days when the village of Black Rock was competing with the village of Buffalo. The building later served as a church for three congregations, an Odd Fellows hall, a children's detention center (iron bars still remain on some of the windows), and as a reception center for Chinese immigrants traveling from Canada.

In 1922 the building was bought by Harry Stritt, a local piping contractor, and John W. Priebe, head of piping products for a local wholesaler. They formed a partnership and opened their new wholesale distribution company at 44 Breckenridge Street in September 1922.

But within six months Stritt died, and Priebe and his wife, Clara, bought out Stritt's share. They never changed the name of the company because to the frugal Priebes that constituted an unnecessary expense. Over the years, that family tradition of thrift and value along with service has kept the business going when others like it have failed.

The firm changed its products to keep abreast of new developments in the industry, such as the introduction of plastics. In recent years, Stritt & Priebe decided not only to sell pipes, valves, and fittings, but to offer a repair service and a fabricating shop for valves and instruments as well. It also became the only company in the state to earn the National Board of Pressure Vessels and Boiler Inspectors' approved certificate to set and repair boiler valves.

As the business approached its 60th anniversary, it was still owned by members of the Priebe family. John W. Priebe headed the company until his retirement in 1957. He was succeeded by his son, John L. Priebe, until 1971, when the third generation assumed control of the business. John L. Priebe, Jr., who joined the venture in 1953, became president in 1971. His brother, J. Henry Priebe, joined the company in 1963 and serves as vice-president. Their mother, Susan V. Priebe, is chairman. Oscar Kemp, a salesman, has worked for Stritt & Priebe since 1924.

From the beginning operation, which took up only half the building, Stritt & Priebe has had to expand twice at its site. It has grown to a business with more than 20 employees and annual sales of more than $3 million.

WSF INDUSTRIES, INC.

WSF Industries, Inc., grew from a simple idea. Welder Frank J. Leofsky noticed that a great deal of time and labor was used to get into sealed metal vessels. Because the vessels needed to be closed tightly, they were sealed with many large bolts which were manually unscrewed.

Working on the notion that there should be some way a vessel could be fastened shut without all that effort, Leofsky's small welding company designed a system to lock and unlock containers in seconds. The design, registered under the name Rapidoor, uses a system of rotating locking lugs.

For some time the company didn't make full use of its achievement. Between 1955 and 1960, only 20 of the special doors were made. But even without widespread use of the Rapidoor, the company was steadily growing.

Leofsky had founded the Welding and Steel Fabrication Company, Inc., in May 1941. Despite the long name, the operation was basically a one-man welding shop on Niagara Street. But within a few years, Leofsky expanded operations into a converted airplane hangar at 2085 Military Road in the Town of Tonawanda. When in 1959 construction of the Youngmann Highway forced him to move again, Leofsky bought six acres of vacant land and this time built a new 18,000-square-foot plant. The firm moved into the facility at 7 Hackett Drive in Tonawanda and has stayed and expanded on the site.

The start of Welding and Steel Fabrication's rapid growth and diversification can be pinpointed to 1960, when Henry J. Piegza joined the company. The engineer who later became president had met Leofsky through a mutual friend and was ready to act on his interest in the Rapidoor. Welding and Steel Fabrication pushed ahead with designing and producing its own process equipment. By 1962 the firm had come up with a heat-setter system that fixed synthetic fibers so they could be woven into stretch fabric. More than 500 have been built.

WSF Industries built this large continuous sterilizer for one-liter plastic packaged intravenous solution in 1976.

The U.S. Navy contracted with WSF Industries to build this vessel to simulate deep-sea conditions.

Generally, however, industry was still skeptical that the Rapidoor seal was strong enough to withstand high pressure. The company set out to prove it could. By the mid-1960s, Welding and Steel Fabrication was making autoclaves, high-pressure systems to do such tasks as curing tubing and covered cable and sealing building materials so they would be more resistant to fire and decay. The firm now makes a wide range of products. It has built huge sterilizers that cut the time of sterilizing dramatically and has made vessels to sterilize intravenous solutions—the largest sterilizers of that type in the world. The firm supplied equipment to the U.S. Navy for simulation of ocean depth, and has even come up with a system to make beer less cloudy.

Because the company's business was no longer restricted to welding jobs, the name was changed to WSF Industries, Inc., in 1973. The name kept the initials of the original name which had earned the reputation as one of the leading designers and manufacturers of autoclave systems, pressure and vacuum vessels, sterilizers, vulcanizers, reactors, heat exchangers, and other specialized equipment.

Just prior to his 70th birthday, Leofsky sold the business to John L. Hettrick, a former top officer of Marine Midland Bank, Inc. Hettrick has been owner and chief executive officer since January 8, 1978.

F. WARDYNSKI & SONS, INC.

In one of the yellow brick walls at Wardynski & Sons Inc. headquarters, a red brick stands out. It came from the Kazimierz, Poland, birthplace of founder Frank Wardynski and symbolizes the company's links to the traditions of the Old World.

Since 1919, the Wardynski family has been making and selling sausage and other meat products in Western New York. The recipes, brought by Frank Wardynski from Poland, have changed only slightly over the years.

Frank Wardynski came to Buffalo from the small town in central Poland in 1914 at the age of 22. As he was learning the ways of his adopted country, he held a number of jobs including working as a helper in a meat store on Buffalo's east side. He bought that store in 1919 and a year later expanded it into 336 Peckham Street. That same year he married Lottie Tomczak, the daughter of a local bottler. Together they made and sold the sausages, weiners, and bologna in their small shop.

Little by little the demand for the high-quality products grew and the couple began making their products for other shops to sell. Even after the births of their children, Raymond, Edmund, and Alice, the hard-working Wardynskis worked in the market from 5 a.m. until 10 p.m. The family of five lived behind the store in a small apartment consisting of a living room, kitchen, and bedroom. Everyone worked. Eldest son Raymond, now president, recalled stoking the log fire to smoke hams when he was just 10 years old. His brother also learned the business at an early age. He is now secretary of the company. Edward Posluszny, husband of sister Alice, is sales manager.

The family ended its retail business in 1954 to concentrate on making and wholesaling its products. That year marked one of

Members of the Wardynski family pose for this 1926 holiday picture with their staff. That's young Raymond F. Wardynski at the extreme left, his mother Lottie in the center, and Frank Wardynski in the overcoat at right.

the expansion years of the company and its formal incorporation. The first expansion had been in 1937 and wasn't an easy decision. No one knew for certain if the country was finally coming out of its Depression. But the family decided to move ahead and its decision proved auspicious. By 1972 the business had expanded four more times. Wardynski's facilities were now more than 20 times the size of the original shop. They were also more modern, with such changes as automated smoke houses replacing the burning logs.

Despite the intense competition in the meat industry, the Wardynski family remains committed to its old traditions. And as it entered the 1980s, a third generation, Raymond Michael Wardynski, joined the family business to carry on its work.

The entire Wardynski family—Edmund, Raymond, Alice, Lottie, and Frank—posed for this formal portrait in 1928.

WEHLE ELECTRIC COMPANY, INC.

A look at the Wehle Electric Company, Inc., headquarters at 475 Ellicott Street gives an indication of the firm's growth since it moved to Buffalo in 1945.

Five times the Buffalo offices had to be expanded to make room for the growing staff. During this same 35-year period, Wehle Electric grew more than twentyfold in sales. Today the company is considered the state's largest independent electrical wholesaler.

The firm's roots go back to 1923, when Edwin C. Wehle was a founder of the Southern New York Electrical Supply Company in Binghamton, New York. It sold everything from light switches to electric appliances. Within two years the successful business expanded into Elmira and years later into Rochester and Buffalo.

Wehle's son, Richard J., joined the growing company in 1928. At first, young Wehle made deliveries on his bicycle after school. Then he began acquiring more experience in a number of jobs ranging from shipping clerk to salesman. After graduating from college in 1938 he came to Buffalo to work in the company's branch office. In 1945, when his father turned the reins of the business over to his son, Richard Wehle moved the main office to the Queen City.

The name had been changed to Wehle

Richard J. Wehle, president of Wehle Electric Company, Inc.

Electric Company, Inc., back in 1938. And in that name lies another story. To help customers pronounce the name "Wehle," the family came up with the idea of using a trademark of a whale followed by the letter "E"—Whale E. Influenced by the family logo, Richard Wehle's young daughter Patricia made her father a papier mâché whale. That was the start of a whale collection more than a quarter of a century in the making.

Wehle has what is believed to be one of the largest private collections of whale and whaling artifacts in the world. The presentation, which fills more than two rooms of a museum in the company's headquarters, includes some of the world's finest examples of scrimshaw on whale teeth, whale harpoons, and dozens of handcarved whale bone items. Two of the most magnificent pieces in the collection are a huge jawbone of a whale which practically fills an entire room by itself, and a wall-sized painting of a family of sperm whales by Richard Ellis, well-known sea-life artist.

The Wehle Electric Company, Inc., Buffalo building, which was enlarged in 1972 to provide much-needed extra warehouse space for the firm's expanding business.

WESTERN NEW YORK SAVINGS BANK

Since its founding 150 years ago, the appearance of Buffalo has changed dramatically. Antiquated streetcars have been replaced by modern buses and a new Light-Rail Rapid Transit system. The waterfront's grain mills have given way to new developments of residential and commercial structures. And the patches of a decaying downtown are being revitalized through restoration of the theater district and new office developments. Except for two short decades of Buffalo's early history, Western New York Savings Bank has been an important part of the changes and development of the city.

As Buffalo's second savings bank, Western first opened for business on August 25, 1851, in a temporary office on Seneca Street near Main Street. The first depositor was Stephen D. Allen, who put $10 into the bank's safe. He was from Detroit, living temporarily in Buffalo. By the end of the first week, the bank listed assets of $408 in bank notes, $63 in gold, and $2 in change.

Western's main office in 1904 shows banking was a relatively simple operation. As Western expanded, it became one of the first banks in the area to computerize its services and offer point-of-sale banking.

Within six years, the bank, known to area residents as the Western Savings Bank of Buffalo, reached $100,000 in assets. Relocation brought it to larger quarters at 11 East Genesee Street. By March 1, 1872, the bank's assets climbed to over one million dollars. The trustees decided it was time for a permanent headquarters.

The northwest corner of Main and Court streets was purchased for $44,000 and a new 3-story building marked the landscape. The structure was remodeled in 1899 and 1933. In 1964 construction of the 12-story marble and glass building marks Buffalo's skyline today.

The growth of Western parallels the vivid growth of Buffalo. With the postwar construction boom into the suburbs, Western was the first savings bank in the state to apply for a branch office outside of the city limits. The Cleve-Hill office at Kensington and Eggert Road was established in 1946. More than 25 years later, during a movement to revitalize the city, Western again was the first local savings bank to apply for a new branch within the city limits in 27 years. In 1970 the bank changed its name to Western New York Savings Bank to convey its diversification and outstanding growth.

According to a little-known story of 1884, a Western trustee and prominent attorney named William Clement Bryant was disturbed to hear that the famous Buffalo Indian Red Jacket had been placed on the Cattaraugus Indian reservation in an unmarked grave. Bryant persuaded the warrior's family that he deserved more historical acknowledgement than the unmarked grave. He personally carried Red Jacket's remains in a 4-foot cedar box into Western's vault in 1884. Shortly after, Bryant had raised enough money for a monument to be erected in the Forest Lawn Cemetery where Red Jacket rests today.

During the course of Western's history, the bank has seen 13 presidents. The first was Gaius B. Rich, and today, during the bank's 130th year of operation, it is Charles Diebold III, president and chairman. His father, Charles R. Diebold, Jr., had been president before him and his grandfather, Charles Diebold, had been president from 1924 to 1948.

From that initial $10 deposit, Western New York Savings Bank has grown to more than one billion dollars in assets and secured a place not only in Buffalo's history, but also Buffalo's and Western New York's future.

Western Savings Bank has been a landmark at the corner of Court and Main streets since 1872. Since this 1930s photograph, expansion and modernization has taken place.

WESTWOOD PHARMACEUTICALS INC.

Westwood Pharmaceuticals Inc., a subsidiary of Bristol-Myers, is headquartered in Buffalo. Westwood is a national leader in the development and marketing of dermatologic products. Among the most successful of its nearly 50 products are Alpha Keri Bath Oil, the world's largest selling therapeutic bath oil; Keri Lotion, a therapeutic moisturizer for treating dry skin; a complete line of Pre-Sun sunscreen products; Sebulex medicated shampoo; several acne treatment products, including Fostex; and a number of prescription pharmaceutical products for treating dermatological problems.

Westwood is a descendant of a company started in 1876 by a Buffalo entrepreneur, Orrin E. Foster, to market patent medicines. Dr. Thomas' Eclectic Oil was the company's first product. Incorporated in 1884 as the Foster-Milburn Company, the organization began to grow rapidly with the introduction of Doan's Pills. Products such as Burdock's Blood Bitters and Dr. Wood's Extract of Wild Strawberry followed.

As medical care evolved in the 20th century, so did the direction of Foster-Milburn's business. Moving away from patent medicines and into the professional medical area, the company established a surgical supply division known as Westwood Pharmacal Corporation in the 1940s. Located on Main Street in Buffalo, it provided drugs, medical instruments, and medical equipment to area hospitals and physicians.

In 1949, the Westwood Pharmaceuticals Division of Foster-Milburn was founded by the company's research chemist, Charles A. Oclassen. Under his direction, Westwood Pharmaceuticals began creating the line of dermatologic products for which it is so well known today. In fact, Oclassen himself developed the company's first product, which is still marketed successfully—Lowila Cake, a soapless cleanser for patients with soap-sensitive skin.

Through the 1950s Westwood continued to distinguish itself in the field of dermatology, with Fostex Cake and Cream created for the treatment of acne and dandruff. In 1959, Alpha Keri Bath Oil for dry skin therapy was introduced, and within a decade, sales of this product grew from $153,000 to $4 million. The company's own scientists, working at the same Buffalo location since its founding, have developed the many other products for which Westwood is known today.

In 1969 Westwood Pharmaceuticals Inc. became a subsidiary of the Bristol-Myers Company, which produces and markets pharmaceutical, health-care, nutritional, and consumer products. Bristol-Myers con-

Products currently manufactured by Westwood Pharmaceuticals.

tributes significant resources toward Westwood's continuing research and development of new products in three important growth areas—acne therapy, topical cortico-steroids and dry skin care—and has laid the foundation for new expansions of research in dermatological therapy.

Westwood's long-term commitment to research and development, as well as to the Buffalo area, is evidenced by the company's new research and development building. This $5-million structure adds approximately 55,000 square feet of laboratory and administrative space to Westwood's original facility on the city's west side.

Westwood Pharmaceuticals' expanded research and development facility and administrative offices, featuring distinctive architectural panels.

WILLIAMS GOLD REFINING COMPANY, INC.

The rich history of the Williams Gold Refining Company, Inc., is filled with adventures in the Klondike gold mines to pioneer uses of gold and other metals.

The Williams story starts in northeast Canada, where John Scott Williams, like his father, was a gold miner. John Scott's son, Alexander D. Williams, followed the family path of gold mining and went off to work a claim during the famous Klondike Gold Rush of 1898. Play out of the claim sent Williams to the United States.

By 1907 he and a partner started a company in Kansas City that made use of the glittery metal. The new venture's product was a special dental gold filling material. Within five years Williams bought out his partner and moved the business to a second-floor office at 700 Main Street in Buffalo. A few years later he bought 2978 Main Street, the Norton Abrasives Company factory, formerly a stagecoach stop. The family-owned business has remained at this site, expanding as needed to adjacent properties.

A.D. Williams' brother, Malcolm Cameron Williams, meanwhile was recruited in 1917 to start up another plant in Fort Erie, Ontario, to serve Canada. His grandson, Malcolm A. Williams, still carries on that operation. The Canadian company manufactures one of Canada's best-selling fishing lures. The Williams Wabler uses real gold and silver and is highly reflective.

By the 1920s, Williams Gold already had the reputation as a leading producer of gold alloys for dentistry. But its status took a major leap under the direction of Reginald V. Williams, son of Alexander. Working with a professor at Princeton University, Reginald Williams developed the first commercial application of induction melting in 1926. This melting method allowed for a more homogeneous quality in the final gold alloys. Other manufacturers finally utilized the induction method 40 years later.

Williams' emphasis in research resulted in a wide range of developments, including the ability to roll a gold alloy as brittle as glass to one-sixth the thickness of a human hair. Use of a spectrograph to check for the impurities in raw materials became another important first for quality manufacturing.

Williams Gold took the dental industry lead in the 1930s by starting an educational department to teach new procedures to dentists and dental laboratories today. The

John Scott Williams, holding the miner's pan, stands with fellow miners outside a Klondike gold mine.

Alexander D. Williams brought his company to Buffalo in 1912.

Reginald V. Williams stressed research and development.

Horses and carriages wait in front of a travelers' stop at 2978 Main Street prior to its conversion to Williams Gold Refining Company, Inc., offices.

department demonstrates new uses of gold, porcelain, and other related products.

In 1958 Reginald Williams turned management of the U.S. operations over to his sons. John A. Williams, a Yale University business graduate, was named president and R.V. (Vic) Jr., a Princeton University graduate, was named executive vice-president.

Up until this generation, the business was almost entirely dental related. The new management focused on precious metals manufacturing expertise and moved the company into alloys for the electronics business.

When gold prices skyrocketed in the 1970s, Williams successfully developed new alloy systems containing less gold, as well as alloys based on palladium-silver. About 95 percent of the dental materials made at Williams Gold today did not exist in 1970. The company is a recognized leader in developing new materials and alloys for dentistry and electronics.

The organization has also grown into other business lines. In the early 1980s Williams entered the jewelry supply business, and continued to expand its refining business.

In the 25 years of third-generation management, Williams Gold has grown from 70 employees and one million dollars in sales to 270 employees and more than $90 million in sales. From its small start in Kansas City, Williams Gold is now one of the largest privately owned businesses in the dental products industry.

Although Williams Gold has been run by the family, the company credits much of its success to numerous dedicated employees. Longtime employees, one of whom spent 62 devoted years with the firm, combine with an energetic younger group to form an active, progressive team. It is because of its employees and its deep roots in Buffalo that Williams Gold continues to prosper and grow.

Williams Gold Refining Company, Inc., is now managed by the third generation. John A. Williams is president, and emphasizes expansion and diversification.

R.V. "Vic" Williams, Jr., is executive vice-president.

WORTHINGTON GROUP
McGRAW -EDISON COMPANY

When the retired U.S.S. *Little Rock* and the U.S.S. *The Sullivans* made the trip to their new home in Buffalo's Naval and Servicemen's Park in the late 1970s, they were of historical interest to Worthington since both ships were originally equipped with Worthington Buffalo-made compressors. Those compressors were among the more than 1,200 special compressors built in Worthington's Buffalo plant for installation on board battleships, aircraft carriers, and other naval vessels during World War II. A compressor of this type was given to the Naval Park as a display in 1981 to commemorate Worthington's 131 years of service to the U.S. Navy.

In the 1960s Worthington was taking part in another major effort—putting Americans on the moon. As early as seven years before Apollo 11 landed on the moon on July 20, 1969, Worthington received orders for compressors and expanders to make liquid hydrogen for the space fuel.

In the years before and since these two events, Worthington has made reciprocating compressors and parts for a wide variety of uses. Its products have ranged from pumping engines in municipal water works in the late 1890s to compressors that put the bubbles in champagne in the 1980s.

The company's beginnings in Buffalo go back to 1889. James Snow and Daniel O'Ray, two executives of Standard Oil Company, realized that the increasing industrialization of the United States would mean a greater need for small single and duplex steam driven compressors and power pumps. They raised $100,000 almost exclusively from the citizens of Buffalo and used part of the capital to erect a single 3-story brick building to house the machine shop, foundry, pattern shop, and office of their new firm, the Snow Steam Pump Works. The site chosen was to the southeast of downtown Buffalo, about a half-day round trip by horse-drawn car from the center of the city.

The brick building is still standing and is part of the sprawling Worthington complex at Clinton and Roberts streets. Today Worthington is only several minutes by expressway from downtown.

The Snow Steam Pump Works was an im-

This is the former Snow Steam Pump Works as it looked in 1893 before its acquisition by Worthington in 1899. The present company is located on this site.

mediate success. The plant was working at capacity by the end of its first year of operation. Within five more years, Snow was one of the city's single largest employers. About 600 employees were working in shifts around the clock to fill the orders pouring in.

In 1899 Snow and four other firms were merged into the Henry R. Worthington Company. The name chosen for the con-

This Snow gas engine-driven gas compressor, built in 1902, is a predecessor of the modern Worthington compressors.

In 1980 Worthington furnished three 2,250-horsepower BDC compressors to Petroleos Mexicanos in Mexico for a refrigeration application. The three compressors shown compress ammonia gas and propane.

solidation was the International Steam Pump Company. The Worthington Company had been in operation for more than 50 years before the merger. It was founded in 1845 in New York City by Henry R. Worthington, who designed the world's first direct-acting steam pump.

Three of the other companies merged into International Steam Pump and were relocated to Buffalo to be consolidated with the Snow plant. The first moved was the Holly Manufacturing Company of Lockport, New York. Holly, formed in 1859 and moved to Buffalo in 1902, made pumping engines for water works. In 1927 the Blake & Knowles Steam Pump Works of Cambridge, Massachusetts, was consolidated into the Buffalo operations. A third firm, the Laidlaw-Dunn-Gordon Company of Cincin-

Worthington furnished compressors for the U.S.S. George Washington, and first atomic submarine to launch the Polaris missile, and for the Trident submarine program in the 1980s.

nati, Ohio, manufacturers of steam pumps and air and gas compressors, was partially moved to Buffalo in 1932. Four years later one of the Cincinnati buildings was completely dismantled and relocated to Buffalo. That building is still in use.

The firm has had several names in its history because of mergers and reorganizations. After 17 years as the International Steam Pump Company, the business was reorganized and named the Worthington Pump and Machinery Corporation. In 1952, after years of diversifying its products, the newly adopted name was Worthington Corporation. When Worthington merged with the Studebaker Company in 1967 the name reflected the change—Studebaker-Worthington Inc. In 1979 McGraw-Edison Company acquired Studebaker-Worthington, and by the end of 1980 the Buffalo plant was known as the Buffalo operation of the Worthington Group, McGraw-Edison Company.

Along with its names, the corporation's product line has also changed over the years. Today the Buffalo plant makes compressors for the natural gas, process, air power, marine, and government markets.

The gas engine-driven gas compressor, the predecessor of Worthington's modern line, was developed in 1902. Over the years, the plant had other significant accomplishments. For example, in 1911 James Snow built the first completely American-designed diesel engine in Buffalo.

Other noteworthy developments include building the first oxygen compressors in 1921, manufacturing the world's first turbocharged dual fuel engine in 1945, supplying 25 generators to power the "Voice of America" radio station in 1952, supplying air compressors for atomic submarine service in 1954, introducing the oxygen-type compressor for steel making in 1957, providing hundreds of compressors for offshore drilling beginning in the late 1960s, building a giant reciprocating compressor weighing more than 500,000 pounds to produce rocket fuel for the Space Shuttle program, and building reliable compressors to operate the foghorns at San Francisco's Golden Gate Bridge.

As Worthington nears 100 years of operation in Buffalo, the plant's products are in use all over the world, from the oil fields of Mexico to fertilizer plants in India, from a synthetic fuel plant in Canada to the subways of New York.

PATRONS

The following individuals, companies, and organizations have made a valuable commitment to the quality of this publication. Windsor Publications and the Buffalo and Erie County Historical Society gratefully acknowledge their participation in *Buffalo: Lake City in Niagara Land*.

Abigail Fillmore Chapter, Daughters of the American Revolution
Accountants of Buffalo, Inc.
Adam, Meldrum & Anderson Company*
Airport City
Albrecht, Maguire, Heffern & Gregg, P.C.
American Precision Industries Inc.*
American Steamship Company*
Anaconda Industries, Brass Division
Andco Incorporated
A.E. Anderson III
ARA Coffee System of W.N.Y.
Arcata Graphics, Buffalo Division*
Arcata Graphics Corporation
Armstrong-Roth-Cady Co., Inc.*
Arvin/Calspan Advanced Technology Center (ATC)*
The Bank of New York Western Region*
Bell Aerospace Textron*
Blair, Martin & Messina
Blue Cross of Western New York, Inc.
Buffalo Brake Beam Company*
Buffalo China, Inc.*
Buffalo Color Corporation
Buffalo Courier-Express*
Buffalo Electric Co., Inc.
The Buffalo Evening News*
Buffalo Forge Company*
Buffalo General Hospital*
Buffalo Hilton*
Buffalo Kiwanis Club Foundation, Inc.
Buffalo Mack, Inc.
Buffalo Marriott Inn
Buffalo Museum of Science
The Buffalo Sabres Hockey Club*
Buffalo Savings Bank*
Buffalo Stallions
Bufkor, Inc. - Irving Korn, President
F.N. Burt Co., Inc.*
Canisius College*
Cannon Design Inc.*
Chef's Restaurant of Buffalo, Inc.
Chevrolet Tonawanda Forge
Clarklift of Buffalo, Inc.
Clayton's Gifts & Toys, Inc.
Columbus McKinnon Corporation*
Computer Task Group, Inc.*
The John W. Cowper Company, Inc.*
Cox, Barrell, Walsh, Roberts & Grace
D.B.M. Control Distributors, Inc.
Harry R. Defler Corporation

Delaware North Companies, Inc.*
Diem & Buerger Agency Inc.
Division Tire and Auto Parts, Inc.
Dow & Company, Inc.
Downtown Nursing Home, Inc.
D'Youville College*
Eaton Office Supply Co., Inc.
Eberl Iron Works, Inc.
Ecology and Environment, Inc.
Empire State News Corp.
Erie Savings Bank*
Erie Savings FSB
Ethox Corp.
Federal Bakers Supply Corp.
Ferguson Electric Construction Co., Inc.*
Ferro Corp. - Specialty Ceramics Group
First Line Hockey Equipment, Inc.
Edw. J. Fischer Oil Co., Inc.
Fisher-Price Toys, A Division of The Quaker Oats Company*
S.M. Flickinger, Inc.*
Forest Lawn Cemetery*
G&W International Forwarders, Inc.
General Mills, Inc.*
Gioia Macaroni Company, Inc.*
Graphic Controls Corporation*
Greater Buffalo Press, Inc.*
Gurney, Becker & Bourne, Inc.
Hale Northeastern Inc.
Hydraulic Servocontrols Corporation
International Chimney Corporation
Irish Welding Supply Corporation
Jaeckle, Fleischmann & Mugel
The Jewett Refrigerator Company, Inc.*
Keystone Corporation
Kittinger Company*
Fred H. Koehler Sons, Inc.
Laverack & Haines, Inc.
Lawley Service, Inc.
Liberty National Bank and Trust Company*
Lucidol Division, Pennwalt Corporation
Mrs. Harris McCarthy
Donald G. McGrath
M&T Bank*
Manor Oak Skilled Nursing Facilities, Inc.
Manufacturers Hanover Trust Company/Western, N.A.
Marine Midland Bank N.A. - Western Region*

Matthews, Bartlett and Dedecker, Inc.*
Medaille College
The Mentholatum Company, Inc.*
Mercy Hospital*
Miserendino, Krull & Foley, Attorneys
Mollenberg-Betz Machine Company*
Moog Inc.*
Multiple Parking Services, Inc.
Mutual Life Insurance Company of New York
National Fuel Gas Company*
Niagara Frontier Services*
Niagara Mohawk Power Corporation*
Albert William Noworyta
O-Cel-O Division of General Mills, Inc.*
Oehler Industries, Inc.
Benedict James Pancamo
Carmen M. Pariso, Inc.
Periodical Data Services, Inc.
Phillips, Lytle, Hitchcock, Blaine & Huber*
Posting Equipment Corporation
Pratt & Letchworth Division of Dayton Malleable Inc.*
Rich Products Corporation*
Safety Services, Corp.
The Salvation Army
Peter J. Schmitt Co., Inc.
Schneider Design Associates
Seneca Industrial Center, Inc.
Sen-Wel Industries, Inc.*
Servotronics, Inc.*
Dr. and Mrs. Walter F. Stafford, Jr.
Stimm Associates, Inc.
Stritt & Priebe, Inc.*
Suburban Design Inc.
U.S. Ethicare Corporation
Urban Raiff & Sons, Inc.
W & F Mfg. Co., Inc.
WIVB-TV
WSF Industries, Inc.*
F. Wardynski & Sons, Inc.*
Wehle Electric Company, Inc.*
Western New York Savings Bank*
Westwood Pharmaceuticals Inc.*
S.B. Whistler & Sons, Inc.
Williams Gold Refining Company, Inc.*
Williamsville Water Mills
Dr. Robert M. Wilson, Lockport, New York
Wittburn Enterprises, Inc. - Electrical Construction Division
Worthington Group, McGraw-Edison Company*

*Partners in Progress of *Buffalo: Lake City in Niagara Land*. The histories of these companies and organizations appear in Chapter 13, beginning on page 250.

ACKNOWLEDGMENTS

The persons who helped in the preparation of this book are too numerous to mention as individuals, but special acknowledgment must be paid to the efficient staff of the Buffalo and Erie County Historical Society—particularly to the picture editor, Mrs. Clyde Eller Helfter, who is the Society's Curator of Iconography. In addition, Robert L. Damm, Director of the Society, and the professional staff contributed to the project from the start. They include Wilma C. Bertling, Charles E. Brooks, Bodo Foitzik, Patrick W. Gabor, Mary Ann D. Hickey, Raymond J. Hughes, Kristin B. Keough, JoAnn Morgan, Herman Sass, and Lester W. Smith. Judith A. Caie, Louise Culkowski, and Linda M. Marks provided office services. Staff photographers Robert P. Green and Patricia A. Brazill and contemporary photo coordinator Donna Binder also participated in the venture, as well as other part-time staff members.

Also we would like to thank the efficient employees of Buffalo's newspapers, most notably Harvey Elsaesser of the *Buffalo Evening News*. The staff at the Buffalo and Erie County Public Library proved most helpful. Noteworthy, too, was the cooperation we received from persons associated with Buffalo's leading industrial, financial, and cultural institutions.

While the final words and judgments are those of the two authors, in their respective sections, this book is in a very real sense a cooperative effort by many people.

NOTES ON SOURCES

Readers wishing to know more in general about Buffalo's past should turn to *Niagara Frontier*, the journal of the Buffalo and Erie County Historical Society; to the *Adventures in Western New York* series published by the Society; and to the *History of Erie County, 1870-1970*, edited by Dr. Walter Dunn. The Sunday October 12, 1980, edition of the *Buffalo Evening News*, commemorating the 100th anniversary of that newspaper's publication, contains interesting material on the past, present, and future of the City on the Lake.

Histories of Buffalo have been authored by Robert W. Bingham, Henry Wayland Hills, William Ketchum, Frank H. Severance, J.N. Larned, James Sheldon, H. Perry Smith, and George W. Clinton. Dr. John T. Horton wrote a history of Buffalo for *The History of Northwestern New York* series, Vol. I.

Other books relating to Buffalo history are *Millard Fillmore: Biography of a President*, by Robert Rayback; *Grover Cleveland As Buffalo Knew Him*, by Charles Armitage; *Grover Cleveland, A Study in Courage*, by Allan Nevins; *Grover Cleveland, A Man Four-Square*, by Denis Tilden Lynch; *The Man Who Shot McKinley*, by A. Wesley Johns; *Stars in the Water*, by George E. Condon; *Niagara Power*, Vols. I and II, by Edward Dean Adams; *Niagara's Pioneers*, by Merrill Denison; *A Law Firm and a City*, by Bob Watson; *Reformers in Search of Yesterday: Buffalo in the 1890s*, by Brenda K. Shelton.

In addition to the files of the *Buffalo Commercial*, the *Buffalo Evening News*, the *Buffalo Courier-Express*, and the *Buffalo Times*, there are the Roy Nagle collection of historical papers and documents, the William Hodge, Jr., papers, Louis L. Babcock's books and papers, and Samuel Welch's "Recollections of Buffalo."

THE MAYORS OF BUFFALO

Dr. Ebenezer Johnson . . . . 1832 and 1834
Major A. Andrews 1833
Hiram Pratt. . . . . 1835 and 1839
Samuel Wilkeson 1836
Dr. Josiah Trowbridge 1837
Pierre A. Barker. 1837
Ebenezer Walden. 1838
Capt. Sheldon Thompson 1840
Issac R. Harrington. 1841
George W. Clinton. 1842
Joseph G. Masten . . . . 1843 and 1845
William Ketchum. 1844
Solomon G. Haven 1846
Elbridge G. Spaulding 1847
Orlando Allen. 1848
Hiram Barton . . . . 1849 and 1852
Henry K. Smith 1850
James Wadsworth 1851
Eli Cook. 1853-1855
Frederick P. Stevens. 1856-1857
Timothy T. Lockwood 1858-1859
Franklin A. Alberger 1860-1861
William G. Fargo 1862-1865
Chandler J. Wells. 1866-1867
Maj. Gen. William F. Rogers. 1868-1869
Alexander Brush. . . . . 1870-1873 and 1880-1881
Louis P. Dayton 1874-1875
Philip Becker. . . . . 1876-1877 and 1886-1889
Solomon Scheu 1878-1879
Grover Cleveland. 1882
Marcus M. Drake 1882
Harmon S. Cutting 1882
John B. Manning 1883
Jonathan Scoville. 1884-1885
Charles F. Bishop. 1890-1894
Edgar B. Jewett 1895-1897
Conrad Diehl 1898-1901
Erastus C. Knight 1902-1905
James N. Adam. 1906-1909
Louis P. Fuhrmann. 1910-1917
George S. Buck. 1918-1921
Frank X. Schwab. 1922-1929
Charles E. Roesch. 1930-1933
George J. Zimmerman. 1934-1937
Thomas L. Holling 1938-1941
Joseph J. Kelly. 1942-1945
Bernard J. Dowd. 1946-1949
Joseph Mruk. 1950-1953
Steven Pankow. 1954-1957
Frank A. Sedita . . . . 1958-1961 and 1966-1973
Chester Kowal 1962-1965
Stanley M. Makowski. 1973-1977
James D. Griffin 1978-present

INDEX

Published Books in Windsor Local History Series

St. Paul: Saga of an American City, by Virginia Brainard Kunz (1977)

The Heritage of Lancaster, by John Ward Willson Loose (1979)

A Panoramic History of Rochester and Monroe County, New York, by Blake McKelvey (1979)

Syracuse: From Salt to Satellite, by William Roseboom and Henry Schramm (1979)

Columbia, South Carolina, History of a City, by John A. Montgomery (1979)

Kitchener: Yesterday Revisited, by Bill Moyer (1979)

Erie: Chronicle of a Great Lakes City, by Edward Wellejus (1980)

Montgomery: An Illustrated History, by Wayne Flynt (1980)

Charleston: Crossroads of History, by Isabella Leland (1980)

Baltimore: An Illustrated History, by Suzanne E. Greene (1980)

Omaha and Douglas County, by Dorothy Deveneux Dustin (1980)

The Fort Wayne Story: A Pictorial History, by John Ankenbruck (1980)

City at the Pass: An Illustrated History of El Paso, by Leon Metz (1980)

Tucson: Portrait of a Desert Pueblo, by John Bret Harte (1980)

Salt Lake City: The Gathering Place, by John McCormickn(1980)

Saginaw: A History of the Land and the City, by Stuart D. Gross (1980)

Cedar Rapids: Tall Corn and High Technology, by Ernie Danek (1980)

Los Angeles: A City Apart, by David L. Clark (1981)

Heart of the Commonwealth: Worcester, by Margaret Erskine (1981)

Out of a Wilderness: An Illustrated History of Greater Lansing, by Justin Kestenbaum (1981)

The Valley and the Hills: An Illustrated History of Birmingham and Jefferson County, by Leah Rawls Atkins (1981)

River Capital: An Illustrated History of Baton Rouge, by Mark T. Carleton (1981)

Chattanooga: An Illustrated History, by James Livingood (1981)

New Haven: An Illustrated History, edited by Richard Hegel and Floyd M. Shumway (1981)

Kalamazoo: The Place Behind the Products, by Larry Massie and Peter Schmitt (1981)

Mobile: The Life and Times of a Great Southern City, by Melton McLaurin (1981)

New Orleans, by John Kemp (1981)

Regina: From Pile O' Bones to Queen City of the Plains, by W.A. Riddell (1981)

King County and Its Queen City, Seattle: A Pictorial History, by James Warren (1981)

To the Setting of the Sun: The Story of York, by Georg Sheets (1981)

Springfield of the Ozarks, by Harris and Phyllis Dark (1981)

Charleston and the Kanawha Valley, by Otis K. Rice (1981)

Albany: Capital City on the Hudson, by John J. McEneny (1981)

Selected Works-in-Progress

Dallas: Portrait in Pride, by Darwin Payne (1982)

Heart of the Promised Land: An Illustrated History of Oklahoma County, by Bob L. Blackburn (1982)

Winnipeg: Gateway to the New West, by Eric Wells (1982)

City of Lakes: An Illustrated History of Minneapolis, by Joseph Stipanovich (1982)

Rhode Island: The Independent State, by George H. Kellner and J. Stanley Lemons (1982)

Calgary: Canada's Frontier Metropolis, by Max Foran and Heather MacEwan Foran (1982)

Evanston: An Illustrated History, by Patrick Quinn (1982)

Norfolk's Waters: An Illustrated Maritime History of Hampton Roads, by William L. Tazewell (1982)

Hartford: An Illustrated History of Connecticut's Capital, by Glen Weaver (1982)

Pikes Peak Country: A Social History of Colorado Springs, by Nancy E. Loe (1982)

At the Bend in the River: A History of Evansville, by Kenneth P. McCutchan (1982)

Cape Fear Adventure: An Illustrated History of Wilmington, by Diane C. Cashman (1982)

Chicago: Commercial Center of the Continent, by Kenan Heise and Michael Edgerton (1982)

Windsor Publications, Inc.
History Books Division
21220 Erwin Street
Woodland Hills, California 91365
(213) 884-4050

THIS BOOK WAS SET IN
ORLEANS AND BENQUIAT BOOK
CONDENSED TYPES,
PRINTED ON
80 POUND MEAD OFFSET ENAMEL
AND BOUND BY
WALSWORTH PUBLISHING COMPANY.
COVER AND TEXT DESIGNED BY
JOHN FISH
LAYOUT BY
JOHN FISH
AND LISA SHERER
PARTNERS IN PROGRESS
LAYOUT BY MELINDA WADE

Photo by Paul Pasquarello.